SLOGGING
OVER AFRICA

Other Michael Barthorp books published by Cassell:

BLOOD-RED DESERT SAND: The British Invasions of Egypt and the Sudan 1882-1898

AFGHAN WARS: And the North-West Frontier 1839-1947

THE ZULU WAR: Isandhlwana to Ulundi

SLOGGING OVER AFRICA

THE BOER WARS 1815–1902

MICHAEL BARTHORP

"We're foot-slog-slog-slog-sloggin' over Africa –
Foot-foot-foot-foot-sloggin' over Africa –
(Boots-boots-boots-boots-movin' up and down again!)
There's no discharge in the war!

Rudyard Kipling, "Boots".

CASSELL&CO

Cassell
Wellington House, 125 Strand
London WC2R 0BB

First published in Great Britain as *The Anglo-Boer Wars,* 1987
This edition 2002

British Library Cataloguing-in-Publication data:
A catalogue record for this book is available from the
British Library

ISBN 0-304-36293-X

Printed and bound in Slovenia by Mladinska knjiga tiskarna d.d.,
Ljubljana by arrangement
with Prešernova družba d.d.

CONTENTS

CHRONOLOGY

EVENTS PRECEDING AND BETWEEN THE BOER WARS

1652 Dutch East India Company establishes settlement at Cape of Good Hope, then inhabited only by aboriginal Bushmen and Hottentots.

1779 First conflict between Cape Dutch and Kaffir (Bantu) invaders from north-east.

1795–1802 Revolutionary France occupies Holland and establishes puppet Batavian Republic. Britain, at war with France, occupies Cape. Minor insurrection by Cape Dutch (Boers).

1803 Cape returned to Batavian Republic after Peace of Amiens.

1805 Britain, again at war with Napoleonic France, re-occupies Cape.

1812 British and Boers combine to resist further Kaffir invasion on eastern frontier. (Five more Kaffir Wars followed until 1877.)

1814 Napoleon abdicates. Holland cedes Cape Colony to Britain.

1815 Boer uprising at Slachter's Nek. Six leaders hanged for insurrection.

1820 British immigration to Cape.

1824 British traders settle in Zululand, at Port Natal (Durban), with Zulu permission.

1826 Cape Colony extended northwards to Orange River.

1834 Abolition of slavery at Cape alienates Boers.

1835 British Government refuses petition of Durban settlers for annexation.

1836 Great Trek of Boers from Cape Colony north across Orange and Vaal rivers; also into Natal after defeating Zulus (1838).

1838–9 Temporary occupation of Durban by British troops.

1841 Instability of Boer republic in Natal. British re-occupy Durban and are attacked by Boers.

1843 Natal annexed as British colony. Most Boers leave for Transvaal.

1845 British troops cross Orange River to protect Griquas from Boers. Boers dispersed at Zwartkopjes (30 April).

1846 British Resident appointed at Bloemfontein. Action against Boers at Vet River.

1848 Trans-Orange territory annexed to Cape Colony as Orange River Sovereignty. Boers rebel but defeated at Boomplaats (29 August).

1852 Britain recognizes independence of Transvaal.

1854 Britain recognizes independence of Orange Free State (OFS).

1868 Basutoland annexed as British Crown Colony.

1871 Kimberley (OFS) annexed to Cape Colony after discovery of diamond fields. De Beers Mining Co. founded (1880) by Cecil Rhodes.

1872 Cape Colony granted internal self-government.

1876 London Conference to discuss federation of Boer Republics and British Colonies; thwarted by opposition of Cape Government.

1877 Transvaal, bankrupt and threatened by Zulus, annexed as British Colony.

1879 The Zulu War.

1880–81 THE FIRST BOER OR TRANSVAAL WAR. Transvaal granted internal self-government, Britain retaining control of its foreign affairs. Paul Kruger began first of four Presidential terms.

1884 London Convention grants Transvaal (South African Republic) greater independence. Germany annexes South-West Africa.

1885 Bechuanaland annexed by Britain to prevent westward and eastward expansion by Boer Republics and German SW Africa respectively.

1886 Gold discovered in Witwatersrand (Transvaal); influx of British and foreign immigrants ('Uitlanders').

1887 Zululand annexed by Britain to prevent Boer expansion to east coast.

1890 Cecil Rhodes's British South Africa Co. occupies and establishes Rhodesia (Matabeleland and Mashonaland) on Transvaal's northern frontier. Rhodes Prime Minister of Cape Colony.

1895 Britain links Cape Colony to Natal and blocks Transvaal's access to Indian Ocean by annexation of Kaffraria (1875), St Lucia Bay (1884), Pondoland (1893) and Togoland (1895). Pretoria-Delagoa Bay (Portuguese East Africa) Railway opened.

1896 Jameson's Raid into Transvaal in support of Uitlanders defeated. Rhodes resigns as Cape Premier.

1897 Sir Alfred Milner appointed British High Commissioner at Cape. Military pact between Transvaal and OFS. Transvaal re-arms.

1899 **March.** British Uitlanders petition, with Milner's support, for British Government intercession. **June.** Bloemfontein Conference (Kruger-Milner). Milner breaks off negotiations. **August.** Uitlanders begin leaving Transvaal. **September.** British Government authorizes 10,000 reinforcements for Natal garrison. Transvaal and OFS mobilize. **October.** 1st Army Corps mobilized in Britain. Kruger issues ultimatum, expiring 11 October.

1899–1902 THE SECOND BOER WAR.

FOREWORD

This book is the fourth in a series of illustrated narrative histories of the British Army's colonial campaigns in the last century. It seeks to outline, within the confines of one volume, Britain's attempts to deprive the Afrikaners of the independence they had striven for since the seventeenth century, not only during the Anglo-Boer War of 1899–1902 but also in the earlier clashes between Briton and Boer since Britain acquired the Cape of Good Hope in the Napoleonic War.

This is primarily an account of military operations and, since both protagonists endeavoured to maintain a policy of 'a white man's war', the reader will find little mention of the black South Africans who dominate today's headlines. Although the Anglo-Boer Wars may appear to have little relevance to those headlines, they nevertheless reveal the influences that have moulded the Afrikaners and their tenacity in opposing the might of the British Empire, thus affording some insight into the national character and determination of their descendants.

To assist the reader to visualise the stern and stubborn Afrikaners of earlier generations, together with the British, Canadian, Australian, New Zealand and British South African soldiers who confronted them in the nineteenth century, the text is complemented by a large number of illustrations from a variety of sources which are listed in the Picture Credits. For help in their assembly and in other matters the author must acknowledge a debt of gratitude to the following: Major D. Baxter, Mr René Chartrand, Miss Alison Foster, Mrs M. Harding, Mr I.J. Knight, Mr R.J. Marrion, Brigadier J.P. Randle, Miss J.M. Spencer-Smith, Mr Peter Stanley, Colonel P.S. Walton, Mr M. Willis and Miss Clare Wright. Thanks are also due to Mr Barry Gregory for proposing the work, Mr Michael Burns for editorial assistance, Mrs Sheila Watson for supervising the author's interests and to the London Library for its excellent service.

M.J.B.
Jersey,
Channel Islands

1. THE IRRECONCILABLES
1815—1880

Five days before Christmas in the year 1880 part of a largely Irish regiment, the 94th Foot, was marching peacefully through the Transvaal towards the capital and seat of the British administration, Pretoria. The column, led by the colonel and the band, was completed by some ox wagons and mule carts, laden with baggage and soldiers' families. From a distance the white helmets, red coats faced with green and white equipment made a brave if conspicuous show against the surrounding grasslands, but a closer inspection would have revealed how travel-stained the soldiers were. They had been marching across the veldt, sometimes under heavy rain, sometimes under a brilliant sun, for a fortnight.

Fifteen months before they had stood in the square at Ulundi, pouring volleys into the faltering and final charges of the Zulu impis. Three months later they had helped to flush out the Bapedi chief, Sekukini, from his stronghold north of Lydenburg. Since then, however, their lot had been garrison duties in the scattered 'dorps' of the Transvaal, small, sleepy, tin-roofed townships with their sullen, brooding Afrikaner inhabitants, where boredom drove a soldier to drink or thoughts of desertion. Two weeks before they had set out from one such dorp, Lydenburg. But now there were only 40 more miles to go, it would soon be Christmas, and Pretoria could hardly be a worse station than Lydenburg. The 94th's spirits lifted as they tramped along, sucking at peaches they had earlier gathered from an orchard. When the track began to descend to a stream where they were to halt for the night, the band struck up a popular tune of the day, 'Kiss me, Mother, Kiss your Darling'.

Although the bandmaster's choice of music can hardly have been inspired by a sense of foreboding, within half an hour he and 56 of his comrades were dead and nearly 100 had been wounded, 20 of them fatally. The sentimental words so carelessly sung to the band's music such a short while before now had a savage truth:

Tell the loved ones not to murmur,
Say I died our flag to save,
And that I shall slumber sweetly
In the soldier's honoured grave.

As the column approached the stream, a party of 200 armed Boers suddenly rode over a ridge to its left. The Boer leader informed the British commanding officer, Lieutenant-Colonel Anstruther, that the Transvaal was now once again a Republic, and that any further advance by the troops would be an act of war. Anstruther refused to turn back and ordered the ammunition to be distributed. The Boers rode forward to within 200 yards, dismounted and opened a heavy fire into the packed ranks of the astonished and ill-prepared column. Fifteen minutes later, with all his officers dead or wounded, the dying Anstruther ordered the remains of his regiment to surrender. And so, at Bronkhorst Spruit, were fired the opening shots of the Transvaal War or, to the Boers, the First War of Independence. Here, some twenty years later when war again covered the land, peach trees, fertilized by the fruit in the dead soldiers' haversacks, blossomed over 'the honoured graves.'

The short campaign that followed the ambuscade at Bronkhorst Spruit was not the first passage of arms between Briton and Boer since the two white races had first confronted each other at the beginning of the 19th century. The Boers, convinced of their racial superiority over the indigenous inhabitants—the progeny of Ham and his son, Canaan, condemned to be 'servant of servants'—were often to regret that white men should fight each other in South Africa. Yet it was almost inevitable that the two should conflict. Britain had acquired the Cape from the Dutch Government during the Napoleonic Wars to protect the route to its possessions in India. British interest in the area, therefore, was at first strategic

and commercial. For the Boers it was their own land where they had been settled for generations, which they had fought for and carved out of a wilderness. The British were benevolent and even-handed towards the natives. But the Boers regarded the aboriginal Bushmen and Hottentots as inferiors, to be used as slaves or servants and accordingly looked after but kept firmly in their place, and the Kaffirs and Zulus from the north as implacable enemies who threatened their homes, farms and families. The British favoured an orderly, progressive and financially sound administration. The Boers, by contrast, were almost anarchic, disdaining anything that interfered with or threatened each individual's freedom and way of life. Even when danger forced them to combine in their commandos, each remained his own man, coming or going as he pleased. Indeed nothing afforded a greater contrast between the two races than their military methods. The Boer wore no uniform, drew no pay, provided his own horse and weapon and fought in very democratic, loosely structured formations. The British in the colonies relied chiefly on infantry—uniformed regulars, armed with rifle and bayonet but usually more proficient with the latter, formed into rigid, hierarchical battalions which drew their strength from discipline instilled by close-order drill. The sight of British soldiers marching in step to shouted

Scene of the action at Bronkhorst Spruit on 20 December 1880 between the Transvaalers and Anstruther's 94th Regiment.

commands astonished, even disgusted, the Boers, whose confidence was built upon self-discipline, skill at arms and horsemanship bred in each family since birth. The British soldier fought for pay and because he was under orders; the Boer for love of his land and the need to survive.

The Boers' self-confidence in their military prowess in the first half of the 19th century stemmed from the robust, often dangerous lives they led daily on the frontiers of civilization, the defeats they had inflicted on numerically superior, though primitive, enemies and the certainty that God was on their side. Yet in their early skirmishes with the British the Almighty did not always favour their cause. The first event to herald the approaching discord between the white races occurred in 1815, four months after the Battle of Waterloo. A Boer named Frederick Bezuidenhout, living alone on a remote farm, was summoned to answer charges of ill-treating a Hottentot servant. Unwilling to risk his property while travelling to the nearest town, he ignored the summons. Some locally enlisted Hottentot soldiers were sent to arrest him and in the ensuing struggle he was killed. A body of armed burghers, led by his

9

Mrs. Smith, wife of the Bandmaster, 94th Regt, at Bronkers Spruit. 1880.

Cigarette card from a series 'Heroic Deeds' depicting the tending of the 94th's wounded under fire at Bronkhorst Spruit by Mrs Smith, wife of the regiment's bandmaster, who was killed.

erupted after 1834, following the abolition of slavery with inadequate compensation for the owners. From 1836 some 12,000 Boers, men, women and children, trekked north across unmapped country to find new lands where they could live according to their own principles and beliefs. Though technically they were all British subjects, the Cape authorities did nothing to stop them, confident that privations and death would ensure their return. But the Boers, with little but their Bibles and muskets to sustain them, beset by hunger, thirst and fever, attacked by wild animals and ferocious savages, pressed on against all odds, fanning out across the Orange and Vaal rivers, searching for their promised land like the Israelites of the Old Testament with whom they so strongly identified. Among the wagons was a family named Kruger with their ten-year-old son Paul, whose experiences in this great exodus were to mould him into one of the most outstanding leaders of his race.

From the top of a whale-shaped height they called Spion Kop, or Look-Out Hill, some gazed down across the River Tugela at the fertile, rolling countryside of Natal. Here they encountered Dingaan's Zulus, the most feared tribe in Africa. After the treacherous murder of their leader, Piet Retief, and some of his followers while under promises of safe conduct, the Boers led by Andries Pretorius sought revenge. On 16 December 1838, at Blood River, 500 Boers fought 11,000 Zulus, killing 3,000 of them and forcing the remainder to flee back to Zululand. This group of Boers then settled in the land they had won and established the Republic of Natalia.

But even here they were not free of the British. Since 1824, a small British trading settlement had existed under Zulu sufferance at Port Natal, later Durban. The settlers had made periodic requests to the Cape for the annexation by the Crown of their settlement, but to no avail. However the discovery of coal in Natal and the strategic value of a port at Durban caused the British authorities to reconsider. Reports of Boer ill-treatment of the natives in Natalia—with the consequent possibility of dispossessed tribes making for the Cape—led to the despatch of two companies of the 27th (Inniskilling) Regiment with two guns under Captain T.C.Smith, a Waterloo veteran. He marched north up the coast and in May 1842 arrived near Durban, fortifying a laager.

After all they had endured, Pretorius and his followers had no intention of submitting again to

brother, set out in pursuit of the Hottentot soldiery to exact revenge, but were captured by a troop of British Light Dragoons. The burghers were put on trial for insurgency, all admitted their guilt and six ringleaders were hanged at the place where they had assembled—Slachter's Nek.

Memories of Slachter's Nek, political equality for the natives and other instances of what the Boers regarded as British interference all built up a head of steam in the Boer consciousness which finally

British rule. Negotiations having failed, Pretorius led a commando against Smith's troops. Outnumbered by three to one, Smith fell back to his laager, sending a young white hunter, Dick King, riding south for reinforcements from Grahamstown. King had 458 miles of difficult and dangerous country to cover, but he accomplished the journey in nine days. More troops were sent up by sea and, exactly one month after King had set out, they fought their way ashore to Smith's laager, which was still holding out. Dismayed by this turn of events, the Boers dispersed. Britain formally annexed Natal in the following year; British immigration to the new colony was intensified and the discouraged Boers trekked back over the Drakensberg into the Transvaal.

Those Boers who had established the Orange Free State north of the Orange River also found the Imperial arm longer than they had anticipated. Again the cause was friction between the Boers and the local inhabitants, in this case the Griquas, a collection of mixed race settlers who were recognized as British subjects. In April 1845 fighting broke out and the 7th Dragoon Guards under Lieutenant-Colonel Richardson were sent up from Fort Beaufort to restore order. Encountering a 400-strong commando at Zwartkopjes, Richardson rapidly drove the Boers from their position and all fighting ceased. A British Resident, Major Warden, was appointed at Bloemfontein with a troop of Cape Mounted Rifles[1] to keep order. Apart from a successful skirmish against some disaffected Boers at the Vet River in June 1846, the country remained quiet.

On 3 February 1848 Sir Harry Smith, Governor at

Typical Boer family with black servants on a farm close to Bronkhorst Spruit.

the Cape, annexed the Free State as the Orange River Sovereignty. The Free Staters reluctantly submitted until down from the Transvaal came Pretorius with 200 burghers to rouse them to arms. Joined by 800 Free Staters he forced Warden to evacuate Bloemfontein and, riding south, took up a position at Boomplaats to ambush the British advance he was sure would come.

Smith, a former Rifleman of the Peninsular War and Waterloo, accepted the challenge and marched north across the Orange with 600 men[2] on 26 August. Pretorius had concealed his burghers along a ridge of low hills which formed a horseshoe around the road up which Smith had to advance. Behind this position were a stream and higher hills on which Pretorius placed a party with a gun to make Smith believe this was the main position and to which his forward burghers could fall back if necessary. On 29 August Smith approached. Riding forward to scout the hillocks on the right of the road the advanced guard of Cape Mounted Rifles came under fire from the Boer left. At the same time the Boer centre opened fire. Smith withdrew the CMR to his left and sent forward the 45th and Rifle Brigade covered by artillery to outflank the Boer left. The Boer right rode out from cover to attack Smith's wagons but were driven back by gunfire and the CMR. Meanwhile, the infantry on the right had advanced so rapidly that the Boers opposing them were unable to regain their horses and

11

had to run back towards their centre under fire from the artillery which had come quickly into action on the captured position. All the Boers now fell back to make a stand above the stream, but Smith's infantry continued to press forward covered by the guns and, one hour after the first shots had been fired, the Boers were in full retreat. They made some attempt at a rearguard action but were continually pressed and finally dispersed. Despite their mobility, marksmanship and sound choice of ground they had been unable to resist Smith's coordination of guns and infantry and the speed of his attack. The apparent ease with which small British Regular forces had by this date overcome superior numbers of armed farmers on three separate occasions bequeathed a legacy among the British of contempt for the Boers' fighting quality.

After Boomplaats, Boer insurgency in the Orange River Sovereignty collapsed. Pretorius escaped back to the Transvaal, determined to halt any further British encroachment into his territory. However an anti-colonial mood now gripped the British Government, which was concerned at the cost of South African operations against the Boers and the Kaffirs, who were again threatening the eastern frontier of Cape Colony. Sir Harry Smith was recalled and in 1852 the independence of the Transvaal was recognized, followed two years later by a similar undertaking for the Orange Free State. At last, it seemed, the purposes of the Great Trek would be fulfilled and the Boers would be allowed to live their simple pastoral lives unfettered by the machinery of governments and insulated from the outside and, to their minds, sinful world.

But there were too many pressures and influences at work in the second half of the 19th century for them to exist undisturbed. In the Transvaal, where the backwoods mentality was more pronounced than in the increasingly more sophisticated Free State, the nomadic nature and racial attitudes of the Boers provoked endless disputes over land with warlike native tribes. These disputes could at any time boil over into widespread uprisings. Furthermore the Boers' fierce independence, contempt for regulations and narrow religious views bred disunity and controversy among themselves, making the establishment of a centralized government almost impossible. Not until 1864 was the Transvaal welded into a single Republic with one President, but even then few

Contemporary pencil drawing showing the difficulties of the march of the 27th Regiment under Captain T.C. Smith from Grahamstown northwards in 1841.

burghers saw any reason to change their uncooperative attitudes. Thus it was surprising when, in 1872, T.F. Burgers was elected President, because Burgers was a man of European education and manners, with progressive and enlightened ideas for turning the Transvaal into a modern State. When the Transvaalers began to appreciate what changes to their traditional way of life Burgers' plans would entail, the Boer capacity for pig-headed stubbornness asserted itself and Burgers' well-intentioned measures were thwarted at every turn.

Meanwhile other portentous events were happening. Small traces of gold had been found in the Transvaal before Burgers took over but, far from exploiting this discovery to relieve their State's near-penury, the Transvaalers, believing that no good could come of it, did their best to hush it up. Then diamonds were discovered in huge quantities around Kimberley, near the joint borders of the Transvaal, Free State and Cape Colony. At the Cape's instigation the land was claimed by and, after somewhat dubious arbitration, allotted to a Griqua chief who then allowed it to be declared a Crown Colony. This was subsequently annexed to the Cape, which paid compensation of nothing like the true value to the Free State. This piece of sharp practice did nothing to improve relations between the British territories and

the Boer Republics, but it transformed the economic prospects of the Cape, which in 1872 was granted internal autonomy. Furthermore the ensuing diamond rush attracted an influx of immigrants all bent on self-enrichment which endangered the status quo of an already sensitive area and whose morals and behaviour outraged the Boers' strict Calvinism.

Though an alternative route to the East was now available to Britain through the Suez Canal, South Africa still commanded the Indian Ocean and therefore had to be denied to foreign powers; to its strategic value was now added the potential wealth of its new-found minerals. Yet the tensions stemming from the diversity of its peoples and territories—colonies, republics, native states and tribal lands—made for instability and conflict, threatening the security of the whole region with the consequent certainty of increased expenditure and military effort if British interests were to be maintained. It seemed to the Home Government that the best policy to achieve peace and order at minimum cost was to work towards a federation of self-governing territories, including the Boer Republics, as had recently been achieved in Canada. This had been mooted unsuccessfully by the Liberal administration before

1874, but the Conservative Colonial Secretary, Lord Carnavon, persevered, despatching a mission under General Sir Garnet Wolseley to pave the way with the different territories. Notwithstanding the generally unfavourable response accorded to Wolseley, Carnavon called a conference in London in 1876. The Transvaal refused to attend, the Free State was only interested in discussing its loss of the diamond fields, and the now prosperous Cape was unwilling to yoke itself to the others with their weak economies and troublesome native problems.

The failure of the London Conference was aggravated by the Transvaal's apparent incompetence to manage its own affairs. It was bankrupt and disunited, President Burgers having failed to convince his countrymen of their civic responsibilities; it had been unable to subdue the rebellious Bapedi chief, Sekukini; and it was in dispute with the even more dangerous Zulus over some territory on the Blood River. Sekukini's success could well

13

Statue at Durban of Dick King. With one Zulu companion, he avoided his Boer pursuers and covered the normally three-week-long journey from Durban to Grahamstown in nine days to summon help for Smith.

citizens and without bloodshed. After four months of cunningly exploiting the disunity and impoverishment of the Transvaal Government, Shepstone formally annexed the country on 12 April 1877 with the apparent, if private, acquiescence of Burgers and most of his ministers and to the satisfaction of many merchants and traders in the capital, most of whom were of British extraction.

By August 1879 a British army, after initial reverses, had eliminated the Zulu threat; by the end of the year it had disposed of Sekukini. Apart from a few individuals, the Transvaalers had contributed nothing to the destruction of their two chief native enemies. They had preferred to watch British blood being spilled and, indeed, had drawn considerable satisfaction from the vulnerability of British troops early in the Zulu War. But even before then it had become clear that the annexation was by no means as popular in the Transvaal as Shepstone and Carnavon had believed, or wished to believe, particularly among the outlying burghers.

Resentment against British occupation and administration began to crystallize around the one-time boy of the Great Trek, Paul Kruger, who before annexation had been elected Vice-President to oppose Burgers' policies. Kruger had the sympathy of the Orange Free State and of Liberals in England, where he led two delegations to protest against annexation. On the second occasion he armed himself with a petition opposing annexation, signed by over 6,000 burghers out of a male suffrage of 8,000. Although the British Government undertook to consider local autonomy for the Transvaal in the future, it made clear that complete independence would not be restored. Kruger returned rebuffed and revengeful. Boer indignation increased apace, fed by British administrators' insensitivity towards Boer customs and sympathy towards the interests of the Africans. Nor was it in any way diminished by the appointment of Colonel Owen Lanyon to be Shepstone's successor as Administrator of the Transvaal. Lanyon was an overbearing, slow-witted man whose dark complexion, the result of service in the West India Regiment, raised serious doubts in Boer minds about his racial origins. The trouble was that, while the Boers were concerned about his antecedents, he was unconcerned about their aspirations.

Far from being grateful for the crushing of the

encourage the Zulus into belligerence, with dire results not only for the Transvaal but for Natal as well. So fragile did the Transvaal's position seem to be that Carnavon was persuaded that its only hope lay in British protection and sound administration via annexation, which later could serve as a renewed step towards federation. Accordingly he sent to Pretoria Sir Theopilus Shepstone, an experienced colonial administrator then responsible for native affairs in Natal, ostensibly to report on the situation but also with powers to annex the Transvaal if this could be done with the agreement of a majority of its

Action at Zwartkopjes, 30 April 1845. In the centre a troop of 7th Dragoon Guards is firing from the saddle to cover the advance of another troop on its left, supported by Griqua levies in the right foreground.

Zulus and Sekukini, the Transvaalers maintained that the removal of these threats meant that British military occupation of their country was no longer justifiable. Mass meetings protested against the occupation and the British denial of legitimate Boer rights. Sir Bartle Frere, the High Commissioner for South Africa, appreciating that Boer individualism was turning into nationalism, urged upon the Home Government the need to grant some self-government to the Transvaal if armed rebellion was to be averted. However Frere was out of favour at home for precipitating the Zulu War and his responsibilities for the Transvaal were handed over to Wolseley[3], who lost no time in reminding the Boers that 'the Vaal River would flow backwards through the Drakensberg sooner than the British would be withdrawn from the Transvaal'.

By the end of 1879 the nationalists had become more militant, with open defiance of the Queen's authority. Wolseley disposed of only 3,600 troops, all infantry except for the King's Dragoon Guards, to cover the whole Transvaal, an area almost twice the size of England and Wales. He now ordered redoubts to be built at eight locations spread over the country. These were to be garrisoned by infantry companies, while a movable column was to be stationed at Pretoria; this force, he considered 'amply sufficient to destroy any forces the Boers can collect'.

However the Boers, led by Kruger and Piet Joubert, still believed they could achieve their aims peacefully. In March 1880 Gladstone and the Liberals, who in opposition had repeatedly denounced the annexation, replaced the Conservative Government which had been in power in Britain since 1874. Confident that independence would soon be granted, the Transvaal quietened down. In the belief that his show of force had cowed the Boers into submission, Wolseley asked for, and was granted, permission to hand over his duties to his protegé, Major-General Sir George Pomeroy-Colley. Encouraged by the apparent calm, assured by the obtuse Lanyon that the Boers would not fight, and urged by the new Government to make economies, Colley reduced the outlying garrisons to five and the entire force in the Transvaal to two infantry battalions, each consisting of eight companies and one Mounted Infantry (MI) company. These were the 2nd Battalion 21st Royal Scots Fusiliers, which, apart from one company in Natal, was held mainly in Pretoria, and the 94th Regiment, which was spread

Bloemfontein, capital of the Orange Free State, in the mid-19th century.

through the outstations. One of the regiments withdrawn was the King's Dragoon Guards, so the officer in command of troops, Colonel Bellairs, had no mounted force available to him except the two weak companies of MI.

Bellairs had expressed misgivings about these withdrawals and by November his fears were proved right. Gladstone had found that undertakings pledged in opposition proved inexpedient to fulfill in office. His Cabinet was divided over the Transvaal, some believing that only continued British rule could protect the Africans, others that the Boers' demands should be met, while a third element wished to maintain British prestige, albeit at minimum cost. For Gladstone, preoccupied with the Irish problem, Cabinet unity and retention of office were more important than the grumblings of some disaffected farmers thousands of miles away, however much he deplored Tory Imperialism. Reassured by the complacent reports of officials on the spot he informed Kruger that 'the Queen cannot be advised to relinquish her sovereignty over the Transvaal'.

Kruger and Joubert now realized they had no choice but to fight for independence. Well aware of the force reductions and the precise deployment of the remaining garrison, they secretly prepared their men, allotting no more than were necessary to contain the scattered outstations and Pretoria so as to leave a sufficient force to halt British reinforcements from Natal.

At Pretoria Lanyon was absorbed in a scheme for more efficient tax collection, totally oblivious to the likely effect of Gladstone's decision and incredulous of such reports that reached him of the Boers' intention to fight. On 14 November his complacency received a mild jolt. Armed burghers rode into Potchefstroom to prevent the auction by a magistrate of a wagon seized in distraint from a man named—in an ominous echo of Slachter's Nek—Piet Bezuidenhout, who had been summonsed for tax arrears. Lanyon's unworried response was to order two companies of the 2/21st with two guns and some MI to Potchefstroom to restore order and build a redoubt. Bellairs, more prescient than his superior, urged the withdrawal to Pretoria of some of the 94th from the more distant stations of Marabastadt and Lydenburg, but Lanyon took a week to agree. Still he maintained 'there was not much cause for anxiety', though he did ask Colley to send reinforcements from Natal.

Sir Henry Bartle Frere, High Commissioner for South Africa.   Viscount Wolseley.

Paul Kruger, President of the Transvaal.   General Piet Joubert.

Sir Harry Smith's defeat of the Boers at Boomplaats, 29 August 1848. The Boers are retreating as the 45th and Rifle Brigade advance firing towards the stream.

On 13 December some 4,000 Boers assembled between Potchefstroom and Pretoria. Appointing a triumvirate of Kruger, Joubert and ex-President Pretorius (son of the famous Andries) as their leaders, they pronounced the Republic re-constituted and swore to fight for their freedom. Two days later Piet Cronje led 500 armed burghers into Potchefstroom to have the proclamation of independence run off on the town's printing press. The 2/21st companies from Pretoria were taunted by the burghers with cowardice and shots were fired. Outnumbered, the troops retired to their redoubt and were immediately invested by Cronje.

Lanyon had been sufficiently alarmed by the Boer gathering to declare it illegal, but he was still unable to understand 'what can have so suddenly caused the Boers to act as they have'. Even so, he reported to Colley, 'I do not feel anxious for I know these people cannot be united'. But his complacency was jolted again when the Boers demanded the keys of the Government offices within 24 hours, and finally shattered when he heard the appalling news of the near-decimation of Anstruther's column at Bronkhorst Spruit on 20 December[4]. Had Anstruther marched from Lydenburg with more despatch he could have reached Pretoria safely, as had his company and MI from Marabastadt, which had

arrived on 10 December. Three companies of the 58th Regiment, which Colley had released from Natal, had marched up to the southernmost garrison towns, but there was nothing else Lanyon could do: like all the Transvaal garrisons, he was now himself besieged.

The Boers had managed to muster 6–7,000 men under arms. Joubert took 2,000 to the Natal frontier, leaving the remainder to invest the garrisons. These were spread over the country from Wakkerstroom and Standerton in the south to Marabastadt (some 230 miles away) in the north, and from Potchefstroom and Rustenburg in the west to Lydenburg (a similar distance) in the north-east. All, except Rustenburg, were over 100 miles from the central garrison at Pretoria and the nearest any two garrisons were to each other was 50 miles—and that as the crow flies. The strength of the garrisons ranged from some 1,700 effectives (including irregular volunteers) with two guns at Pretoria to the 50-odd left behind by Anstruther at Lydenburg. The others had from one to three infantry companies each, with few or no mounted men and no artillery.

The morale and discipline of all these troops in the scattered garrisons had not hitherto been high— these were some of the most isolated and unpopular stations in the world. Now, besieged in each case by equal or superior numbers and without hope of support from each other, they had no choice but to buckle down to their own defence in the hope that relief would come up from Natal. In the Forties their forebears had proved more than a match for the Boer farmers. Surely history would repeat itself?

2. UNFIT FOR A CORPORAL'S GUARD

JANUARY–FEBRUARY 1881

The man to whom the Transvaal garrisons looked for relief was Sir George Pomeroy-Colley who, in addition to his political duties as High Commissioner for South-East Africa, was in overall command of all troops in Natal and the Transvaal. Then aged 45, this Protestant Irishman had reached his local rank of major-general after a career of great promise. He had passed out top from Sandhurst, seen active service as a junior officer at the Cape and in China and graduated from the Staff College with the highest marks ever achieved. Scholarly, interested in the Arts, he had earned Wolseley's high regard and became a member of Wolseley's famous 'Ring' for his work as a staff officer during the Ashanti campaign in 1874. Thereafter, apart from a spell as Military Secretary to the Viceroy of India, his career followed at Wolseley's right hand. A modest and chivalrous man of much charm, he endeavoured always to emulate his hero, the great Confederate Robert E. Lee, who combined eminent military qualities with a gentle and kindly nature. But his reputation as 'the best instructed soldier' and 'the incarnation of intelligence' was based solely on his work as a staff officer, much of it of a quasi-political nature, and he had never held an independent command of troops. Though undoubtedly ambitious, he was deeply sensitive and possessed a need for reassurance. It remained to be seen whether his recently acquired wife, who had inherited many of the forceful attributes of her father, General 'Tiger' Hamilton, and was as ambitious as her husband, might compensate for this infrequently observed weakness in his character.

Colley had no doubts about the quality of the British soldier; he had asserted in India that '500 men with breech-loaders could ordinarily overcome any opposition' on the North-West Frontier. He now had to show that double that number could do the same in the Transvaal. Reinforcements had been summoned,

seasoned regiments from the Afghan War (where his assertion had proved fallacious), but it would be mid-February before they could reach him from India and Colley doubted whether the besieged garrisons could hold out that long. He was particularly concerned at the shortage of food at Potchefstroom. He decided that an attempt must be made to reach at least the nearest garrisons at Wakkerstroom and Standerton with the troops he had available in Natal, in the hope that an advance north would force the Boers to divert men from the other sieges to confront him. He was aware that he could muster immediately only some thousand men but, recalling the Boers' poor performance at Boomplaats and against Sekukini, he assessed that the risk of not waiting for reinforcements was worth taking. Orders went out for a concentration at Newcastle, 25 miles from the border at Laing's Nek.

The main element of Colley's force was 11 companies of infantry—five of the 58th (Rutlandshire) Regiment, five of 3rd Battalion 60th Rifles and one of the 2/21st. He was very weak in mounted troops, having only an *ad hoc* squadron of 150 men— 25 men of the King's Dragoon Guards, left behind when that regiment sailed for India, some Mounted Infantry, Army Service Corps drivers and Natal Mounted Police—under the command of Major Brownlow KDG. The artillery, from which much was expected because it was thought the Boers would not stand shell-fire, was a makeshift battery, hurriedly organized by Captain Greer RA, of four 9-pounders and two 7-pounders drawn from store in Durban and manned by mixed crews of Royal Artillery and infantrymen. Finally there were 120 men of the Royal Navy with two Gatlings and three rocket tubes under Commander Romilly RN, rushed up from HMS *Boadicea* lying off Durban. Excluding non-combatants, Colley thus had only some 1,200 men to fight their way through, at most, 7,000 Boers in order

19

to relieve about 2,000 soldiers spread all over the Transvaal. Furthermore Colley's speed of action was limited to the marching pace of an infantryman; the Boers' to that of a good horse.

One criticism later levied against this Natal Field Force was that its infantrymen were all products of the controversial short-service system, introduced in 1870 as part of Cardwell's reforms and strongly supported by Wolseley, whereby men enlisted for only six years with the Colours and six on the Reserve. The long-service engagement that the new system replaced was still favoured by conservative elements in the Army, including Wolseley's chief rival, Sir Frederick Roberts, who had recently achieved fame in the Afghan War with long-service soldiers. But although Colley's battalions contained a number of recently joined young soldiers, they contained also experienced campaigners, because both battalions had taken part in the latter stage of the Zulu War. Nor were the men reluctant for the task ahead. Private Tuck of the 58th noted in his diary: 'Our men are now very eager to advance and relieve our other men who are already up there'. Their stamina proved their spirit—despite a long uphill march to Newcastle from central Natal, with torrential rain churning the road into a quagmire and the cumbersome ox-drawn wagons slowing them down, they still managed to average 18 miles a day. On Christmas Day itself they covered 20 miles—a feat for which each man received a quart of beer.

By 24 January 1881 the Field Force had completed its concentration and the advance to the frontier began. Boer patrols had been spotted observing the troop movements from high ground for over a fortnight and when the column reached its last camping ground at Mount Prospect, three miles from the frontier, the Boer numbers had greatly increased and some could be seen building schanzes[5] astride the road where it passed over a col about 300 feet high at Laing's Nek. To break through into the Transvaal along this axis from Mount Prospect Colley's men would have to cross a grassy, undulating plateau which, as it approached Laing's Nek, was channelled into a crescent of high ground with a steep ascent on the Natal side. At the western end stood the flat-topped Majuba Hill, 6,600 feet above sea level, from which spurs ran back and down to Laing's Nek. East of the road rose a table hill, which bent slightly to the south-east and stood some 600 feet above the plateau,

Major-General Sir George Pomeroy-Colley, in the dress he wore during Wolseley's Ashanti campaign of 1874.

the highest point being at its eastern end. Connected to the table hill by a col, and still in a south-easterly direction, was a detached conical hill from which the ground fell away to the Buffalo River, flowing in a deep ravine, which then marked the Transvaal border. At the foot of the heights were lateral watercourses, fed by smaller tributaries from the high ground. Two of these descended to the plateau on either side of a spur running down from the eastern end of the table hill.

The Natal Field Force on the march to the frontier. Engraving from *The Graphic*.

Not only were the approaches from Mount Prospect completely overlooked by this high ground, but the Transvaalers had established their wagon laagers out of sight behind it, so that it was difficult for Colley to assess their strength. In the account he later wrote for Wolseley, the only specific reference to Boer numbers is one of 'probably 200 men' holding the conical hill to his right. He realized that the Boers, whom he guessed to be about 2,000 in all, were extended all along the high ground—a wide deployment he claimed to have forced on them by the central position he had taken up at Mount Prospect, which left them in doubt as to his point of attack.

With the small force at his disposal he decided against first dealing with the conical hill, as ideally he would have wished to do, as this would have allowed the enemy time to reinforce their left from their centre and right. He therefore settled for a frontal attack covered by artillery upon the high, eastern end of the table hill, which he conceived to be the key of the position. He decided to use the 440 bayonets of the 58th, with their right flank protected

21

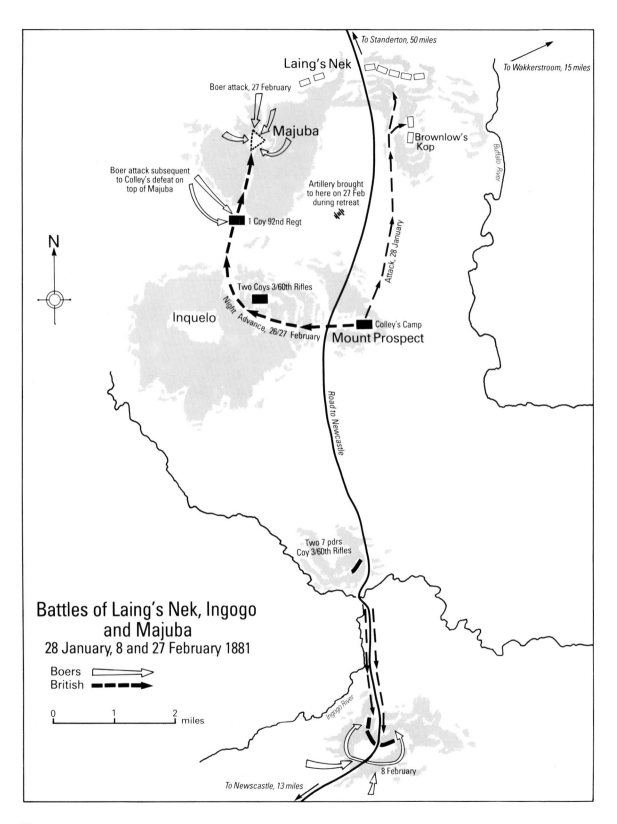

To Standerton, 50 miles

To Wakkerstroom, 15 miles

Laing's Nek

Boer attack, 27 February

Majuba

Brownlow's Kop

Boer attack subsequent
to Colley's defeat on
top of Majuba

Artillery brought
to here on 27 Feb
during retreat

Attack, 28 January

1 Coy 92nd Regt

Two Coys 3/60th Rifles

Inquelo

Night Advance, 26/27 February

Colley's Camp

Mount Prospect

N

Buffalo River

Road to Newcastle

Two 7 pdrs
Coy 3/60th Rifles

Battles of Laing's Nek, Ingogo
and Majuba
28 January, 8 and 27 February 1881

Boers
British

0   1   2
miles

Ingogo River

8 February

To Newcastle, 13 miles

from the conical hill by the mounted squadron, holding the 60th Rifles in reserve. One 60th company and the 2/21st company with the Gatlings were to guard the camp.

Colley's chief staff officer, Colonel Deane, who was appointed to lead the attack, believed the 58th to be 'one of the best [battalions] in the service'. As such, though without three of its companies and with a steep, uphill and exposed assault to make, it was doubtless capable of overcoming any number of undisciplined Boer farmers who would probably run away. Colley must have been aware of his mentor Wolseley's dictum that, against a well-trained British battalion in a defensive position, 'twice, nay thrice its numbers of the very best troops in the world would be easily destroyed by it'. He seems to have believed that if the battalion was attacking and the defenders were only armed civilians,[6] it could still overcome thrice its strength.

On the morning of 28 January the force advanced from Mount Prospect and at 9.15 a.m. halted on a low ridge just out of rifle range from the heights. Colley pushed out the Royal Navy detachment with its rockets and a protective company of the 60th to a walled enclosure just to the right of the road, whence the rockets opened fire at Laing's Nek itself and the reverse slopes behind. The six guns went into action against the Boer schanzes on the table hill from a central position amid the remaining three companies of the 60th and 70 Natal Mounted Police. As the guns began to get the range the 58th and Brownlow's mounted squadron were ordered to the attack.

To the Boers watching from the heights it must have been an astonishing sight. Five companies of 'Rooibaadjes' or Redcoats advancing parallel to one another, each in its column of fours, their white helmets and scarlet coats brilliant against the green of the plateau, and in their midst, as had always been the custom of British infantry going into action, the Colours unfurled—two large, heavy standards nearly six feet square, the Union flag for the Queen's Colour and St George's Cross on a black ground for the Regimental, each carried by its ensign. Tempting though such a target was, the guns were keeping the Boers' heads down so they held their fire and lay low behind their schanzes.

As the 58th marched steadily towards the foot of the spur leading up to the eastern end of the table hill, Brownlow went prematurely into action. Colley's intention had been that, when the 58th had ascended that part of the spur which, owing to its convexity, was in dead ground from the top, Brownlow was to make for the col between the table and conical hills and then either attack the latter or continue his advance, whichever would best protect

Mount Prospect camp with Laing's Nek on the skyline beyond and Majuba Hill to the left.

TABLE HILL 600.FT

POINT OF FINAL
REPULSE X JAN 28.1881

10th RIFLES

Panorama of the attack at Laing's Nek showing, centre
background, the table hill assaulted by the 58th, the light-
coloured col to its right, and the conical hill, right. Brownlow
halted at the point marked 'O'.

the 58th's right. Either these orders had been unclear
or Brownlow had misunderstood them, because he
charged the conical hill before the 58th had even
begun to climb the spur. The leading troop, mostly
King's Dragoon Guards, neared the top only to be
met by a heavy fire from the Boers. Brownlow was
unhorsed and his subaltern killed. Troop-Sergeant-
Major Lunny got in alone among the Boers, firing his
revolver until he too was killed, as were two other
men. Private Dougan, though wounded, dismounted
to offer his horse to Brownlow and was hit again.
Seeing this reverse, the second troop turned about
and galloped downhill. The Boers, who had been
about to mount up and ride off, returned to their
positions, now with a perfect field of fire into the
right flank and rear of the 58th as they ascended the
spur.

Troubles began to multiply for the infantry. As the
lower part of their climb was out of sight of the crest,
the companies were still in close formation. The
intention was that they would deploy into attack
formation on reaching a ledge near the top of the
spur, which was within charging distance of the
crest, and go in with the bayonet. With their right
flank now exposed, they not only began to suffer
casualties, but command of the battalion was taken
out of the hands of the acting commanding officer,
Major Hingeston, and his regimental officers by
Colonel Deane and his four staff officers. Being
mounted, the latter kept urging the battalion on at a
pace which the infantrymen, laden with some 50 lbs
of equipment, found increasingly difficult to sustain
on the steep grassy slope made slippery by the
January rains. Nevertheless they reached the ledge,
albeit in some disorder, and flung themselves down
to regain their breath before the final charge. But
they were to have no respite or time to reorganize, for
Deane immediately ordered them to press on with the
bayonet. The artillery fire, from which the Boer
commander, Joubert, later admitted 'we suffered
heavily', had ceased so, as the 58th scrambled over
the ledge to charge, there was nothing to prevent the
Boer riflemen opening rapid fire into their ranks at

about 50 yards range. Deane and three of his staff
were killed and Major Hingeston severely wounded.
Captain Lovegrove, the acting second-in-command,
led the men on, but he too fell wounded. The Colour
party attracted much fire and Lieutenant Baillie with
the Regimental Colour went down, shouting to his
fellow ensign, Peel, 'Never mind me, save the
Colours'. Peel gathered up both Colours but fell into
an ant-bear hole. Thinking he had been hit, Colour-
Sergeant Bridgestock seized the Colours and, under
heavy fire, bore them away down the hill to hand
them over to the Quartermaster.[7]

Every attempt to get to grips with the Boers
withered under the devastating musketry, though
Joubert afterwards said that some 'came so near that
the dead on both sides fell in amongst each other'.
But he had now brought up more men to the
threatened point and Major Essex, the sole surviving

The 58th's attack at Laing's Nek. Lieutenant Monck, the
Adjutant, whose horse was shot, being encouraged by a fellow
Etonian, Lieutenant Elwes (Staff), who was then killed. Etching
after the painting 'Floreat Etona' by Lady Butler.

25

Boer defences astride the road through Laing's Nek. Looking west towards Majuba in background.

staff officer, seeing that the 58th had no chance as most of their officers were casualties, ordered them to retire. Hitherto the Boers had not left cover but, seeing the rearward move, they ran forward to fire down the slope, supported by their comrades on the conical hill, who fired into the flank of the hapless battalion. Covered by two companies, the remainder of the 58th fell back down the spur in good order, doing what they could for their wounded. Lieutenant Hill tried to carry the wounded Baillie down but the ensign was hit again and killed. Hill got another wounded man on to a horse and led him to safety, thereafter returning up the hill to rescue another casualty. Private Godfrey assisted Major Hingeston and Captain Lovegrove into the cover of a gully, remaining with them until help came to carry them to an ambulance. For these acts Hill was later awarded the Victoria Cross and Godfrey the Distinguished Conduct Medal, the latter award going also to Colour-Sergeant Bridgestock and Sergeant-Major Murray who, though twice wounded, remained behind to encourage the rearguard. The Victoria Cross was also granted to Private Dougan KDG.

At the foot of the hill the senior surviving regimental officer, Lieutenant Jopp, reformed the remains of the 58th behind the 3/60th whom Colley, seeing the attack's failure, had deployed to cover the final withdrawal. Captain Marling of the 60th, who had watched the whole attack, wrote afterwards: 'The 58th behaved with great gallantry. If the command of the Battalion had only been left in the hands of the Regimental officers, I firmly believe they would have carried the position'. Colley later admitted that, when Brownlow's charge failed, he had wanted to call off the infantry assault but felt it was too late to recall the 58th. As it was, one of his two battalions had lost a third of its strength and the Boers still blocked his route north. He concluded that the only course open to him was to return to Mount Prospect and await reinforcements.

That evening in camp Colley addressed his men, congratulating the 58th and characteristically taking all blame for the repulse upon himself. He was undoubtedly correct in accepting responsibility for his plan's failure, though Deane's conduct had been more like that of a reckless subaltern than a prudent staff officer. Deane's gallant, if foolhardy, death, however, absolved him from blame. Whether Colley was wise in publicly admitting his failure to men who had just suffered a bruising defeat and lost many of their comrades is questionable. He wrote to Wolseley that 'the troops are as cheery and confident as possible and only keen to go at it again', but the war correspondent T.F. Carter, joining the force next day, found 'a gloom around the camp'. Captain Lovegrove wrote after the battle that an attack such as the 58th had been called upon to undertake, relying on the bayonet against entrenched marksmen, was doomed to failure and was against 'the recognised principles of warfare'. This does not say much for Colley, 'the best instructed soldier'. The Victorian soldier was, in the main, a stoical creature who did not lose his morale on the strength of one defeat, but if the Natal Field Force's confidence in their general was not yet lost, it must have been shaken. Much would depend on what happened next.

The Boers, justifiably elated at their victory, had made no attempt to pursue and indeed Joubert demonstrated his humanity by agreeing to a truce so that the killed and wounded could be collected from the battlefield. In this lull the troops found that, though some of the younger Boers showed an arrogance and a callousness towards the wounded, the older men deplored the loss of life and restrained the others but at the same time making clear their determination to defend their country. With Colley's small force now attenuated by casualties, Joubert, still with some 2,000 burghers in arms,[8] might have risked an attack on Mount Prospect before reinforcements could arrive. However a vital principle impressed on all Boer commanders was the conservation of manpower, so Joubert decided to hold firm on the frontier but at the same time to disrupt Colley's line of communications back through Natal. Accordingly a 300-strong commando under Nicolas Smit was despatched to raid the road between Mount Prospect and Newcastle.

Colley first learned of this threat to his rear on 7 February, when his mail was ambushed at the Ingogo River crossing, five miles to the south, and its police escort reported that nearly a thousand Boers were lurking in the vicinity. It was imperative that the road be kept open for the reinforcements and, more immediately, for a convoy of supplies due to leave Newcastle on 8 February. Ordering out the 60th Rifles with 38 Mounted Infantry and four guns and taking command himself, Colley marched down to the Ingogo crossing to clear away the commando and

Colours of the 58th carried at Laing's Nek with, left and right, Colour-Sergeant Bridgestock and Private Godfrey, both awarded the DCM. Centre, Private Osborne, who won the VC at Wakkerstroom. All three also wear the Zulu War medal. Their tunics have white facings, changed from black after July 1881.

escort the convoy back to Mount Prospect. Unbeknown to him the convoy's departure had been delayed by the local commander at Newcastle.

Having detached one company and two guns to command the crossing, Colley advanced on to a low triangular plateau on the far side. As the Riflemen ascended the rise some hundred mounted Boers were seen about a thousand yards away across a ravine. It was now 12.30 p.m. and the remaining two 9-pounders at once went into action from the centre of the plateau. Their opening rounds went high and the Boers, instead of dispersing as expected, galloped forward, dismounted and began to encircle the plateau, opening fire from good covered positions on the gun-teams and the four companies hastily deployed around the rock-fringed rim. In their dark green, almost black, uniforms, and silhouetted against the skyline, the Riflemen made prime targets for the concealed Boer marksmen firing uphill and casualties quickly mounted.

Colley realized that his troops were faced with a fight for survival. He hurriedly sent two men riding for Mount Prospect to bring out three companies of the 58th to reinforce the detachment he had left north of the river. He was just in time, for Smit had brought up reinforcements and the plateau was quickly surrounded. It was now a question of who could win the fire fight. Though the numbers were about even and Colley had the guns, the Boers were the better shots and their firing positions were difficult to spot. The Riflemen, suffering casualties and increasing thirst from the hot sun, held fast to whatever cover they could find, but the gun-crews were terribly exposed. Both officers were hit and the guns could only be kept in action by replacing casualties with Riflemen. The horses of the gun-teams and the MI suffered severely as for them there was no cover. The most vulnerable part of the position was the eastern corner, which had no rocky fringe from which to fight. A party of Boers managed to get up close here to engage the guns and a company had to be doubled across the open to block the gap. Only one officer and 13 men survived the fusillade that greeted their dash, but they held the perimeter intact. Late in the afternoon the Boer fire slackened and the Boers were seen to be removing their wounded. But any hope that they might be breaking off the fight was soon dashed. Smit had been joined by more men and the firing again intensified.

Confident that it would be only a matter of time before the British either surrendered or were annihilated, Smit made sure of none getting away and of no help arriving by sending a party to seize the crossing. This was fired on by the company left there in the morning. At that moment the 58th companies summoned from Mount Prospect arrived and the Boers rode away.

Storm clouds had been gathering as the afternoon waned and as dusk began to fall Smit called on his burghers for an assault. But the guns and Riflemen were still firing from the plateau and with the storm imminent the Boers declined to come on. Smit believed that Colley would not risk a night withdrawal with so many wounded and would be unable to move his guns with so few horses remaining. Leaving patrols to watch the position he disengaged and allowed his men to seek shelter.

As darkness fell the storm broke. Soaked and chilled, Colley's exhausted men had no shelter on the plateau. They had no greatcoats because they had marched in light order, not expecting to be out all night. They had no food, ammunition was low and medical supplies almost finished. Seventy-six men had been killed and another 67 were wounded, some severely. It was impossible to move the wounded without ambulances and the Ingogo was rising rapidly. Even though the Boers had apparently withdrawn, they might still ambush a night retreat. On the other hand to stay and continue the fight in the morning held out little hope and, above all, Colley feared for Mount Prospect, now with only three weak companies to defend it. He decided to risk the march back.

Harnessing the remaining horses to the guns and leaving the wounded as comfortable as possible, the column set out. The noise of the storm concealed their departure. The river could be crossed only by forming a human chain; even so eight men were swept away. The horses were now so weak that, once on the other bank, the drenched and exhausted Riflemen had to pull the guns. It took until nearly dawn to cover the five uphill miles to the camp. The day had been a complete fiasco, redeemed only by the steadiness of the Riflemen and the gunners.

So fraught had been the river crossing that only a cursory attempt had been made to inform the four companies installed above the drift of the withdrawal. When morning came they were still there, having endured a wretched night and uncertain of the situation. Realizing that the column had gone, they marched rapidly for camp, catching up Colley's stragglers. Later that morning ambulances were sent down to the battlefield under a flag of truce to collect the wounded.

Of the original 1,200 men of the Natal Field Force, some 340 were now casualties. Colley had barely sufficient strength to hold his camp, let alone patrol the road. To his acute sense of failure was added deep personal grief and an increased burden of work, both caused by the loss of all his personal staff save two, his wife's brother, Lieutenant Bruce Hamilton, and the seemingly indestructible Major Essex, who had escaped from Isandhlwana, in the Zulu War, and who

Transvaal commanders in 1881 including Piet Joubert, centre, Nicolas Smit, top centre, and Piet Cronje, who besieged Potchefstroom, top right. Right of Joubert is J.M. Kock, who had fought at Boomplaats and was to be killed in 1899.

29

Part of the ground held by 3/60th Rifles near the Ingogo on
8 February, with remains of the artillery and MI horses.

had now survived Laing's Nek and the Ingogo.

The losses incurred during another setback, the
continuing rainy weather, plus the sight of distant
Boers hovering like vultures, cast a pall over
everyone. Colley made another of his noble speeches
to the 60th but, although everyone doubtless
recognized his personal courage and courtesy, it
cannot have escaped his two battalions that he had
now twice publicly confessed to defective generalship. However, a week later, Tuck of the 58th was
recording in his diary that 'our men are in high
spirits'—though whether this was due to news of the
reinforcements having reached Newcastle or merely
to jolly cricket matches with the 60th is unclear.
Captain Marling, on the other hand, had come to the
conclusion that Colley 'ought not to be trusted with a
corporal's guard'!

Distressed though Colley was, the fires of ambition
still burned within him, stoked by his desire to
restore Britain's and his own reputation, by
heartening letters from his wife in Pietermaritzburg,
by the approach of the longed-for reinforcements
and, not least, by the imminent arrival of his
designated second-in-command, the energetic and
popular Brigadier-General Sir Evelyn Wood, a V.C.,
another of Wolseley's 'Ring' and a proven field
commander; thus a rival by whom Colley had no
intention of being superceded.[9] He had already
written to welcome Wood to Natal and to outline a
plan whereby Wood would lead a flanking column
while, he, Colley, went on to Pretoria, insisting 'you
will understand that I want to take the Nek myself'.
Colley was also desperate to resume the offensive as
soon as possible as he had become aware since 3
February of peace negotiations that the Colonial
Secretary, Lord Kimberley, had begun with the
Transvaalers through the offices of President Brand
of the Free State, even before Laing's Nek. In the

Battle of the Ingogo. Standing left is Colley with Lieutenant-Colonel Ashburnham 60th. To the right, lying against the rock, is the wounded Lieutenant Parsons RA talking to Lieutenant Wilkinson, Adjutant 60th. A red-coated mounted infantryman lies dead, centre foreground. Watercolour by C.E. Fripp.

absence of Governmental instructions resulting from these talks, Colley had conceived it his duty to attack at Laing's Nek. This had incurred Gladstone's disapproval—particularly as he had failed. Further disapproval followed when Colley interpreted as a demand for unconditional surrender by the Boers, a message from Kimberley for Brand that the future relationship between Britain and the Transvaal would be discussed once armed opposition ceased. Brand pressed for clarification on this interpretation but the Government was dithering in early February: Gladstone, as usual, more preoccupied with domestic matters and antipathetic to military measures, the Radicals generally pro-Boer, and the Whig element ready to negotiate but preferably not before Colley had re-asserted British authority. Notwithstanding Wolseley's assurance that Colley could finish the job once reinforced, the politicians' confidence in Colley

was further lowered by news of the Ingogo and their will to continue military action was weakened by fears that the Free State might enter the war if hostilities continued.

Feeling the sands beginning to shift beneath his feet, Colley put the best gloss he could on his reverses. His performance so far had elicited little enthusiasm in the British Press but there were those who took a more supportive line. Since, much to everyone's surprise, the Transvaal garrisons were still holding out, Colley's endeavours, it was argued, must have contributed to their successful stands.

3. THE HILL OF DOVES

FEBRUARY–AUGUST 1881

By the middle of February 1881 hostilities had been continuing for eight weeks, but Colley was still no nearer bringing succour to the garrisons. He may have been comforted by Kimberley's assurance that he had 'indirectly' contributed to their resistance but in truth his operations had had little effect. Some Transvaalers had joined Joubert on the frontier, but this was more out of boredom than necessity; others had simply drifted off home for the same reason. Siege warfare, being static and likely to lead to costly assaults, did not suit Boer military methods and principles. Rather than trying to overcome the small, isolated posts, they were content to keep them bottled up until a shortage of supplies forced them to give in. They were well informed of each garrison's strength and thus deployed no more men than were necessary to blockade, rather than to besiege. If anything it was the garrisons' existence which tied down manpower that could otherwise have been used by Joubert, thereby assisting Colley's field force, rather than the other way round.

The sieges, on the whole, were desultory, uneventful affairs, characterized for the besieged more by discomfort from cramped conditions and in some cases food shortages than by any great danger. Most of the beseiged, together with loyalist civilians, women, children and native servants, were crammed into small forts outside the townships. The fort at Lydenburg measured 78 yards by 20 yards; that at Potchefstroom was 30 yards square. The latter, being garrisoned only just before the outbreak of war, was the least well-prepared both in fortifications and provisions. Food had to be rationed from the first day of the investment by Cronje and his 500-strong commando and to be further reduced by the end of January. Despite his precarious situation in one of the most anti-British areas of the Transvaal, Lieutenant-Colonel Winslowe and his two companies of the 2/21st put up a sufficiently determined resistance for

Cronje to refuse to detach men for Joubert. At Rustenburg another 21st officer, Captain Auchinleck, though disposing of only one company of his regiment and being thrice wounded, kept the Boers at a distance by leading sorties against their trenches whenever they tried to sap forwards. In the entire siege of Marabastadt, held by Captain Brooke with a weak company of the 94th, some civilian volunteers and native police, the garrison sustained only five casualties, the Boers one. The fact that Lydenburg held out owed more to the leadership of the doctor, Surgeon Falvey, and the chaplain, Father Walsh, and to the bright courage of the young wife of the commander, than to the commander himself, the inexperienced and supine 22-year-old Lieutenant Long. Only recently transferred to the 94th from a cavalry regiment, Long had failed to win the confidence and esteem of his 53 men, who were the cast-offs and undesirables of the 94th, left behind when Anstruther marched away to his doom.

The largest garrison, at Pretoria, where Bellairs commanded, consisted of four companies of the 2/21st, one of the 94th and its MI, two Royal Artillery guns and some Royal Engineers. In addition, Bellairs had five guns that had belonged to the Transvaal Republic and 570 loyalist volunteers. Of the latter the most useful and reliable were two troops of mounted men known as the Pretoria Carbineers and Nourse's Horse. The services of these mounted troops were constantly required because the Boers invested Pretoria by means of a chain of laagers and posts 6–8 miles out from the town. Bellairs tried to maintain an aggressive defence by frequent patrolling and sorties, in the hope of breaking out to link up with Potchefstroom. His first attack, using the mounted volunteers and the 21st carried forward in mule wagons, achieved some surprise and the only Boer surrenders in the whole campaign. On succeeding occasions, the Boers were ready for them and the

2/21st Royal Scots Fusiliers in the Transvaal. Apart from diced bands on their Glengarries, this regiment was then uniformed as English infantry.

raids failed, forcing Bellairs to discontinue them.

In the south, at Standerton on the main Pretoria-Natal road, Major Montague conducted an energetic defence with three companies of the 94th and one of the 58th. Before Laing's Nek it had looked as though Joubert might attack with the main Boer force, rather than leave the post in his rear, but he decided against it. Without any mounted troops there was little offensive action Montague could take, but by maintaining a disciplined fire response from his fort as far as his ammunition reserves would allow, he successfully enagaged the attention of his besiegers, who would otherwise have joined Joubert. The chief danger at Wakkerstroom, held by Captain Saunders and two companies of the 58th, was its close proximity to the main Boer force at Laing's Nek, from which an attack was constantly expected. However, the Boers were content to cordon off the fort; the siege developed into an exchange of long-range rifle fire and occasional raids by both sides to capture provisions.

The siege casualties on both sides were low. At Potchefstroom 24 of the defenders lost their lives and at Pretoria 17, both places having roughly double these numbers wounded, but in none of the other places did the numbers of killed reach double figures. Despite the slow tempo of the operations, there were some moments of acute danger—attested by the awards of three Victoria Crosses to the defenders: to Corporal Murray of the 94th and Trooper Danaher of Nourse's Horse at Pretoria and Private Osborne of the 58th at Wakkerstroom, all for saving wounded men under heavy fire during sorties from the forts.

The need for continued resistance by the garrisons was brought into question on 14 February. The Cabinet in London received an offer from Kruger, via Colley, that the Transvaal would accept a Royal Commission to investigate its case, and abide by its findings, if British troops were immediately withdrawn from the country. Two days later the Cabinet, though dodging the last proviso, instructed Colley to inform Kruger that, providing the Boers ceased hostilities, a Commission would be appointed. Colley was to halt his operations if these terms were acceptable to Kruger.

Colley was alarmed by the Government's conciliatory attitude, particularly now his reinforcements were at hand. He was further incensed on the 17th, when he met Evelyn Wood at Newcastle, by the latter's news of the Government's decision in principle to revoke the annexation, restoring the Transvaal's independence though retaining sovereignty over the native border districts—a scheme devised without any consultation with him as High Commissioner. Wood had arrived with three regiments from India: the 15th Hussars, 2/60th Rifles, sister battalion to that already in Natal, and the 92nd Highlanders; the 6th Dragoons and the 83rd and 97th Regiments were marching up from Durban. Therefore it seemed inconceivable to Colley not to wipe out the reverses with this much stronger force and then negotiate from strength. He temporized on the Kruger offer, wiring back to Kimberley his opposition to the Government's plan and enquiring

33

Defenders of Lydenburg, the 'undesirables' of the 94th with, centre, Lieutenant and Mrs Long. On her left is Surgeon Falvey.

what he was to do about the distant garrisons and the Boer forces in Natal territory, in the event of Kruger agreeing to an armistice. Kimberley's answer was specific: if the armistice was agreed, Colley was not to occupy Laing's Nek nor march to relieve the garrisons; he was also to 'fix a reasonable time within which an answer must be sent by the Boers'.

While waiting for this reply Colley had sent Wood to reconnoitre the country east of the Laing's Nek position towards Wakkerstroom. He had thoughts of detaching part of his enlarged force under Wood and sending it in that direction from Newcastle; the reconnaissance also got Wood out of the way while the interchange of telegrams went on. On Wood's return to Newcastle, reporting no major force to the east, Colley asked him to go back to Pietermaritzburg in order to, in Wood's words, 'expedite the transport of provisions of which there were at Newcastle only thirteen days' supply'—a surprisingly menial and time-consuming task, it might be thought, for a deputy commander at a time when he had been nominated to command a flanking column in the event of the offensive being resumed. Wood obligingly departed on the 21st, but not before extracting a promise from Colley that he would not move from Mount Prospect before Wood returned.

Left to his own devices Colley then drafted a reply

for Kruger, repeating Kimberley's assurances about the appointment of a Royal Commisson once the Boers ceased hostilities. He added that he had authority to suspend his own operations 'upon this proposal being accepted within forty-eight hours'. Deciding not to despatch this until back at Mount Prospect, he marched north with the three regiments Wood had brought up, taking with him, as Chief of Staff, Lieutenant-Colonel Herbert Stewart, another of Wolseley's protegés.[10]

Crossing the Ingogo on the 22nd he learned that in his absence the Boers had been strengthening their positions astride the Nek, which would make any attempt against it even more costly than the first, notwithstanding the extra troops. Thinking it unwise to have all his force concentrated so close to the border under Boer observation, he sent the 2/60th with one squadron of the 15th back to Newcastle, taking on the 92nd and the other squadron to strengthen the garrison at Mount Prospect.

The message for Kruger reached Smit at Laing's Nek on the 24th but he replied that no answer would be possible within 48 hours as Kruger had gone off to a distant part of the Transvaal and could not be reached for at least four days. In the event Kruger was to receive it on the 28th, and accept its terms, but by then it had been overtaken by events.

Colley had reassured the Secretary for War on the 23rd that he would not engage the Boers before Kruger's reply was received 'without strong reason', but he could not sit idly by waiting for it. As a loyal servant he had to comply with Government policy, however much he disapproved of it, but he would be failing in his duty as local commander if he did not consider his future course of action should Kruger rebuff Kimberley's offer. In that case, and in the light of the strengthened defences on the Nek, it seemed that the only way into the Transvaal was round the Boers' left flank via the route reconnoitred by Wood. The latter, knowing the ground, could effect this from Newcastle with the regiments coming up, while the force at Mount Prospect could hold the enemy's attention in front. Such a plan would take time to implement and the credit would have to be shared with Wood. Though he and Wood were friends that thought, with two defeats to redeem, cannot have been easy to stomach.

As he pondered the situation with Stewart, Colley's eye was increasingly drawn westwards, to

Pretoria. Major Campbell, Provost Marshal, in front of Fort Royal redoubt with three of his military police and, left, two 94th MI.

the towering, flat-topped bulk of Amajuba, 'the hill of doves', dominating all the land around—his camp, the Boer defences astride the Nek and their laagers behind. He reconnoitred the hill circumspectly, examining its steep rock- and scrub-covered slopes and questioning natives about its summit. The Boers had made no attempt to include it in their defensive semi-circle, merely using it as a daytime observation post from which they withdrew at night. As the days passed, with no reply from Kruger, Colley became more and more obsessed by its dominance. On the 26th, when the 48 hours had expired, he spent all afternoon covertly examining it through binoculars. That evening, after dark, without divulging a hint of his intentions to anyone but Stewart, he ordered a detachment to parade at 9.30 p.m. equipped with greatcoats, picks and shovels, waterproof sheets and three days' rations.

The detachment, carefully selected by Colley, consisted of two companies of the 58th, two of the 3/60th, three of the 92nd and 64 men of the Royal Navy; no guns, Gatlings or rockets were to be taken. It was therefore approximately of battalion strength but without the cohesion of the battalion organization, resulting in a scratch force for his hazardous enterprise and likewise for that left to protect the camp, in the charge of Colonel Bond of the 58th,[11] to whom nothing was imparted. Furthermore there was much dissimilarity between the components. The newly arrived 92nd were Highlanders, a type of infantry greatly esteemed by the public and even

more greatly by themselves. Unlike the 58th and 60th, smarting from two defeats, the 92nd were fresh from a victorious campaign in Afghanistan, heroes of Roberts' great march from Kabul to Kandahar. Due to return home, they had been diverted to Natal as the result of a curious example of the Victorian Army's methods—a secret telegram had been sent by Lieutenant Ian Hamilton and the subalterns, imploring the authorities to send the battalion. Again, unlike the other two battalions in their now soiled and crumpled scarlet and green, the 92nd looked fit for anything in serviceable Indian khaki above their flaunting Gordon kilts. Whereas the English battalions' musketry had compared unfavourably with the Boers', the 92nd had been the best shooting battalion in India through the efforts of the same Hamilton as musketry instructor, although they had had no shooting practice for six months. The military critics at home had ascribed the failures at Laing's Nek and the Ingogo to the short-service soldiers of the 58th and 60th—unfairly since both battalions had behaved well under hopeless circumstances. The 92nd, on the other hand, having been in India since 1868, was still predominantly filled with the mature, experienced long-service men of the type so eulogized by opponents of the new system. Cocky, confident and patronizing to the younger English soldiers, the Highlanders had no doubt the Boers would give them little trouble.

Why then, as was asked at the time and afterwards, did not Colley take this fresh and apparently excellent battalion entire, instead of the mixed force he selected? As one of Wolseley's reformers he may not have wanted a long-service battalion to gain all the credit. More likely he simply wanted all three battalions and the sailors to have a share in his plan. If so, the 58th at least were unenthusiastic about it; as one of the company commanders, Captain Morris, later reported to Colonel Bond, 'the men had lost confidence in Colley and had an idea they would be led into another trap'. Hamilton heard some of the 58th say to his men 'they wished we had brought the whole Regiment'.

When the night march began at 10 p.m. not a man had been told where he was going or what was expected of him, except that he was to show no lights and to keep absolute silence. After an hours' march westward the two 60th companies were detached to picquet Inquelo Hill, two miles south of Amajuba. At the foot of Amajuba itself Robertson's company of the 92nd was left. With the line of communication back to Mount Prospect thus secured, the remaining four

Defending a redoubt at Standerton. Engraving from *The Graphic*, after C.E. Fripp.

companies and the sailors began to climb the hill. In pitch darkness, with the narrow, rocky track more difficult to find the higher they went, it was a tiring and nerve-wracking business. Not until dawn was breaking did the last man scramble up to the top of the track where it emerged at the south-west corner of the summit.

At the top they found a plateau shaped roughly like an isosceles triangle, of which the base line, some 500 yards long, faced north-east overlooking Laing's Nek, 2,000 feet below and over a mile away. From the south-east and west sides, each about 425 yards long, the ground fell precipitously from the rim of the plateau into a tangle of tree- and scrub-covered ravines, but the north-east rim sloped down more gently to a terrace about 100 yards wide, beyond which another precipice fell to a lower terrace. Towards the northerly end of the west face rose a small hillock from which a low rise, about 20 feet higher than the rim, ran towards the north-east face, then curved right round the perimeter, rising slightly at the south-east angle, back to the south-west corner, thereby enclosing a hollow about 350 yards all round. At the north-west and south-west angles, and separated from each by about 100 yards, were two knolls, both slightly lower than the rim.

After detaching a reserve of 120 men from all three units, Colley disposed the remaining 240 around the perimeter: the 58th between the south-east and south-west angles, the sailors on the west face up to the hillock including the south-west knoll, and the 92nd from the hillock right round to the south-east corner. The hillock on the west was placed in charge of Lieutenant Hector MacDonald, who had been commissioned from the ranks of the 92nd for gallantry in the Afghan War. The north-west knoll, though exposed, was picquetted by 15 men of the 92nd since it commanded the slopes of the north-east face, much of which was in dead ground from the rim. No other consideration was given to the relative accessibility of the different faces, so the remaining 92nd under Hamilton on the north-east had to be spread as much as twelve paces apart to reach the south-east corner. The reserve was stationed in the central hollow where a hospital was also established. Having made these deployments Colley, a slightly bizarre figure in tennis shoes with his uniform breeches tucked into his socks, seemed content to wander round without issuing any further orders.

Captain Froom's company of the 94th, part of the Standerton garrison. Most men are wearing full dress tunics (8 buttons), others the serge frock (5 buttons) usually worn in the field.

'We could stay here forever', he remarked gaily to Stewart. An officer enquired whether the men should fortify their positions but Colley thought they were too tired after their climb and said they should rest. So the soldiers, apart from some who piled a few loose rocks in front of them, slept.

By his daring night march Colley had established a force on the extreme west of, and overlooking, all the Boer positions including their rearward laagers. But with no weapons on the hill other than Martini-Henry rifles which, though sighted to 1,450 yards, had an effective range of only 400 yards, and with insufficient troops left at Mount Prospect to make any sort of frontal demonstration against the Nek, Colley's five companies could achieve no more than a picquet of five men could have done—they could only observe.

After a while, bored with inactivity and not as fatigued as Colley surmised, some of the Highlanders began shouting insults at the Boers far below. One or two fired their rifles, which Colley at once forbade. Taken completely unawares, the Boers in the laagers made frantic preparations to move while those on the Nek began to leave their positions, all expecting a bombardment at any moment. But, as the minutes passed and no gunfire came, the bolder Boer spirits

determined to fight. Collecting some 50 burghers, Commandant Ferreira and Field-Cornet Roos rode hard for the tree-covered base of the hill and dismounted. While some men opened long-range covering fire at the rim, the others split into two groups and began to climb towards the north-east face. Once convinced he was threatened by no more than infantry on the hill, Joubert sent Smit riding round Amajuba to the west to cut off Colley's retreat and ordered more men to the hill, some to support Ferreira and Roos on their left, others to attack up the west side. Taking advantage of every piece of cover, with any move always covered by fire, the stealthy ascent went on. By 7 a.m. some 300 Boers were in action, half on the hill, half firing from below.

On the summit the fire did little damage, but it compelled the defenders to keep their heads down. In the hollow the reserve slept on undisturbed and Colley appeared quite unconcerned, doing little more than send messages to Mount Prospect by heliograph. At 9 a.m. he ordered the 15th Hussars and 2/60th to

37

Sir Evelyn Wood VC. Photograph *c.* 1900.

South-west knoll on Majuba Hill, showing the track by which Colley ascended. Here a Royal Navy detachment was posted.

be summoned from Newcastle, though without giving any indication of what they were to do when they arrived. He circled the perimeter, chatting to the men and discussing the future siting of some redoubts with his staff. At 11 a.m., while standing at the south-west corner, his friend, Commander Romilly RN, fell mortally wounded at his side. Colley's mood abruptly changed. The fire by now was intensifying but to Hamilton's reports about the Boers' progress he appeared distant, merely repeating that they were to hold on for three days. Henceforth his grip on the situation seemed to deteriorate, for he shortly sent another signal saying the Boers were still firing heavily but had broken up their laagers and were moving off. He then lay down to sleep.

Meanwhile Ferreira's men, still under cover, were approaching the north-west knoll while Roos' detachment was moving up to his left. Owing to the configuration of the ground at the rim, the Highlanders at the north-east face and on the knoll had to expose themselves to fire at the enemy. Suddenly some of Ferreira's men stood up and fired a volley at the knoll while Roos engaged it from the flank. Most of its garrison were killed at once, the few survivors running back to the rim. Ferreira manned the knoll, opening a heavy fire which enabled Roos to reach the north-east rim, so that in places Boers and Highlanders were within feet of each other, shooting furiously. Someone ran back for reinforcements but the reserve, its men intermingled and some abruptly awakened, responded slowly and reluctantly to the frantic shouts of officers who were unfamiliar to them. As they went forward over the low rise they collided with the Highlanders running back. Hamilton later claimed that the reserve, having come up, then broke, forcing his men to retreat, but Stewart maintained there had been 'complete panic in the front line; they retired and the reserves being advanced at the same time, the greatest confusion resulted'. The northern part of the plateau was now lost and Highlanders and reserve all bolted back to take cover behind the boulders lining the low rise

above the hollow. Within a few minutes the relaxed, confident mood of the morning had been transformed into one of acute anxiety.

After a brief lull, during which more burghers joined them, Ferreira's and Roos' men opened rapid and accurate fire at the low rise from all round the northerly apex of the plateau at ranges between 30 and 100 yards. From the western hillock MacDonald, reinforced by some 58th, maintained a flanking fire across the front of the rise, but he soon began to lose men from Boers ascending the west face. Behind the rise the men were ordered to fix bayonets; had a charge then been made, though casualties would have been inevitable, the charging line should have been on the Boers before they could reload. But Colley declined to give the order and the fierce firefight continued. From the right of the north-east face, at the right rear of the rise, men began to leave their posts, drifting in to join their comrades behind the rise itself as though following some herd instinct—a fatal weakening of the position as at that moment more Boers were clambering up to that very point. Hamilton, acutely aware of how critical things were, implored Colley to order a charge but was again refused. In the view of Morris of the 58th, Colley 'seemed to have lost his head, to be overwhelmed by the appearance of affairs'.

In contrast Roos, whose position was closest to the rise, sensed that the Boers' moment had come. Waving his hat, he shouted, 'Come on you chaps! The English are flying!' His men sprang over the rim and ran forward firing. Ferreira came forward on his right and the party to his left emerged on the right rear of the rise. T.F. Carter, the correspondent, watching from the hollow, heard 'a sudden piercing cry of terror' and saw the right start to crumble. Panic spread rapidly and the whole line behind the rise gave way, the men racing for the south-west corner to get away from the Boers' devastating rifle-fire. All over the plateau the broken troops raced for safety, most making for the track, some leaping over the precipices, as the Boers ran forward to shoot them down. Colley fell, shot through the head, midway between the hospital and the west face. Some survivors said afterwards that he was trying to rally the men, others that he was waving a white handkerchief in surrender, while a third theory held that he had shot himself. Whatever the manner of his death, he can have had little wish to live.

Only from the western hillock was resistance kept up. Of the men thereon, MacDonald later wrote: 'Their gallantry was beyond praise, for even when

R. Caton Woodville's impression of the final moments on Majuba, with 58th, 92nd and sailors all mixed up along the low rise above the hospital, foreground. Colley stands centre left, pointing.

they were surrounded by the Boers and half their number killed or wounded and saw the others disappear from view,they did not move or murmur'. Seeing the hopelessness of the situation, MacDonald at last told the survivors to escape if they could, but all were shot except him and Sergeant Giles of the 58th, who were taken prisoner.

In the fury of the Boers' final assault not even the hospital was unscathed. Surgeon Landon was mortally wounded and Lance-Corporal Farmer, Army Hospital Corps, stood up unarmed under a heavy fire waving a white bandage over the wounded until shot through both arms. He was later awarded the Victoria Cross. All the wounded and prisoners might have been despatched in the heat of the moment had not the older Boers intervened.

Of the 365 alive on the summit that morning, 285 were casualties;[12] many fell to Boer riflemen as they

fled down the slopes. Despite the 92nd's proud shooting record in India, only two Boers lost their lives and four were wounded—a tribute to their amazing skill at fieldcraft and fire and movement, a practice then unknown in the British Army.

The sight of the troops streaming off the hill was watched with stunned disbelief from Mount Prospect and by the three companies left to guard the route the night before. Robertson of the 92nd soon found his position threatened by the Boers but determined to make a stand, summoning the 60th companies in his rear to support him. However the latter marched off to Mount Prospect and Robertson was signalled to withdraw by Colonel Bond who, now in command, needed every man to defend the camp. Robertson had to fight his way back but managed to reach camp covered by the guns.

The camp was not attacked but that night there was much inter-regimental acrimony. The 92nd blamed the 58th for not supporting them, the 58th, whose forebodings of disaster had proved only too true, countered with the Highlanders' failure to hold the first attack. The Rifles, who had been spared the worst, claimed that had they been on top matters

The hillock on the west face held by MacDonald, seen from the sailors' northernmost position. The first Boer attack came over the skyline to the right. Colley fell to the right of the rocky patch on the right edge of the photograph.

would have taken a different course. The soldiers' only common ground was to blame the sailors. Scottish apologists for the 92nd would later claim Majuba Hill as a saga of 'Highland heroism', but in view of the regiment's pre-battle reputation they were bound to protest—perhaps too much. All such arguments were pointless, if understandable. Carter, who had no axe to grind, wrote of the men's wavering, 'Who it was in particular held back I defy anyone to say' while Stewart, a cavalryman, asserted: 'There was no difference in the conduct of any of the troops engaged'. Both Scottish and English musketry had been woefully inaccurate and unsteady. Both Scots and English had been demoralized by the Boer tactics, and they had for most of the fight been all mixed up together, not under their own officers. One regiment had been over-confident, the other pessimistic, and from first to last they had been kept in the dark by their general as to what was expected of them.

It is hard to know what exactly was in Colley's mind, before and during the battle. Some said he was inspired by Wolfe's landing behind the French lines at Quebec, but Wolfe had immediately attacked his enemy. Others claimed he was trying to emulate Roberts' flank approach at Peiwar Kotal in the Afghan War, but Roberts had combined this with a frontal assault. Colley, once on Majuba, had summoned reinforcements from Newcastle but, as Hay of the 92nd said, 'either he was a day late in sending for them or he moved a day too soon'. Stewart, who was in the best position to know, thought Colley reckoned, by preying on the Boer fear of being outflanked, that he could force them to abandon the Nek without firing a shot, never imagining they would risk an assault on such a dominant position. If successful he could have claimed he had kept his undertaking not to resume hostilities before the Boers replied to the peace offer. It is possible that, worn out by over-work and a feeling that he had been deserted by the good fortune that had hitherto attended his career, he had lost confidence in himself and this, added to a pre-

41

The flight off Majuba as seen from the 60th picquets on Inquelo Hill. Sketch by Melton Prior from an eyewitness description.

sentiment of death, began so to unhinge him that, as events continued to oppose him, while outwardly preserving his customary calm demeanour, he had actually lost touch with reality. Whatever Colley's state of mind, the fact remained that he had gambled for high stakes and lost—his battle, his reputation and his life.

Yet his memory continued to exert a strange fascination on those who had known him. Years later, when nearly 80, Ian Hamilton, who had been captured at Majuba and had little cause to think well of Colley as a commander, wrote that, during the annual two minutes' silence for the Great War dead, the first thought that always came to his mind was of 'Sir George Colley, stretched out, exactly as the effigy of a knight lies in a cathedral, upon the flattened summit of Majuba. There he lay upon a site which might have been selected by Valkyries for a hero's grave, midway between the Transvaal and Natal with an eagle's outlook over both'.

Although the Transvaal garrisons still held out and more troops were ordered out as soon as the news of Majuba reached London, the disaster effectively ended the First Boer War. Evelyn Wood assumed Colley's appointment and on 6 March a truce was arranged with the Transvaal. Wood was all for playing for time until his military strength could be built up so that, before negotiations began, he could achieve 'decided, though lenient action' against the Boers to salvage prestige and reputation. But when Gladstone learned of Kruger's conciliatory reply, he decided enough was enough.

The Royal Commission was appointed and the provisional peace terms grudgingly negotiated by Wood were ratified by the Convention of Pretoria in August 1881. In return for its independence, the Transvaal had to accept the Queen's suzerainty, a British Resident to supervise the Africans' interests, continued British control over native districts on the eastern border and British approval of its foreign relations. Three years later the British Government, pre-occupied with Ireland and the Sudan, agreed to a fresh convention, of London, whereby the Transvaal managed to rid itself of the first two of these qualifications.

In terms of duration and numbers engaged on both sides—less than a thousand in all—Majuba Hill was little more than a skirmish, albeit a military object lesson in minor tactics and morale. Yet its effects were far-reaching. For the victors each individual Boer's yearning for unfettered personal independence became transformed into an aggressive and unified Afrikaner nationalism all over South Africa. On the vanquished it inflicted a festering wound of bitterness and humiliation which could be healed only by revenge. Majuba would no longer be remembered as the tranquil home of doves, the harbingers of peace, but rather as the eyrie described by Hamilton, with eagles brandishing the thunder-bolts of war.

4. USING THE UITLANDERS

1884—1899

After the First Boer War a former Conservative Colonial Secretary, Sir Michael Hicks-Beach, claimed that Gladstone's Government had secured 'not only that peace shall not be lasting, but that it shall be the precursor of infinitely worse trouble than any from which their weak yielding has for the moment delivered them'. Prophetic words, but in the war's immediate aftermath the British Government merely reacted to events in South Africa, rather than initiating them, the prime movers being Cape Colony under Cecil Rhodes and the Transvaal, or South African Republic as it became after 1884, under Paul Kruger.

Rhodes, a Hertfordshire vicar's son, who had made a fortune in the Kimberley diamond fields and was to make another in gold, had entered the Cape Parliament in 1881 with a dream of 'painting as much of Africa British red as possible', envisaging the spread of British dominion from the Cape to Cairo. The base for such an expansion would be a federated, self-governing South Africa under the Crown, but in Rhodes's view the impetus towards this should come from Cape Colony, not the British Government.

He appreciated that his design could be accomplished only by co-operation between the two white races, but Majuba had hardened Afrikaner attitudes. Despite the mid-century establishment of the two Boer republics, the idea of Boer nationhood had not begun to take root until the 1870s, when it was chiefly propagated by Afrikaner intellectuals in the Cape through a cultural organization called the Afrikander Bond. After the war the Bond grew more political but at the same time became divided within itself, one faction favouring an Afrikaner-dominated South Africa, the other, more moderate, ready to accommodate all white South Africans and confining its activities to Cape Colony. Rhodes cultivated the moderates to such good effect that in 1890 he became Prime Minister of the Cape with their support.

In the Republics the Bond did not flourish; neither President Brand nor President Kruger wanted his authority questioned. Having fought for and won his independence from Britain, Kruger set about making the Transvaal a strong, Afrikaner state with enlarged boundaries. Between 1884—7 Transvaal attempts to overflow into native territories westwards and eastwards were thwarted by the British annexation of Bechuanaland and Zululand. From 1890 expansion to the north was blocked by the operations of Rhodes's British South Africa Company across the Limpopo River in what was to become Rhodesia. By not resisting this move, Kruger hoped to gain British acquiescence to his securing an outlet to the Indian Ocean between Portuguese East Africa (now Mozambique) and the only remaining unoccupied littoral territory of Tongaland. Negotiations broke down over the Transvaal's refusal to agree to a customs union with the British territories and in 1895 Tongaland was taken over as a British protectorate effectively barring the Transvaal from the sea.

If the Transvaal had failed to expand territorially, its economy had undergone a dramatic transformation. In 1886 gold was discovered in quantity in the Witwatersrand, leading to an influx of immigrants, most of whom were British subjects, to work the mines and create the town of Johannesburg, which soon was the richest and most populous in South Africa. The gold revenues made the Transvaal's traditional near-bankruptcy a thing of the past, but so numerous were the immigrants, or Uitlanders, and so different culturally and socially from the pastoral Boers, that the latter, long threatened from without, soon felt threatened from within, aware that in time they might become the minority whites in their own country.

To retain control Kruger imported Dutchmen, Germans and Cape Afrikaners to run his administration, since his fellow-countrymen not only

Cecil Rhodes.

Joseph Chamberlain.

Dr Leander Starr Jameson.

Sir Alfred Milner.

Johannesburg from the north, *c.* 1895.

deplored the gold boom on moral grounds—though not always averse to its rewards—but most were ill-suited to administration. Living and working costs were made high for Uitlanders by imposing mining and customs duties and by granting monopoly rights to concessionaires of the Government's choice. Uitlanders received no State support for English schooling and, though liable to taxation, no political representation. No Uitlander could vote in the Presidential or Volksraad[13] elections unless he was a naturalized Transvaaler and had lived in the Republic for 14 years. By the mid-Nineties the Uitlanders formed a substantial proportion of the Transvaal population; they ranged from rough labourers, skilled artisans, professional men and entrepreneurs, to gold magnates like Julius Wernher and Alfred Beit,[14] the friend and partner of Rhodes. All had come to the Transvaal to enrich themselves. Some were not much concerned about the lack of franchise, but on the other hand all were being deprived of political rights by people often less intelligent and certainly less politically sophisticated than themselves. In 1892 some founded a movement to press for reform by constitutional means.

Meanwhile, at the Cape, Rhodes had been growing restive at the threat posed to his federation plans by the enriched Transvaal, which clearly was opposed to both economic and political union. In 1895 Kruger closed the Vaal crossings to the passage of Cape goods, with the aim of diverting traffic to his newly completed railway from Pretoria to Delagoa Bay in Portuguese territory. This was a setback to the Cape's trade, but Rhodes found an ally in the new Colonial Secretary, Joseph Chamberlain, who had recently taken office in Lord Salisbury's Conservative Government. A Birmingham industrialist, Chamberlain had been a member of the Cabinet that had made peace in 1881 but, having broken with Gladstone over Irish Home Rule, he had founded the Liberal Unionists, who in 1895 formed an alliance with the Conservatives. Extremely able and vigorous, he arrived at the Colonial Office at a time when the European 'scramble for Africa' was at its height and he had no intention of presiding over any reduction of British Imperial power in that continent and in South Africa in particular. His response to Kruger's tariff campaign against the Cape was to register a strong protest to the Transvaal Government, backed by the threat of military force. Kruger re-opened the Vaal crossings.

With a committed Imperialist in the Colonial Office, Rhodes now embarked upon a plan to bend the Transvaal to his will before his ill-health forced

The Jameson Raiders' last stand at Doornkop, 2 January 1896.
Dr Jameson (long coat) amid his staff and the Rhodesian police.
Painting by R. Caton Woodville.

him to retire. By exploiting the Uitlanders' dis-content, he intended with Beit's connivance to en-gineer an uprising in the Transvaal to be supported by a force of his own, whereupon the British Government would have to intervene on behalf of its subjects, and the subsequent granting of the franchise to all Uitlander males would ensure a friendly Transvaal Government receptive to federa-tion. Chamberlain was aware of the plot but, though prepared to allow Rhodes a base in the Bechuanaland protectorate for his support force, he insisted that the preparations and the execution must be a matter for Rhodes and not the Home Government.

When the time came for the rising, in December 1895, the whole devious scheme collapsed. Uncertain whether to fight for their rights under the Union Jack or the Transvaal 'Vierkleur', distrustful of Rhodes's motives, the Uitlanders prevaricated. On the border Rhodes's henchman, Dr Jameson, with 500 Rhodesian mounted police, waited with growing impatience. When no rising occurred in Johannesburg Chamber-lain threatened to revoke the British South Africa Company's charter unless Rhodes forbade Jameson to move. Rhodes did so but Jameson, hoping to goad the Uitlanders into action, went in. Instead of rising, the Uitlanders began negotiations with Kruger and Jameson was forced to surrender to a commando at Doornkop on 2 January 1896.

This fiasco had far-reaching consequences. The leading Uitlanders were charged with high treason and fined heavily. Jameson and five of his officers were sent for trial in England and imprisoned. Rhodes had to resign as Cape Premier and the Afrikander Bond severed its alliance with him, going on to win the Cape elections in 1898 by a narrow margin. Henceforth the sympathies of the Cape Afrikaners and, even more important, of the hitherto uncommitted Orange Free State (which had kept out of the 1881 war) were entirely with the Transvaal, all united in common distrust of Britain.

Kruger's prestige was greatly enhanced, in Europe as well as South Africa, and he took the opportunity of restricting the Uitlanders' political activity more rigorously than before. He increased his police and began importing modern arms in large quantities from Europe. In 1897 he concluded a treaty of mutual assistance with Martinus Steyn, the newly-elected President of the Free State, a highly intelligent and dedicated man of much greater political sophistic-ation than Kruger. Far from curbing Afrikaner power, the Jameson Raid had strengthened and unified it. A

47

suspicion began to grow among British South Africans and at home that there was an Afrikaner conspiracy to replace British dominance with its own. In fact Kruger was merely consolidating his position and taking precautions to defend it in future. At all costs he was determined that Boer voters must never be outnumbered by Uitlanders and that the latter must be kept out of the Volksraad.

In Britain Chamberlain, having successfully exonerated himself from complicity in the Raid, was equally determined to maintain British supremacy in South Africa and to give justice to the Uitlanders, but henceforth by peaceful means. He appointed as High Commissioner Sir Alfred Milner, a brilliant administrator and a fervent and ruthless Imperialist. Milner was neither an exploiter nor a mere expansionist, but he sincerely believed in the British Empire, particularly its white territories, as a power for good in the world, provided they spoke with one voice. South Africa as a whole had an important part to play in his philosophy but at present it was disunited and fissile.

Milner set himself to work up a crisis over the Uitlanders, whose grievances had been inflamed afresh by the murder by a policeman of an English artisan. He intended, by exerting constant and increasing diplomatic pressure, to force Kruger to make voting concessions to the Uitlanders. Chamberlain agreed to this strategy, believing it would yield a settlement satisfactory to all parties. But, as time passed, the impatient Milner's private intention, disclosed only to a few influential friends, was to secure the support of a united Uitlander movement including the important gold magnates and then to demand so much from Kruger, ultimately backing his demands with the threat of force, that the Transvaal would be compelled to fight, which must in due course lead to its re-annexation and a unified South Africa. At the same time he would have to convince the Home Government that he was committed to a diplomatic solution, while constantly keeping the Uitlanders' supposed plight uppermost in its mind.

Early negotiations led to a meeting in May 1899 between Milner and Kruger at Bloemfontein under the aegis of President Steyn. By demanding what he guessed Kruger would not concede, Milner managed to break up the conference despite Chamberlain urging him to be patient. Kruger's chief adviser at this meeting, the clever young Cape lawyer, J. C.

Smuts, sensed that Milner planned to seize the Transvaal but for the moment enjoined continued negotiation. Milner, rebuffing each concession as inadequate and side-stepping offers of mediation by Cape Afrikaners and the Free State, insisted to Chamberlain that Kruger would yield more providing the pressure for a still better deal for the Uitlanders was kept up and the British garrison in South Africa was strongly reinforced.

Milner was far from happy with the state of military preparedness. Not only did the GOC, General Sir William Butler, have pro-Boer sympathies and great distrust of the Uitlander movement, but there were only 10,000 Regular troops spread between the Cape and Natal against an estimated 50–55,000 men of military age in the two Republics who might be joined by several thousand Cape rebels. Milner had Butler recalled, but in London there was disagreement over the number of troops needed to safeguard the two colonies. Wolseley, now Commander-in-Chief, still pugnacious but a shadow of his former self after the failure of his Nile Expedition in 1885, demanded an immediate reinforcement of another 10,000 and the mobilization in England of an Army Corps of some 30,000. Lord Lansdowne, the cautious and cost-conscious War Secretary, favoured no more than 5,000 initial reinforcements as suggested by the recently appointed GOC in Natal, Major-General Sir Penn Symons—an unrealistic figure as it would take four months to deploy the Army Corps in South Africa, should it be needed.

Before any decision was made Kruger presented another offer which went beyond Milner's demands at Bloemfontein but was conditional on Britain refraining from future interference in the Transvaal's internal affairs. Milner, fearful that this would torpedo all his efforts but now secretly assured of the gold magnates' support, even in the event of war and consequent loss to the mines, insisted to Chamberlain that the conditions were unacceptable and that, with more troops at his back, he could force Kruger to climb down peacefully. Won over by Milner's eloquence, Chamberlain warned the Cabinet on 8 September that, unless Kruger's bluff was called by the threat of force, the whole British position in South Africa would be put in question and with it 'the estimate formed of our power and influence in our Colonies and throughout the world'. Reluctantly the Cabinet agreed. On 17 September 10,000 men of all

General Sir George White VC.

General Sir Redvers Buller VC.

Major-General Sir W.Penn Symons.

Colonel Ian Hamilton.

arms, from the Mediterranean and Indian garrisons, began embarking for Natal. To command them Lansdowne selected the 64-year-old General Sir George White, an Afghan War V.C. with much Indian and Burmese experience but none in South Africa.

By now Kruger was sure war was inevitable. A massive exodus of Uitlanders was leaving the Transvaal. Smuts recommended an immediate invasion of Natal to capture Durban before the British reinforcements arrived and while the Boers still enjoyed a five-to-one superiority. But Kruger could not act without the Free State and Steyn still believed Chamberlain would compromise. Then came news that the 1st Army Corps was mobilizing in England for despatch to South Africa. On 28 September the Transvaal mobilized, followed four days later by the Free State. The commandos moved towards the frontier and on 9 October, two days after White and the first troops from India were landing at Durban, Kruger issued an ultimatum. Unless British troops were withdrawn from the borders and all reinforcements halted within 48 hours, war would follow. Milner had forced Kruger's hand—into a declaration of war on the British Empire. All that was needed now was for the soldiers to trounce the Boers and the Union Jack would then fly from Cape Town to the Zambezi.

5. REMEMBER MAJUBA!

12 OCTOBER–22 NOVEMBER 1899

The combination of waiting for the Free Staters and defective logistic arrangements, which had delayed the Transvaal's mobilization, had cost the Boer armies a critical fortnight so that, as their offensive began, the British reinforcements were pouring up by rail from Durban. Though the Boers still planned to invade Natal, they dissipated their immediately available combined forces of some 50,000 by adopting the 1881 strategy of investing detached garrisons, at Mafeking and Kimberley in the west. They sent other contingents to watch the Rhodesian border and the Rhodesia-Cape railway alongside the Republics' western borders. Others were sent into Cape Colony to threaten the important railway junctions and stores depots at De Aar and Naauwpoort and to incite the Cape Afrikaners to join them. Even so these dispositions left about 21,000, including 6,000 Free Staters, to deal with the Natal garrison which, when the reinforcements were disembarked, would total 13,000 Regulars and 1,800 Natal Volunteers before the Army Corps began arriving in early November.

Commanding the Natal invasion was the victor of 1881, Commandant-General Piet Joubert. In the inter-war years he had been the focus of the moderate and progressive elements in the Transvaal and had twice opposed Kruger for the Presidency. Now aged 66, he had been against the war and he struck the young Free Stater, Deneys Reitz, as being 'a kindly, well-meaning old man' who seemed 'bewildered at the heavy responsibility now resting upon him and unequal to the burden'. Certainly the mobilization delays and the caution he was soon to display revealed that he was not the man he had been in 1881.

The bulk of his forces were still much as then, the burgher commandos of mounted riflemen, though each now had a modern magazine rifle, the German Mauser. Every commando elected its own officers and was divided into two or more field-cornetcies each of 150–200 men, which were subdivided into corporalships of about 25 men. These numbers were variable and the strength of a commando depended on the area or town from which it came; the strongest was 3,000 from Potchefstroom, the smallest only 60 from Springs. Among them were units of German, Dutch, Irish and other European and American volunteers. In addition there were nearly 3,000 Regular, uniformed troops: the 1,200-strong South African Republic Police (ZARP), a para-military force which combined the natural military qualities of the burghers with experience of discipline; and both Republics' State Artillery, largely German trained and officered, with 100 guns, mostly modern 75mm Creusot and Krupp field guns with a maximum range of 8,500 yards and the 155mm Creusot, firing a 94-lb shell with a range of 11,000 yards. The Boer forces, therefore, had all the attributes of their 1881 forebears—mobility, marksmanship and motivation, together with greatly improved armaments.

Their potential was largely under-rated by the War Office and most of the Army, in whose collective memory the humiliations of 1881 burned brighter than the lessons. To face a wholly mounted enemy and to fight in a theatre of war having an area slightly more than that of France and the Iberian Peninsula combined, of mostly open rolling country, with few roads and towns of any size and only three main railway lines running south-north, the British sent a force consisting predominantly of infantry. Indeed when Australia and New Zealand offered contingents, they were told that infantry would be preferable—despite most of their forces being trained as mounted riflemen, a role they would reassume not long after their arrival. Canada's first contribution was purely infantry but later contingents were all mounted. The three battalions of the pre-war Natal garrison each had a company of Mounted Infantry and battalions at

The Orange Free State's Winsburg Commando with, in front, two guns of the Free State Artillery.

home were supposed to have some men trained as such. In Natal there were two cavalry regiments, two more were coming from India, and the Army Corps would include a cavalry division of two brigades each of four regiments: under 6,000 cavalrymen in all. Some of the small Natal Volunteer units were mounted, as was the 600-strong Imperial Light Horse, recently formed from refugee Uitlanders. The latter were mounted riflemen, but in the regular cavalry, although every man had a carbine, chief reliance was placed on shock action with sword or lance. Though obviously all were trained to ride, few were as good horsemen as the Boers, whose horses were an extension of themselves.

After the arrival of the reinforcements there would be 11 infantry battalions in Natal, each of between 800 and 1,010 men, and the Army Corps would provide another 24, formed in three divisions, each of two brigades. The single-shot Martini of 1881 had been replaced by a bolt-action, 10-round magazine rifle, Lee-Metford or Lee-Enfield, sighted to 2,800 yards but most effective from 500 to 800 yards; unfortunately its magazine had to be loaded singly whereas the Boer Mauser was loaded with clips of five rounds. In addition to its rifles, each battalion had a mule-drawn Maxim machine-gun, as did each cavalry regiment and MI company.

Most of the British artillery were six-gun 12-pounder horse or 15-pounder field batteries, the latter having 175 men and 137 horses, the former slightly more. RHA gun-crews were mounted, RFA gunners rode on the limbers and the gun axle-tree seats. On the outbreak of war there were three RFA batteries and one 7-pounder mountain battery in Natal and three more field batteries were coming with the reinforcements. The infantry divisions from England each had three field batteries and each cavalry brigade had its own horse battery. The maximum ranges of 12- and 15-pounders were 5,400 and 5,600 yards respectively when firing HE shell but about 1,600 less when firing shrapnel, which was most commonly used in the war. They were thus considerably outranged by the Boer guns, though the latter fired only shell. Furthermore neither pattern of British gun had gun-shields (essential because all firing was by direct, not indirect, fire), the lack of which had cost the gunners dear at the Ingogo. Accompanying the Army Corps were three 5-inch howitzer batteries firing a 50-lb shell with a range of 4,900 yards but initially the Natal force had to rely for heavy guns on the Royal Navy's conversion for land use of its 4.7-inch guns (45-pounders) with a range of 10,000 yards, which were landed at Durban from HM ships *Terrible*, *Powerful*, *Monarch* and *Doris*.

The field experience of the army of the Nineties was confined to mountain warfare against elusive, scattered groups of rifle-armed tribesmen on the

North-West Frontier or desert warfare against largely spear-and-sword masses in the Sudan. The former called for small-scale operations, long-range marksmanship and rapid hill climbing; the latter for close-order formations and volley-fire. Some of the battalions deployed in South Africa had had experience in one or other of these, though neither had much application to the war they were about to fight, except perhaps in developing the attributes required of the individual soldier—skill-at-arms, marching and the ability to look after himself in the field—and teaching junior officers and NCOs the techniques of leadership.

Within the limitations imposed by under-manning and restricted manoeuvre areas, the majority of the troops had been trained in England in accordance with the current manuals, which were drawn up with a European enemy in mind, that is, one that would fight in a broadly similar manner to the British. The brunt of any battle would be borne by infantry, though cavalry, artillery and engineers would be necessary for the former's success. The attack theory, for instance, was based on a preliminary bombardment to soften up the enemy position; once this had been achieved, the guns would cease fire and prepare to accompany the infantry advance. This was divided into three groups: a firing line going forward and periodically firing volleys, supports following behind to keep the firing line built up, and finally reserves. The numbers allotted to each group would depend on circumstances, but a battalion might start its attack with its eight companies deployed two, two and four. In theory the firing line would, as it advanced, achieve such a measure of fire superiority over the enemy that the position could finally be carried by a bayonet charge. As the enemy broke, the cavalry would be let loose in pursuit. Since regimental officers could command only by the power of their voices, by bugle calls and by hand signals, the infantry's attack formations had of necessity to be, if not the shoulder-to-shoulder of Crimean days, at least fairly close and carefully controlled. Section volleys[15] were preferred to independent fire; they were thought more effective and less wasteful of ammunition. Though the use of cover was not forbidden, officers were reminded that it must be 'subordinate to order and cohesion and to the necessity of pressing forward unremittingly'.

Neither savage warfare nor the manuals provided

Gunner of the Transvaal 'Staats-Artillerie' in pre-war full dress with Creusot 155mm gun.

ideal tactics for the battles soon to blaze across the veldt. Had the lessons of the American Civil War been studied as diligently as those of the Franco-Prussian War, the Army might have been better prepared to face a terrain of wide-open spaces and an enemy whose tactical philosophy was based primarily on the hit-and-run principle, whether it be running forward to hit again or running away to fight another day. Most important of all, the running was at a horse's speed whereas the British Regulars were tied to the pace of a laden infantryman, often unacclimatized and not long disembarked from three weeks at sea.

All the Regulars were products of the once-controversial short-service enlistment system; indeed almost half the Army Corps were recalled Reservists,

Transvaal hospital train with uniformed doctors and nurses. Medical assistance came from Germany, Holland and Russia.

which that system had been designed to provide. Later in the war the Regulars would be joined by Britain's second-line, the embodied Militia, the Yeomanry and Volunteers,[16] and specially enlisted volunteer civilians. Of value out of all proportion to their numbers were the Canadian, Australian and New Zealand volunteers. The States of Queensland, Victoria and New South Wales had offered assistance three months before hostilities began, followed by New Zealand in September, and Canada and the other Australian states on the outbreak of war. Not only was this a most heart-warming demonstration of Imperial unity—the very thing Milner set such store by—but many of these men had similar backgrounds to the Boer farmers and were thus good shots and natural horsemen, as of course were the South Africans of British stock who provided the largest element among the Colonials.[17]

Another change from 1881 was that the old numbered infantry regiments had now become battalions of larger regiments embracing Regulars, Militia and Volunteers with territorial affiliations. Among those destined for the seat of war were the descendants of the victims of Majuba, the 58th now 2nd Northamptonshire Regiment, the 3/60th now

King's Royal Rifle Corps (though still known colloquially as 60th Rifles) and the 92nd now 2nd Gordon Highlanders. The latter, coming from India, were to find themselves, as will shortly be seen, in a brigade commanded by their senior subaltern of Majuba days, Ian Hamilton.

No longer did the Army take the field in the scarlet, blue or green of that time but in universal khaki drill, the only splashes of colour being the regimental flashes on the khaki helmets and the kilts and hose of the Highlanders. Though the new dress afforded better concealment from the sharp-eyed Boers, the drill material, while admirable for India or the Sudan, was to prove insufficiently warm or hardwearing and had to be replaced by serge. The long marches would soon reveal that the infantryman's boots simply came apart under South African conditions and a new pattern had to be manufactured. Other deficiencies came to light once fighting began: shortages of saddlery and harness, a lack of transport and hospital equipment and inadequate bridging facilities. Staff duties lacked system, intelligence work was unpractised, many officers had little military knowledge except of close-order drill and their soldiers had not been trained to think for themselves, a grave disadvantage as most Boers had considerable personal initiative. An infantry officer wrote of the average soldier: 'No class or race could equal him in standing firm, shoulder to

54

Troopers of the Natal Carbineers, a permanent volunteer corps embodied on 29 September with 500 all ranks. When mounted the rifle was carried in a bucket attached to the bandolier, a device peculiar to Natal troops.

shoulder, against a mob of howling savages . . . but modern warfare is just a bit beyond him. He has neither the intellect of a highly educated man, the instinct of a savage or the self-reliance of the colonial. He is a good fellow but a terribly thick-headed one'.[18]

Although the Army Corps was organized into divisions and brigades, their commanders, staffs and units had not worked and trained together in peacetime, with the exception of one brigade. The divisional lieutenant-generals and brigade major-generals had all seen active service of some sort but none had experience of commanding large formations in the field apart from Lieutenant-General Gatacre who had led a division, and Major-General Lyttleton a brigade, in the Sudan. The Corps Commander, Sir Redvers Buller, had never held an independent command as a general. Such was the shortage of troops in the theatre when the Corps started to arrive that its organization was broken up and brigades, even battalions, were deployed piecemeal. For example, Hildyard's 2nd Infantry Brigade (the one exception above), though nominally in the 1st Division, was never to serve with it, and Gatacre became completely divorced from the brigades of the 3rd Division he was nominated to command.

This situation arose from the critical developments in Natal and elsewhere since the Boers had invaded on 12 October. Sir George White's task was the defence of Natal and before leaving England he knew

of Buller's view that the best defence line was the River Tugela. But to hold there would mean abandoning half the colony without a fight. He realized that to go north to the frontier, as Colley had done, would risk his force being encircled in the narrow apex of the colony. He therefore decided to concentrate at Ladysmith, an important railway junction and Natal's chief military centre, already supplied for 60 days, ready to fight on the Biggarsberg hills just to the north, though this would mean having on his left rear Van Reenen's Pass through the Drakensberg, whence the Free Staters were likely to come. He then learned that the over-confident Penn Symons had already moved up to Dundee, 45 miles north-east of Ladysmith, with 4,500 men, thus leaving a dangerous gap between himself and the main body of the Natal Field Force concentrating at Ladysmith. White's instinct was to recall Symons but he was persuaded to leave him there as a reassurance for the Natalians who were apprehensive both of the Boers and of a Zulu uprising.

Symons was not only dangerously exposed but

The Imperial Light Horse, 500 strong, raised in Natal from Uitlanders on 8 September, riding out of Estcourt.

was caught napping. On 20 October Lucas Meyer's commando, 3,500 strong, appeared on a ridge to the east, Talana Hill, and began shelling the camp. Leaving 1st Leicesters and one battery to guard the camp, Symons ordered 2nd Royal Dublin Fusiliers, 1st King's Royal Rifle Corps and 1st Royal Irish Fusiliers to attack after a preliminary bombardment, sending the 18th Hussars round behind the Boers to cut off their retreat. As the infantry formed up under cover of a wood, Colonel Gunning of the 60th, with only moments to live, urged his men to 'Remember Majuba!'. When the bombardment ceased, the infantry attack stalled under a storm of Mauser bullets. Symons rode forward to give a lead and was mortally wounded. The guns re-opened fire, enabling the infantry to reach the top and send the Boers running for their horses, but the final charge sustained more casualties from the 'friendly' shell-fire, which did not stop in time. Part of the 18th Hussars, finding themselves engulfed by the retreating Boers, veered north and rode straight into Erasmus's 2,000-strong commando, which had arrived during the fight, and had to surrender. The capture of Talana Hill was hailed by the British Press as a victory but Symons' successor, Major-General Yule, was the next day to find his command almost surrounded. On the 22nd he received orders from White to retreat to Ladysmith by a circuitous route to the south-east.

While the war's first battle was being fought, Kock's Johannesburg commando, which included a German contingent, had ridden south, by-passing Dundee, and captured a supply train at Elandslaagte station, only ten miles north-east of Ladysmith. White had been joined by Buller's Cavalry Division commander, the squat and energetic John French, accompanied by one of his staff, a clever cavalryman named Major Douglas Haig. On the 21st, with the Imperial Light Horse and the Natal Artillery battery, French turned Kock's men out of the station but came under artillery fire and had to withdraw out of range and await reinforcements.

White quickly sent up by train Ian Hamilton with 1st Devons, 1st Manchesters and 2nd Gordons, followed along the road by the 5th Dragoon Guards and 5th Lancers with two field batteries. South of the station was a horseshoe-shaped ridge of high ground, its open end nearest the railway, the eastern arm of which was held by the commando of about 1,000 men with three guns. Detraining his men behind the western arm, Hamilton explained his plan: while seven companies of the Devons attacked frontally across the 2-mile dip between the arms, the four companies of the Manchesters, five of the Gordons and the dismounted ILH were to work their way round the toe of the horseshoe and roll up the Boers from the south, while the cavalry were to follow the railway, ready to cut in behind the enemy. With vivid memories of the Boer musketry, Hamilton impressed on all ranks the need for wide intervals in the assault, three yards between each man in line, and 450 yards between each successive line—a much greater dispersion than anything practised at Aldershot. Excitedly the men, mostly experienced soldiers from India, cheered Hamilton, shouting, 'We'll do it, sir!'

The afternoon was drawing on and the black clouds of a thunderstorm were massing over the Boer position. After half-an-hour's bombardment the Devons, with three companies in line forward, went over the western arm and advanced steadily across the flat in short bounds, pausing to fire volleys. Their extended formation paid dividends against the Boer gunfire and their khaki blended with the veldt and made poor aiming marks for the enemy riflemen. The nearer they got, however, the heavier the fire, until they were forced to take cover while their supporting batteries re-opened fire and the flank attack developed. The latter had been circling the toe but it too came under a murderous fire as it approached the Boer left flank. The Manchesters went to ground and the Gordons suffered severely in their conspicuous kilts as they were halted by some wire fences. At that moment the thunderstorm broke over the battlefield, enabling the advance to be resumed. Hamilton rode up to order the charge, the bugles sounded and the bayonets swept forward to the objective. Most of the Boers fled and a white flag went up. Hamilton ordered 'Cease Fire'. As the soaked, victorious infantry rested, a hidden group of Boers rushed forward firing. Caught unawares, the infantry recoiled. But Hamilton again was there to rally the

15-pounder battery of Royal Field Artillery in Natal. Note gunners seated on limbers and gun axle-tree seats. Photograph by Horace Nicholls.

Firing line of 1st Royal Dublin Fusiliers on manoeuvres in England, showing a mode of firing and lack of dispersion that would soon need rectifying.

men, calling for the pipes and bugles to sound once more. The infantry recovered and charged home. By now the Devons had also crested the ridge and all over the captured position men lifted their helmets on their upheld rifles, shouting 'Majuba! Majuba!'

The surviving Boers reached their horses and made off north-east to escape in the gathering darkness. Suddenly, from their left, one squadron each of the 5th Dragoon Guards and 5th Lancers crashed into them. The Boers were a courageous people but those lance-points and sword-blades coming at them out of the gloom filled them with panic. Some tried to surrender, but for lancers knee-to-knee at full gallop it was difficult to spare one foe and slay another. For a mile and a half the cavalry rode through them, rallied and rode through again until it was dark. About half Kock's commando were casualties and Kock himself, who had faced the British at Boomplaats as a boy of 12, was dying. British casualties totalled 260 killed and wounded, the

Gordons, who lost 25 per cent of their strength, being the chief victims. The survivors, though, were elated at having won a well-fought and well-coordinated battle.

Sadly their elation was short-lived. White, alarmed by reports of the approaching Free Staters, ordered a hurried withdrawal to Ladysmith. Three days later he fought an inconclusive action at Rietfontein to protect the flank of Yule's column from Dundee which reached Ladysmith on the 26th, hungry and dispirited after a 60-mile march in drenching rain. On the same day the Transvaalers, having made contact with the Free Staters, were close to Ladysmith and soon their combined forces of about 24,000 would be able to surround White's 13,000 crammed into the little town.

Still full of civilians, it lay in a dusty, unhygienic bowl overlooked by hills on all sides. It was no place to be locked up in and only 15 miles south, down the railway to Colenso, lay the Tugela on which White had been urged to stand. The route to it, through hilly country suited to a fighting withdrawal, was still open, yet White decided to risk another battle in the hope of decisively defeating the nearer and stronger Transvaalers to the north and east of the

A 12th Lancer at Aldershot in the new khaki service dress, armed with sword, lance and carbine, all to be of little use against Boers.

town before they could concert plans with the Free Staters, who would then be at a numerical and tactical disadvantage.

He devised a complex plan of dividing his force into four unequal brigades for a two-pronged dawn attack after a night approach march, with subsidiary operations on either flank. Even with experienced brigade commanders served by well-trained staffs and battalions practised in night movement and thoroughly familiar with the ground, the plan would have been hazardous given the difficulties of command and control it presented. Hamilton's

Boer commandos at Newcastle, Natal, 35 miles north of Symons' position at Dundee. They include all age groups and many seem to be in their 'Sunday best'. Most have Mausers, but the elderly man seated left has a Martini.

59

1st Royal Irish Fusiliers entraining for the front in Natal. The helmet flashes are a white grenade over 'IF' on red.

brigade, which at least had functioned well at Elandslaagte, had the task of attacking the main Boer position on Pepworth Hill, five miles to the north-east, supported by three field batteries and with the 5th Dragoon Guards and ILH ready to exploit success. Before this attack went in, a five-battalion brigade[19] supported by four batteries was to seize Long Hill, two miles south-east of Pepworth, and then attack the Boer left flank on the latter in conjunction with Hamilton's frontal assault. This brigade was entrusted to Lieutenant-Colonel Grimwood of the 2/60th, for no better reason than that he was the senior battalion commander. Grimwood's right was to be protected by an advance due east to Lombard's Kop by French with the 5th Lancers, 19th Hussars and Natal Carbineers. Finally, and most risky of all, Lieutenant-Colonel Carleton with his 1st Royal Irish Fusiliers, 1st Gloucesters and the 10th Mountain

Battery was to move due north by night, through the Boer lines up the valley between Pepworth and Tchrengula Hills to the west, in order to seize the pass at Nicholson's Nek through which Hamilton's cavalry was to pass in pursuit after Pepworth fell.

From the start things went wrong. Carleton was unable to reach his objective before dawn, and while his force was climbing the Tchrengula Hills the mountain battery's mules stampeded, carrying off the guns and reserve ammunition, and alerting the Boers to the force's presence. Carleton's two battalions soon found themselves pinned down by a party of Free Staters led by Field-Cornet Christian De Wet—a man whose 'fierce eyes and keen determined face' were soon to become famous.

To the east Grimwood found himself at dawn on his appointed start-line, but with half his brigade missing, no sign of French's cavalry and no Boers on Long Hill. As he wondered what to do, his men came under fire from the east where another great name for the future, Louis Botha, had taken over Lucas Meyer's commando and moved it down from Long

Hill to enfilade Grimwood's troops. So critical did their position become that, far from being able to attack Pepworth, Hamilton had to detach battalions to his right to support the luckless Grimwood who, finding the situation beyond him, had lost control. Even 2nd Rifle Brigade, arriving by train from Durban, found themselves rushed into action from the station which, with the rest of the town, was now being bombarded by a 155mm Creusot, or 'Long Tom', which the Boers had emplaced on Pepworth. Adding to the panic thus caused in the town were reports that the Free Staters were preparing to attack from the west.

With his plan in tatters, White ordered a retreat. Completely in the open and outgunned, the 13th and 53rd Batteries RFA put down a barrage of covering fire while the King's and Manchesters formed an intermediate firing line. However Grimwood's other battalions drew such fire from Botha's men that their retreat quickly turned into a rush for the town. French's cavalry, which followed, was no better. On

Tchrengula Carleton's men had been suffering heavy casualties because their volley-firing constantly exposed them to the Boers' snap-shooting. A detached group put up a white flag, some men ran, and Carleton ordered the remains of his two battalions to surrender. Standing nearby Deneys Reitz had a view over the whole battlefield where 'great clouds of dust billowed as the troops withdrew, and the manner of their going had every appearance of a rout'. He heard De Wet mutter 'Loose your horsemen', but the elderly and cautious Joubert, with thousands ready mounted, let the opportunity slip. The Natal Field Force flung itself back into Ladysmith, covered at the last moment by two 4.7-inch guns from HMS *Powerful* under Captain Lambton RN which had just arrived.

1st King's Royal Rifle Corps near Dundee. Note black buttons and equipment of a Rifle Regiment. Centre man wears NW Frontier ribbon for 1897. Photograph by Horace Nicholls.

Firing line of 1st Devons. First, third and seventh figures from right have their helmets back to front to aim better when lying down, when the helmets tilted forwards. Compare with photograph on p. 58.

This day, 30 October, became known as 'Mournful Monday'. It was a battle[20] from which only the Royal Artillery had emerged with credit. The beaten troops had lost 1,200 casualties and nearly a thousand prisoners. White himself was heartbroken and thought his soldiering days were over. By 2 November the Boers cut the railway to Colenso and surrounded the town. French and the 2nd Dublins had managed to get out, but four cavalry regiments, nine battalions and six batteries were now ineffective except to defend Ladysmith. Apart from the Dublins at Colenso and the 1st Borders further south, the only defence White could render to Natal was to tie down as much of Joubert's army around Ladysmith as possible. Fortunately for him the Boers wasted the great chance his fumbling had afforded them and, apart from sending Botha on a raiding reconnaissance south across the Tugela, the rest settled down to a leisurely investment of the town—so leisurely that some of the burghers decided to go home.

Nevertheless there was now a third besieged garrison for Buller's Corps to relieve. In distant Mafeking, 850 miles up the western railway from Cape Town, Colonel Baden-Powell with 1,200 assorted police and volunteers was invested by some 5,000 Boers. His only hope was that he could be reached from the north by the Rhodesian force being organized by Colonel Plumer; he could expect no relief from the south until the railway was cleared and Kimberley secured. At the latter place 7,000 Boers under Piet Cronje of Potchefstroom fame were surrounding Colonel Kekewich, who had just under 600 Regulars, including half his own 1st Loyal North Lancashire, and 2,000 police and volunteers. At neither Mafeking nor Kimberley did the Boers prosecute their sieges with much vigour and both towns were well-provisioned. However both places had a symbolic significance for the Boers, Mafeking because it had been the start-point of the Jameson Raid and Kimberley because of its diamond fields. Furthermore within Kimberley was the Boers' arch enemy—and an increasing thorn in Kekewich's side—Cecil Rhodes. Though Kekewich commanded the garrison, Kimberley was very much Rhodes's town, and he pestered Milner at the Cape with alarmist signals, demanding that its relief be given

Charge of the 5th Lancers at Elandslaagte by Caton Woodville. This was one of the rare occasions when the lance was useful. Trumpeter Shurlock, aged 14, (centre right) became one of the war's first popular heroes for killing three Boers with his revolver.

Boer commanders in Natal. Left and right, Generals Lucas Meyer and Daniel Erasmus, who fought Talana Hill. Later superseded by the then Commandant Louis Botha, centre, subsequently Transvaal C-in-C.

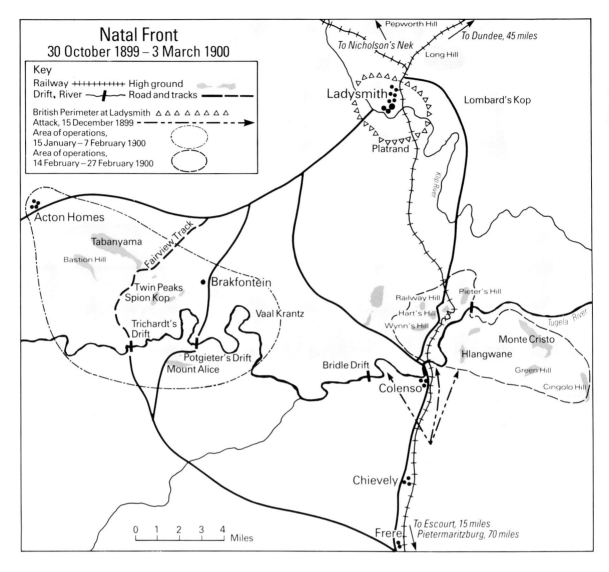

Pepworth Hill
To Nicholson's Nek
To Dundee, 45 miles
Long Hill
Ladysmith
Lombard's Kop
Platrand
Kip River
Acton Homes
Tabanyama
Bastion Hill
Fairview Track
Twin Peaks
Spion Kop
Brakfontein
Vaal Krantz
Railway Hill
Pieter's Hill
Hart's Hill
Wynn's Hill
Tugela River
Trichardt's
Drift
Monte Cristo
Hlangwane
Potgieter's Drift
Mount Alice
Bridle Drift
Green Hill
Colenso
Cingolo Hill
Chievely
To Escourt, 15 miles
Frere
Pietermaritzburg, 70 miles

0 1 2 3 4 Miles

priority. In addition to the besieged towns there was the threat to the railway junctions in the Cape Midlands on whose unfettered use all future offensive operations against the Republics would depend, and for whose defence in late October there were only one cavalry regiment, four battalions and three batteries.

The man to whom all looked to resolve this depressing situation was the Army Corps commander, Sir Redvers Buller. A former 60th Rifleman and a prominent member of Wolseley's Ring, he had been 'magnificent as a major' in the Zulu War, where he had won the Victoria Cross. But, as he had progressed up the promotion ladder, there had been signs that

the higher he climbed the less sure was his touch. He had performed well as a brigade commander in the Eastern Sudan in 1884 but had not shone as Wolseley's Chief of Staff on the Nile Expedition. He had held the great military offices of Adjutant-General and Quartermaster-General and had failed to become Commander-in-Chief in 1895 (in preference to Wolseley and Roberts) only because of a change of Government. In 1897 he had been given the chief home command at Aldershot, but his handling of large bodies of troops in the Army Manoeuvres the following year had been disappointing and indecisive. A senior War Office civil servant described him as having 'a rough exterior and an explosive interior'.

Yule's rain-sodden retreat from Dundee to Ladysmith. 1st Leicesters in greatcoats. Photograph by Horace Nicholls.

If his impressive figure owed more, in 1899, to self-indulgence than to the great physical strength of his earlier years, his whole demeanour, aided by his VC and evocative name, seemed to the general public and lower ranks of the Army, for whose welfare he was always much concerned, to be the epitome of 'the bulldog breed', inspiring a confidence in his abilities shared by almost everyone—except himself. When told in July that he was to have the chief command in South Africa he had been reluctant. He admired the Boers, knowing how formidable they were, he had never exercised such a command, and he thought he would be better employed as a deputy. Later, when he learned of White's and Symons' deployments—against his advice—his forebodings about his task increased. The plan, agreed before he sailed and based on the assumption that White could hold Natal, involved the Army Corps being landed at the Cape ports, prior to a general advance based on the railways through the Free State to Bloemfontein and on to Pretoria. When he landed at Cape Town on 31 October, to find White out of action, Natal and Cape Colony almost defenceless, Milner pressing Rhodes' claims and apprehensive about a rising in the Colony, and Boer activity spread over a front of 400 miles from west to east, the burden of responsibility pressed more heavily than ever upon him. He soon had to agree that the planned advance would have to be postponed and the formations of the Corps deployed as they arrived to deal with the various emergencies.

Thus the Corps was broken up at the very start.

Lieutenant-General Clery, commanding 2nd Division but without either of his own brigades as they had not arrived, was sent off to hold Natal with Hildyard's 2nd Brigade and Barton's 6th (of the 1st and 3rd Divisions respectively). To guard Cape Colony French, safely out of Ladysmith, was despatched with most of his Cavalry Division to the Colesberg area to protect De Aar and Naauwpoort, while Gatacre, without his 3rd Division, was given the Regular battalions already in the Cape to operate from Stormberg. Further mounted units were to be raised locally in Natal and Cape Colony, such as the South African Light Horse which, like the ILH, were mostly refugee Uitlanders. Finally an attempt was to be made by Lord Methuen to relieve Kimberley. Since his 1st Division had already lost its 2nd Brigade to Natal, a new, 9th Brigade was formed from unbrigaded battalions in or arriving at the Cape. The GOC at the Cape, Lieutenant-General Forestier-Walker, who would be responsible for the reception and onward transmission of the incoming troops, had virtually no staff of his own, so Buller had to break up his own Corps headquarters. As Milner said, Buller in his first three weeks 'had done wonders' but, having disposed of his Corps and headquarters, suddenly relinquished his overall responsibility and went to Natal to rescue White, leaving French, Gatacre and Methuen to their own devices.

6. AN INVISIBLE ENEMY

WESTERN FRONT, 21 NOVEMBER–11 DECEMBER 1899

From Methuen's base at Orange River Station it was 75 miles to Kimberley up a single-track railway across a flat, sun-scorched expanse of veldt, broken here and there by occasional rocky ridges and isolated hills, or kopjes, rising abruptly some 200 feet above the plain. Two-thirds of the way to Kimberley the line crossed the Modder River. Before Methuen, then, lay a number of positions from which his advance, which for supply reasons must be tied to the railway, might be disputed and which, owing to the general flatness of the terrain, would give the enemy clear long-range observation of his movements and would also be difficult to reconnoitre closely. Intelligence would be doubly hard to acquire because Methuen's maps were rudimentary and inaccurate, a defect exacerbated by ironstone in the soil which affected compass bearings. Finally, although he had about 10,000 men under command, less than 900 of them were mounted.

He had one Regular cavalry regiment, the 9th Lancers, to whom were attached the first of the Australians, a squadron of the New South Wales Lancers which had happened to be in England on the outbreak of war, the locally-raised 200-strong Rimington's Guides and about a hundred Mounted Infantry. This dearth of mounted troops would also diminish the chances of making wide flanking movements to exploit the Boers' sensitivity about their flanks and rear and make more difficult the protection of the vital railway in Methuen's own rear. These problems would delay the speedy relief so vigorously urged by Rhodes.

On the credit side Methuen had eight good battalions, though the four of Guards[21] and the new 9th Brigade's 1st Northumberland Fusiliers and 2nd Northamptonshire were not long disembarked and had many Reservists in their ranks. Another of 9th Brigade's battalions, 1st Loyals, was at half strength, its other half being in Kimberley. Artillery and engineer support consisted of two field batteries, four Royal Navy 12-pounders and four companies of Royal Engineers.

Methuen was familiar with the area, having led a regiment of mounted rifles in the bloodless Bechuanaland expedition of 1884, and his military outlook was by no means as conservative as his chiefly home service and Guards background might have suggested. Brass buttons and buckles were to be dulled, white equipment stained and, as Lieutenant Barton of the Northamptons recorded: 'Officers are to discard their useless swords and carry rifles or carbines so as to confuse the Boer marksmen. All the old Aldershot Drill Book Tactics are to be abolished and we shall adopt very extended order, men getting quickly from rock to rock, irregularity of line being sought and "regular dressing" avoided'. The Northamptons, aware of how their forebears had suffered in 1881, had devoted much attention to shooting in the inter-war years and now, before the advance began, practised the new field movements, but Barton observed that 'the difficulty was to get the men to keep away from one another; they will get in knots, shoulder to shoulder'. The efforts of drill sergeants on the barrack square proved hard to eradicate, as did the legacy of the relatively close confines of the English training areas.

Such intelligence as Methuen had been able to acquire suggested that the first opposition would be encountered 15 miles up the line at Belmont, where a group of kopjes on the east side dominated the approaches. Having advanced on 21 November, Methuen planned a dawn attack from the west on the 23rd after a night approach march. His plan required both brigades to attack the two westerly kopjes, after which the Guards Brigade on the right was to provide a fire base while 9th Brigade was to swing forward to attack the main hill behind the initial objectives from the north. Each brigade was to be supported by a

Lieutenant-General Lord Methuen, 1st Division.

General Piet Cronje.

Major-General Pole-Carew, 9th Brigade.

Major-General Wauchope, 3rd (Highland) Brigade.

Mounted Infantry of 1st Northumberland Fusiliers reconnoitring near Belmont. MI were accoutred with cavalry bandoliers rather than the normal waistbelt pouches.

battery and the 9th Lancers and Rimington's Guides were to ride left and right respectively round the hills to cut off the Boers once the infantry gained the heights.

Owing to inadequate reconnaissance, faulty maps and inaccurate compass bearings, the attack did not go as planned. 9th Brigade, with Northumberland Fusiliers left, Northamptons right and 2nd King's Own Yorkshire Light Infantry in reserve, deployed on time in the correct position but had to delay its attack as the Guards were late. By the time the attack started it was growing light and the Boers—2,000

Free Staters under Jacobus Prinsloo—opened fire. The distance between the start-lines and the dead ground at the base of the hills proved greater than anticipated and casualties began to fall, particularly among the Grenadiers whose ranks had closed up. Quickening their speed they began to veer off to the right. The Northamptons had to swing left to avoid the Scots Guards, whom they found lying in a mass at the foot of the objective, waiting for the Grenadiers to come up on their right. The latter, however, were now scaling not their own objective but that of the two Coldstream battalions in reserve. 1st Coldstream on the right came under heavy enfilade fire from two small kopjes south of the main hill and diverted to attack these. Meanwhile the Fusiliers and North-amptons, supported by fire from the Scots Guards, who had gained their objective, were meeting very stiff resistance as they clambered up the rocks in small groups. Methuen, realizing his plan was in some disarray, ordered 2nd Coldstream to assist. The assaulting companies, even battalions, had become considerably intermingled, but the men pressed on under the nearest officer until both the original brigade objectives were taken. Only the main hill remained, but with 1st Coldstream threatening the Boer left, the Fusiliers their right, and the Grenadiers and Scots Guards advancing frontally covered by the guns, the Boers abandoned the position and made off on their ponies north-east. Methuen's weakness in cavalry now deprived him of total victory and indeed the Boers rounded on the 9th Lancers who, with tired horses, were enabled to withdraw only by the New South Wales squadron hastily dismounting and opening covering fire.

For most of the soldiers Belmont had been their first action. Above all they had learned what manoeuvres at home had never taught them—how difficult it was to locate the positions of an enemy adept at concealment and using smokeless powder, even at quite close ranges. Sustaining a loss of about 100 casualties and 40 prisoners, the Boers had inflicted 295 casualties, including 75 killed; 45 per cent of these had been borne by the Grenadiers who, according to Barton, 'were crowded to one pace apart' in contrast to his own battalion which 'kept about six or ten paces apart'.[22] The Free Staters had been dismayed by the persistence of the infantry, who for their part now knew that the enemy would run rather than face a bayonet charge, but knew also

that, lacking sufficient and speedy cavalry to cut off the Boers, they could expect repetitions of Belmont at each area of high ground that lay ahead.

So it was two days later at Graspan. Somewhat demoralized by their experience, only some 400 Free Staters were willing to stand on the next group of kopjes to the east of the railway. Their resolve was stiffened by the arrival of a man who was to prove one of the most outstanding figures of the war, Koos De la Rey, with Transvaalers from Cronje's forces besieging Mafeking and Kimberley. This reinforcement, bringing the Boer strength up to nearly what it had been at Belmont, was unknown to Methuen. Employing only 9th Brigade reinforced by a newly-arrived 250-strong Naval Brigade, Methuen attacked after a preliminary and largely ineffectual bombard-

Rimington's Guides or 'Tigers', so-called from the leopard-skin puggarees round their hats. Raised by a Regular officer, Major Rimington, from men familiar with the Republics and fluent in Afrikaans or a native dialect.

Battle of Belmont, 23 November, by Frank Dadd. The Guards Brigade attacking.

ment but soon realized that the hills were more extensively held than he had anticipated. He therefore swung the Naval Brigade half-right to assault the south-east end of the heights. The sailors and Royal Marines, from HM ships *Powerful* and *Doris*, made a most gallant and determined attack which, though successful, cost them dear because of the conspicuousness of their sword-carrying officers and the men's tendency to bunch and refusal to take cover. Again the Boers did not await the bayonets and again the cavalry was launched in pursuit, only to be halted by a determined rearguard. Colonel Gough was removed by Methuen from command of the 9th Lancers and subsequently shot himself.

On the day of Graspan[23] a sortie had been launched by the defenders of Kimberley against their besiegers. Hitherto, apart from a sporadic bombardment, Kekewich had been more troubled by Rhodes than the Boers though the resources of Rhodes's De Beers' company had been useful in providing defence works, ammunition and a water supply. On 23 November Kekewich received a message by African runner to say that Methuen hoped to

reach Kimberley on the 26th. Though he had insufficient troops to sally out to meet the relief column—as demanded by Rhodes—Kekewich determined to harass the besiegers, with the aim of deterring them from sending reinforcements to confront Methuen. Hence the sortie on the 25th which inflicted casualties but failed to destroy any of the Boer guns. In any case, as has been seen, Prinsloo had already been joined by De la Rey. When there was no sign of Methuen on the next day, Kekewich realized he must have been delayed and accordingly ordered another sortie for the 28th. Lieutenant-Colonel Scott-Turner made a dashing attack on some strongly-held redoubts with the Cape Mounted Police and Diamond Fields Horse but exceeded his orders and was killed, together with 25 of his men; another 32 were wounded. The sortie failed to achieve anything and relief was no nearer for Methuen had been halted 25 miles away by 3,500 Boers led by Cronje, De la Rey and Prinsloo.

After Graspan the next most likely positions for a stand lay beyond the Modder River only a dozen miles south of Kimberley on the Magersfontein and Spytfontein ridges. Boers had already been spotted approaching the ridges from the east. Methuen planned to cut loose from the railway and outflank the ridges from the same direction. He then learned

from the station-master at Modder River that the Boers had blown the railway bridge and were digging in along the river banks. This was confirmed by cavalry patrols but whereas the 9th Lancers reported the enemy to be in thousands, Rimington's Guides said there were only 400. The latter figure confirmed Methuen's own appreciation that the main enemy force was at Spytfontein and that there was only a delaying party on the river. Nevertheless this must be dealt with first. So, countermanding the flank march, he ordered a frontal assault astride the railway for the 28th.

Methuen's dispositions were based on the only map he had of the Modder crossing, a sketch drawing which, as it happened, was erroneous. Just east of the bridge two rivers joined, the Modder itself and south of it the Riet, enclosing between them a tongue of land some 1,500 yards long and 700 yards wide, where stood a small hotel amid trees. On either side of the bridge the waterway, some 10 yards wide, flowed westwards between banks about 100—200 yards apart, 30 feet high and topped with bushes and trees. What Methuen's map did not show was that two miles east of the bridge the Riet turned sharply south to run parallel with the railway for just over a mile before bending away south-east, thus flanking the approaches from the south, which sloped very gently down to the crossing over flat, open country affording no cover other than folds in the ground and ant-hills. Methuen was also misinformed about the general fordability of the rivers. In fact the only crossings were one at Bosman's Drift, nearly five miles up the Riet to the south-east, and another two miles downstream from the bridge. This the station-master had reported as not being strongly held. To compound Methuen's faulty knowledge of the ground and misappreciation of the enemy strength—neither of which he tried to rectify by further reconnaissance—was the reception being planned for him by De la Rey.

Prinsloo's failure to resist two attacks had convinced De la Rey that the Boers' traditional use of dominating ground attracted artillery firing shrapnel overhead, which was demoralizing and caused casualties when riflemen raised themselves from cover to see the attackers in dead ground below. Furthermore, such positions made ineffective use of

Searchlight at Kimberley. Operated by Royal Engineers, it was used to signal to Methuen's column.

This he obligingly did. East of the railway advanced the Guards Brigade with, from left to right, 2nd Coldstream, 3rd Grenadiers, 1st Scots Guards with 1st Coldstream in reserve, supported by 75th Field Battery, while on the railway and to the west was 9th Brigade with 1st Loyals, 2nd KOYLI and 1st Northumberland Fusiliers forward. 2nd Northamptons had been left to guard the camp and railway in rear, but in reserve was 1st Argyll and Sutherland Highlanders, the first battalion to arrive of 3rd (Highland) Brigade which was on its way to join Methuen. Supporting 9th Brigade were the Naval 12-pounders and 18th Field Battery was astride the railway. As they breasted a rise the Guards saw three miles ahead the line of bushes and the few houses around the station lying peacefully in the early morning sunshine with not a soul in sight. Thoughts turned to breakfasting in such a pleasant spot, the march for most having begun on empty stomachs at 4 a.m. When three-quarters of the distance had been covered Methuen remarked to Colvile, the Guards brigadier, 'They're not there'.

Almost in answer to his words a blizzard of bullets ripped through the Guards' ranks—such a dense and unceasing volume of fire that all three leading battalions immediately went to ground. Some men tried to return the fire but could see nothing to aim at, others tried to get forward by short rushes or crawling. To the endless rattle of the Mausers were added the shell-bursts of six carefully hidden guns and the incessant throbbing of 1-pounder automatic pom-poms. By lying flat behind the few boulders and ant-hills the Guardsmen were relatively safe, but the slightest movement drew fire. Behind the prostrate infantry the field battery went into action in the open at 1,300 yards, firing shrapnel at the bank and the tree-covered tongue of land between the rivers, trying to search out the Boer guns. Their efforts succeeded in reducing the volume of fire but the Free State Artillery commander, the German Major Albrecht, had prepared alternative gun positions so as never to occupy one emplacement too long.

To get the advance moving Colvile ordered 1st Coldstream to the right to try and outflank the enemy, but the battalion found its way blocked by the hitherto unknown and unfordable north-south stretch of the Riet. The Coldstreamers pushed on down the left bank, only to be halted by Cronje's men at the bend. By 8 a.m. the entire Guards Brigade was

the flat trajectory of modern rifles. Fired at ground level across open ground this could create a much deeper belt of bullets than plunging fire from a height. He therefore persuaded Prinsloo and Cronje to dig in along the south bank of the Modder where, supported by concealed guns and aided by whitewashed stones spread out in front at different ranges, they could lay down an almost impenetrable fire zone across the exposed approaches. The whole plan, of course, presupposed that Methuen would attack frontally.

Maxim of 1st Argyll and Sutherland Highlanders prior to embarkation for South Africa. Mounted is Lieutenant-Colonel Goff, killed at Magersfontein.

pinned down by fire, tormented by flies and ants, and suffering increasingly from thirst as the sun climbed higher in the sky.

Over on the left a similar fate had befallen Pole-Carew's 9th Brigade, who were being engaged not only frontally but also in enfilade from some farm buildings and a rocky outcrop forward of the river. Across a four-mile front eight fine battalions hugged whatever cover they could find to escape the murderous swathe of bullets and shells. The British infantry had been bred in a tradition of ultimately closing with their enemy with the bayonet. In the past the enemy—be they French, Russians or savage hordes—had always been visible. Now, for the first time, the infantrymen lay powerless under a decimating musketry a long way from charging distance and they could not even see the enemy. It was not so much his fire but his invisibility that was so frustrating and disheartening. The more phlegmatic men sought refuge in the British soldier's old standby, sleep.

At least on the British left the farm area provided a recognizable target for the gunners. Holding this position and the river bank trenches west of the bridge were Prinsloo's Free Staters who, after their previous hurried retreats, were less than happy at having the river behind them. Around 1 p.m. a company of Argylls managed to get down a shallow gulley towards the river, thus cutting off the forward position from the trenches. Unnerved by this development and the gunfire, the Boers' firing

diminished. The KOYLI rushed the farm, turning out the Free Staters, who fled across the river by means of a drift and a dam to join their compatriots on the north bank in the village of Rosmead. Led by Pole-Carew, the Loyals and some Argylls followed to seize a bridgehead on the far side. Pole-Carew sent back for reinforcements and tried to push on with the 400 men he had with him through Rosmead to the bridge. He received some fire support from 62nd Field Battery which had just reached the battlefield with foundering horses, having covered as many miles as its battery number in 28 hours. But of infantry reserves none arrived and Pole-Carew's attempts to signal the rest of the Argylls to fight their way up the south bank parallel to him were unsuccessful. Nevertheless he made some headway until De la Rey, now aware that the Free State flank was collapsing, transferred some Transvaalers with guns to the threatened point. At the same time Pole-Carew, without means of signalling his position across the river, came under fire from his own artillery and could get no further. He still hoped to resume the attack before dark, given reinforcements, but all that reached him was a half-company of 2nd Coldstream which crossed the railway bringing news that Methuen was wounded and Colvile was now in command.

73

Infantrymen taking cover at Modder River. They have improved their cover with their entrenching tools, seen lying beside them.

East of the railway the Guards' situation had not changed since morning. Unaware of Pole-Carew's limited success, Colvile planned an artillery bombardment of the whole front, prior to an attack by the Guards at dusk. Informed of this by a gunner officer, Pole-Carew sensibly cancelled any further forward movement on the north bank. It was then represented to Colvile that the Guards were exhausted after a sweltering day without food or water under heavy fire and he postponed the attack until dawn. No word reached Pole-Carew.

When darkness fell De la Rey found that most of the Free Staters had decamped. He was all for continuing the battle next day but Cronje, who was in overall command, and the other commanders refused. Silently the Boers abandoned the position

they had so skilfully held and stole away northwards. The next morning 1st Division crossed the Modder without a shot being fired, but leaving on the south bank nearly 500 casualties, 70 of them killed. The Boers had lost 50 killed and 25 prisoners, as well as an unknown number of wounded. Although the position attacked had been gained eventually, De la Rey was the moral victor of the battle.

Methuen had displayed undoubted personal courage under fire but his generalship had been defective and only Pole-Carew had influenced the outcome. However Kimberley was but 20 miles off, with only the Spytfontein and Magersfontein ridges to bar the way. Had Methuen immediately followed up and had he possessed a sufficiency of mounted troops he might conceivably have caught the Boers off-balance and got into Kimberley. As it was he had to recover from his wound, the railway had to be repaired and reinforcements were awaited. In any case he had learned that Kimberley still had another 40 days' supplies. Twelve days were therefore spent

62nd Field Battery arriving at the Modder River battlefield after
its forced march from Orange River. The gun crews walked
much of the way to lessen the weight of the guns and limbers.

at Modder River, giving the Boers ample time to
prepare their next position. Though Methuen's force
had been joined by the 12th Lancers and another
hundred MI, giving him a total of 1,600 horsemen, so
inadequate was their scouting ability and so open the
country that, despite daily patrols, the extent and
nature of the Boer preparations were not discovered.
Patrolling by night was an unpractised art.

The Boers, reinforced to some 8,000 men with five
each of 75mm field guns and pom-poms, had decided
to hold a line nearly nine miles long running south-
east from just west of the railway near Spytfontein
to Moss Drift on the Modder, six miles east of
Methuen's camp, and centred on the Magersfontein
ridge. This ridge, running north-south, rose abruptly
from the veldt to a height of 170 feet, giving long,
clear views southwards, interrupted only by a small,
lower hill a mile away and another feature, more
extensive but of the same height, roughly midway
between Magersfontein and Modder River Station.
These two eminences became known as Horse
Artillery and Headquarters Hills. South-east of
Magersfontein, after a mile's gap, a low, scrub-
covered rise ran for some three miles down to Moss
Drift. Mindful of the excellent fire effect achieved at
Modder River, De la Rey persuaded Cronje to hold
this line on the flat, just in front of the high ground,
though constructing positions on the latter to deceive
British observers. From Moss Drift up the low rise to
the gap were mixed Transvaal and Free State
commandos behind stone breastworks with three

pom-poms and a 75mm at the Drift. In the
gap was a 50-strong detachment of Scandinavian
volunteers. Magersfontein itself was the key to the
position, since its capture would split the Boer force.
Its defence was entrusted to four commandos, two
from each Republic, with five guns and one pom-
pom, all under Cronje's personal command. At the
foot of the ridge and about 80 yards in front was dug
a narrow trench, 700 yards long, 3–5 feet deep, with
a stone breastwork, to be held by the OFS Hoopstadt
and Kroonstadt Commandos. To their right the other
two commandos constructed low stone defences, all
the positions being carefully camouflaged by scrub.
On the west flank mixed commandos were spread
over four and a half miles under the command of
Cronje's brother, Andries.

All that Methuen's patrols had been able to glean
was that the Boers were preparing to dispute his
advance from between their extreme right west of the
railway and Magersfontein itself. Of the actual
defences Methuen was ignorant; he was even
uncertain whether the ground down to Moss Drift
was held. He decided against trying to outflank the
Boers owing to the lack of water to the west and the
possibility of being taken in flank himself by other
Boers at Jacobsdal to the south-east, but chiefly

9th Lancers scouting before Magersfontein. The flat, open terrain inhibited close reconnaissance of concealed positions.

The Boer trench dug in front of the Magersfontein feature from which the Highland Brigade suffered severely.

because of the vulnerability of his only line of communications. Already Prinsloo and a thousand Free Staters had attacked Enslin Station, 30 miles back down the line, but had been driven off after a six-hour fight by two companies of Northamptons. Realizing that the Magersfontein ridge dominated not only his approaches but also the enemy line to the north-west, Methuen decided to attack it first at dawn after a night advance and thereafter roll up the Boer positions towards Spytfontein. For this task he planned to use Wauchope's recently-arrived Highland Brigade, in support of which part of Pole-Carew's 9th Brigade was to make a diversion up the railway. The Guards Brigade was to be in reserve, Babington's mounted brigade was to protect the Highlanders' right flank and 2nd KOYLI was to guard the rear of the attack by holding a drift between the camp and Moss Drift. The rest of 9th Brigade was to guard Modder River station and the camp while the hitherto unbrigaded 1st Gordon Highlanders[24] was to escort the supply column.

The purpose of a night approach and dawn attack is to gain surprise. Yet on the afternoon of 10 December Methuen deployed his artillery, now reinforced by G Battery RHA, 65th Howitzer Battery and a 4.7-inch Naval gun, to bombard the assumed Boer positions for two hours, most of the fire being directed at the heights. The Boers lay low, lost only three wounded and now knew an attack was imminent.

Half an hour after midnight the Highland Brigade began its 3,300-yard advance from its forming-up place at Headquarters Hill, guided by Major Benson RA on a compass bearing. It was pitch dark and raining heavily, so to avoid men getting lost the brigade's 30 companies were arranged one behind the other in mass of quarter columns, 2nd Black Watch leading, followed in order by 2nd Seaforth Highlanders, 1st Argylls and 1st Highland Light Infantry. This made a block of nearly 4,000 men packed closely together with a front of 42 yards and depth of 170 yards, the left-hand files of each company being connected by ropes. Wauchope

Pipe-Corporal McKay rallying the Argylls at Magersfontein, based on a field sketch by W.B. Wollen of *The Illustrated London News*. Khaki kilt aprons afforded some concealment when men were upright but none when they were lying down.

Group of Boers posing for the camera before taking up firing positions.

intended to deploy before dawn broke at around 4 a.m. with the three leading battalions abreast, keeping the HLI in reserve. The advance took longer than anticipated and it was about 3.30 a.m. when Benson told Wauchope the objective was only half a mile ahead and that he should deploy into attack formation. The rain had mercifully stopped and the bulk of Magersfontein could be dimly perceived ahead. Wauchope however decided to move closer, despite the fact that the deployment was likely to take 15 minutes. After a further delay and some confusion caused by a patch of thorn scrub, it was nearly four o'clock when he halted, now only some 400 yards from the objective.

As the two leading companies of the Black Watch were extending, a furious fire exploded from the unsuspected trench at the foot of the hill. The whole brigade was caught at the worst possible moment. They were bunched up, wet through, tense after the night march and many had never been in action before; now, out of the gloom at close range, came this terrifying fusillade. Some of the Black Watch tried, fruitlessly, to charge, others fled causing panic, the close-packed battalions became mixed up, and Wauchope and two battalion commanders were killed. A group of Black Watch and Seaforth managed to extend to the right, overrunning the Scandinavians in the gap and pressing on to scale the southeast slopes, but were thrown back by a party led by Cronje himself. From 6 a.m. onwards, though attempts were still made to rush the trench, the Highland Brigade was pinioned to the veldt, just as

Black Watch prisoners taken at Magersfontein marching into captivity.

the Guards had been at Modder River. Men hardly dared reach for their water bottles, the dark kilts and shining mess-tins on the back of their belts made perfect aiming marks, and the rising sun scorched the back of their bare knees. A Black Watch corporal later wrote: 'Between 5.25 a.m. and 4 p.m. I don't think I moved one foot either way'. Fortunately the artillery coming into action managed to reduce, though not stop, the density of Boer fire.

Meanwhile the Boers left at Moss Drift had held up the 9th Lancers, who later had to be extricated by 2nd KOYLI from downstream. The 12th Lancers and MI came under fire from the low rise south-east of Magersfontein, which had flanked the Highlanders' advance and, it was now realized, was strongly held. Dismounting, and well-supported by G/RHA, they returned the fire to try and safeguard the Highland right flank and the battery positions on Horse Artillery Hill. However, as the 12th only had carbines, the fire-fight began to go against them, thus putting the batteries at risk, until their firing line was reinforced by half of 2nd Coldstream.

When Methuen realized that the Highlanders' predicament might necessitate their withdrawal, he ordered the Guards Brigade, less the Scots Guards who had got lost in the darkness and later joined the gunners, to this flank as a protective measure. He did not order them, however, to attack the low rise. Thus it was that both Coldstream battalions, reinforced by the Grenadiers, came under fire from the length of the rise and here they were forced to remain throughout the day, in places at very close range. On the far left

Pole-Carew, with only the Northumberland Fusiliers, three companies of Northamptons, Rimington's Guides and with a very long, open approach, had been unable to make much of a diversion, so that Andries Cronje felt strong enough to divert men to the Boer left.

Methuen's plan had depended entirely on the Highland Brigade's success. Now, by 7 a.m., all brigades were committed and all he had left were the 1st Gordons. Instead of using them to assist Pole-Carew or the Guards forward, he made the cardinal error of reinforcing failure by sending them through the midst of the suffering Highland Brigade. At 9 a.m. the Gordons, the heroes of Dargai two years before,[25] attacked. For some 3,600 yards they went steadily forward by rushes across open veldt under heavy fire. Not until they were within 300 yards of the Boer position were they brought to a standstill, flattening themselves to the ground among their fellow Highlanders. Unable now to influence the battle in any way, Methuen could only trust in the endurance of his men to hold on in the hope that the Boers would withdraw at nightfall, as they had at Modder River.

At around midday, seeing Boers starting to outflank them, some of the Seaforth on the right moved to face this threat, but lost heavily. Colonel Downman of the Gordons also tried to form a right-facing flank but was mortally wounded. Noticing these movements, many Highlanders thought they must be withdrawing. Exhausted by their experience, hungry, thirsty and demoralized, they stood up and walked back. The walk turned into a run and the Boer fire redoubled its fury. Everywhere men fell and the withdrawal became a rout. The Black Watch corporal wrote: 'There were some who rallied and re-rallied; others again, the less said about them the better; mind you, there was some excuse'. The Boers shot them down like game but made no attempt to exploit the retreat.

The Guards Brigade and the gunners, joined by a few Highlanders, maintained their positions until nightfall and through the night. If Methuen expected the Boers to leave, he was to be disillusioned. In the morning they were still there. An armistice was arranged for the collection of the wounded and at midday the Guards abandoned their positions, marching back with perfect steadiness under shell-fire.

Methuen's casualties had been 948, of which 210 had been killed. Forty-five officers and 702 men of the total were from the Highland Brigade. But for the courage and skill of the gunners, who fought their guns all day in the open, and the devotion of the RAMC doctors and stretcher-bearers tending the wounded on the fire-swept ground, the losses would have been even worse. The Boers lost around 90 killed and 190 wounded. With Cronje strengthening his position and his own force in some disarray, Methuen had no choice but to return to Modder River and reorganize. Kimberley would have to wait much longer for relief.

Methuen's defeat came as a profound shock in Britain. That the Guards and Highlanders, generally conceived to be the cream of the British Army, had been severely bested by armed farmers was hard to accept. The heavy losses of the Highlanders, so dear to the heart of the British public, were especially distressing and all Scotland mourned its dead and particularly the much-loved Wauchope. What made it even worse was that only the day before, in Cape Colony, General Gatacre, renowned for his work on the North-West Frontier and the Sudan, had suffered a shameful defeat. There was more in store, for this was what came to be known as Black Week.

7. BLACK WEEK

The Free State invasion of Cape Colony, though attracting a number of Cape Dutch adherents, had not been prosecuted energetically and had failed to make the most of its opportunities in a scantily defended area before Buller's deployments took effect. In the north-west French had secured Naauwpoort Junction and with his Cavalry Division had effectively covered the railways back to Cape Town and Port Elizabeth, forcing the Free Staters increasingly on to the defensive around Colesberg. To the east, however, the Boers had occupied the junction set in mountainous country at Stormberg on the East London-Bloemfontein line where another track branched off to the Port Elizabeth line.

Having lost all his division, except 2nd Royal Irish Rifles, to the Natal front, Gatacre had had to await reinforcements. By the first week of December, disposing of three more battalions, 300 Regular MI, two batteries and 1,000 Cape volunteers, he de-

Officers of 2nd Royal Irish Rifles, victims of Gatacre's blunder at Stormberg. Most have rifles in addition to their revolvers and Sam Browne equipment. Note whistles attached to the left brace.

Boer gun firing at Ladysmith from an embrasure of boulders and sandbags. The man on the left of the trail is about to load a shell into the breech.

termined to seize Stormberg by a dawn attack on its surrounding heights after a night march of eight miles from Molteno, where his troops were to detrain.

Gatacre's rhyming nickname of 'Backacher' derived from his passion for physical exertion. Apparently unaffected by fatigue himself he did not countenance it in others. From this in part stemmed the debacle of 10 December; the rest was due to some bad luck but mostly bad judgement. The troops were tired when the night march began owing to mismanagement of the train journey, and the mounted Cape volunteers never even reached Molteno as, due to an oversight, they were not told to go there. Although the 2nd Royal Berkshire was familiar with the region, having been stationed at Stormberg before the war, Gatacre took only the Irish Rifles and 2nd Northumberland Fusiliers (whose 1st Battalion was with Methuen), together with the MI and both batteries. At the last moment before setting out he changed the route and the intended direction of attack, from south to west, but failed to inform his supply and hospital column commander. Having made no reconnaissance of the route or objective, he relied entirely on police guides but did not explain to them his intentions. The guides missed the way, thereby adding another four miles to the march and producing growing uncertainty among the weary troops. By sheer chance they passed the very spot Gatacre was making for, but as the guides did not know this and the general thought they were elsewhere, the march went on. Notwithstanding Gatacre's experience of hill-fighting on the North-West Frontier, daylight found the unprotected column marching in fours, with bayonets fixed, through a pass. The Boers opened fire from the heights and though the three leading companies of Rifles got up a hill to their left, the remainder found the ascent to the right blocked by a precipice. The Northumberlands' colonel ordered a retreat westwards and Gatacre made great efforts to keep the men in hand but there was no stopping the jaded infantry. Thanks to the steadiness of the gunners and MI the shattered column managed to collect itself and retrace its steps, and the Boers made no attempt to follow up. As the troops staggered back to Molteno it was found that 600 men, mostly Northumberlands, had been left behind and had had to surrender.

As the blows of Magersfontein and Stormberg were digested, hopes were now pinned on Buller and the force, equivalent to two divisions, that had been assembled for White's relief at Frere, 12 miles south of Colenso on the Tugela and 25 from Ladysmith. Despite his defeat of White on 30 October Joubert had been unwilling to risk a large force pressing on to Durban while 13,500 British troops remained in his rear, so Botha's advance south of the Tugela, which Joubert accompanied as a restraining influence, turned into little more than a raid towards Pietermaritzburg. It achieved much looting and ambushed an armoured train, in which Winston Churchill was captured,[26] but with the British

Brigadier-General Lord Dundonald, Mounted Brigade.

Major-General Hildyard, 2nd Brigade.

Major-General Lyttleton, 4th (Light) Brigade.

Major-General Hart, 5th (Irish) Brigade.

Boer gun commanding the loop of the Tugela into which Hart's brigade marched. Colenso village in left distance, above gun. The picture shows how exposed were the approaches to the river.

landing in strength at Durban Joubert turned back to the Tugela at the end of November. Meanwhile at Ladysmith White, with eight weeks' supplies, sat tight within his 14-mile perimeter while the surrounding Boers enjoyed an almost holiday-like existence on the dominating hills outside, content to prevent any break-out by the garrison.

The chief military activity was the twice-daily artillery duel and occasional sniping. By the first week in December, aware that Buller was preparing to strike, White authorized two raids on the Boer big-gun positions. The first, by the Imperial Light Horse and Natal Volunteers, destroyed the gun known as 'Long Tom' and a 4.7-inch howitzer, while three nights later 2nd Rifle Brigade blew up another howitzer. Encouraged by these successes, White made plans for a major sortie to assist Buller's attack, once the latter was across the Tugela.

To reach Ladysmith, Buller was faced with a 10-mile approach across open country to the deep, fast-flowing river, fordable only at its various drifts, and backed along its north bank by a range of kopjes, between 500 and 1,000 feet above the river,

stretching back northwards for some five miles. The river made a northerly loop around Colenso village and station on the south bank, having made a similar loop two miles to the west; a mile to the east the river changed course to the north, having on its right bank a hill running parallel to it called Hlangwane, the view from which gave perfect observation along the north bank beyond Colenso.

Faced by this formidable obstacle, and with his task made no easier by poor maps and difficulties over reconnaissance, Buller decided to outflank it by crossing upstream at Potgieter's Drift, a 22-mile march north-west from Frere. But learning on 13 December of Methuen's defeat and deeming immediate action was required, he changed his mind and ordered a frontal attack at Colenso for the 15th, announcing his intention to the Boers by bombarding the hills across the river for two days beforehand.

Botha, who commanded on the north bank, had anticipated this would be the case and deployed nine commandos and the Johannesburg Police, with 12 guns, over a front of $6\frac{1}{2}$ miles, but with his chief strength covering the drifts and the Colenso road bridge which had purposely been left intact. His plan was to open fire when the British were about to cross, or were crossing, the river and then to enfilade their right flank and rear with a tenth commando from Hlangwane, thereby also denying its use to Buller. In view of its vulnerable situation on the right bank, the choice for this task was drawn by lot and fell to the 800-strong Wakkerstroom Commando which occupied the hill on the night of the 14th–15th.

Such reconnaissance as Buller had effected had yielded little information about the well-concealed Boer positions and his orders, issued at 10 p.m. on the 14th, apart from mentioning two suspected camps north of the river, said only that 'the enemy is entrenched in the kopjes north of Colenso bridge', with no mention of Hlangwane. Seemingly unaware of how vital the possession of this hill was for either side, his expressed intention was 'to force the passage of the Tugela' by a two-brigade attack in daylight on the kopjes north of the bridge. On the right Hildyard's 2nd Brigade was to cross in the Colenso loop while to the left Hart's 5th (Irish) Brigade was to force the Bridle Drift half a mile west of the other loop, thereafter marching east to the objective. Half of Dundonald's mounted brigade, with one battery, was to protect the right flank by advancing towards Hlangwane and, if possible, to get on to the hill to enfilade the kopjes; the rest of his brigade was assigned as flank and baggage guards. Dundonald's was therefore a subsidiary, protective role, rather than an essential part of the main attack. The other four field batteries and six naval guns were to support the infantry assault. Lyttleton's 4th (Light) Brigade and Barton's 6th (Fusiliers) were to be in reserve to left and right respectively.

The advance from the camps some three miles south of the river began at 4 a.m. At 5.30 the Naval guns opened fire against the hills north of Colenso. So as not to give away their positions the Boers made no response but, as the British came within range, the tempting targets they presented proved too much for the burghers to heed Botha's orders to withhold fire until the crossing actually began. On the left Hart, a martinet who believed in keeping his Irishmen well in hand, disregarded reports of enemy to his front by patrols of Royal Dragoons and marched forward with his leading battalion, 2nd Royal Dublin Fusiliers, deployed with its companies marching abreast in fours, and the other three in mass of quarter columns behind—the formation used for the Highland Brigade's night advance at Magersfontein. Hart would have been splendid in the Crimea but in an age of smokeless powder and magazine rifles he was a

The other side of the previous picture. 2nd Royal Dublin Fusiliers under heavy fire in the loop. Sketch by René Bull, war artist for *Black and White Budget*.

The destroyed railway bridge at Colenso with kopje beyond held by the Krugersdorp and Vryheid commandos. Another kopje stood to the left of the picture. The intact road bridge was 1,200 yards upstream (left). Photograph taken later with repair work in progress.

dangerous anachronism. At 6.30, misled by his native guide as to the site of the drift, he directed this compact mass into the salient formed by the river bend. When the Dublins were within 200 yards of the bank, the four commandos on the far side opened fire. The Dublins rushed forward but, finding nowhere to cross, had to take cover; some men jumped into the river and were drowned. The second battalion, 1st Royal Inniskilling Fusiliers, tried to deploy to the left out of the loop but were recalled by Hart, who strode about, disregarding the hail of fire, urging the men forward and berating officers who tried to extend. By 7.15 the whole brigade was mixed up and trapped by fire from three directions, having suffered 400 casualties. With more faith in the bayonet than artillery fire, Hart had given his three supporting batteries no orders at all, so it was left to their commander to do what he could to cover the hapless Irish.

Appalled at 'the devil of a mess' Hart had created, Buller ordered Lyttleton to extricate the Irish Brigade from the loop and turned his attention to the right, where already a second fiasco was looming. The artillery commander, another fire-eater called Colonel Long, conscious of the inferior range of his field guns, determined to give the closest possible support to Hildyard's attack by galloping forward the 14th and 66th Batteries RFA to the right of Colenso village. By 6 a.m., leaving his infantry escort and Hildyard's brigade far behind, Long opened fire at 990 yards range from the Boers across the river and in full view, though not in rifle range, of those on Hlangwane. Unable to resist the sight of 12 guns correctly aligned in the open as though at Woolwich, the Boers engaged them with artillery and rifles. At first their fire was inaccurate, but soon they got the range, inflicting casualties particularly among the officers standing up to direct fire. Long himself was shot through the liver. Nevertheless, so devotedly did the gunners serve their guns, that, aided by the sailors' 12-pounders firing from better cover to the left rear, the Boer fire was damped down and by 7 a.m. only the enemy riflemen were in action. By then, however, Long's ammunition was nearly expended and, while an officer rode back to find the supply wagons, the gunners retired to keep under cover in a ditch.

By now the infantry escort of half each of the Scots and Irish Fusiliers had reached the gun positions and deployed as local protection. Hildyard had reached the Naval gun-line, but with Hart stationary on his left, Long's guns out of action, and with no support yet available from the right, he halted rather than risk his brigade in the fire still coming across the river. On the right Dundonald had covered Hildyard's brigade as ordered and then, using the 13th Hussars to protect his right, he dismounted the South African Light Horse, the Composite and Thorneycroft's regiments of MI[27] and sent them against Hlangwane. Most of these had only been enlisted about a month before but they went at the hill like 'veteran soldiers'. However, with one man in four detached as horse-holders, their attacking strength was barely two-thirds that of the defenders and, though they gained a lodgement on the lower slopes, they could not prevail. Dundonald sent across to the reserve Fusilier Brigade for help but Barton would not detach even a company.

It was in any case too late. Buller, disheartened by Hart's failure, had been riding down to watch Hildyard's attack when he learned of Long's predicament. Though neither Hildyard nor Barton were yet committed, he decided to call off the whole attack. Telling Hildyard to get into Colenso village to protect the left of Long's gun-line, he rode on with his staff to see the guns for himself. When the Boers saw 2nd Brigade begin to move they transferred men from their left to meet it, but Hildyard's battalions had been well trained in the use of dispersion and cover and 2nd Queen's and 2nd Devons lost few men as they advanced into the village and opened rapid and effective musketry at the trenches across the river.

Riding forward under fire Buller reached a donga where the battery drivers were sheltering with the gun-horses. Looking out across the 800 yards of open ground towards the silent guns he called for volunteers to save them. Corporal Nurse and some drivers of 66th Battery galloped off, accompanied by three of Buller's staff, Captain Schofield RHA, Captain Congreve Rifle Brigade and Lieutenant Roberts 60th Rifles, the only son of Lord Roberts. Amid a hail of fire they reached the guns and got two away, but Roberts was hit three times. Congreve, also

wounded but aided by Major Babtie RAMC, who had been tending the gunner casualties, managed to drag Roberts under cover. Further attempts to reach the remaining guns proved fruitless because, although the Queen's and Devons were still firing from Colenso, they were unable to subdue the volume of fire that swept the plain. Finally Captain Reed of 7th Battery made a gallant dash of a mile and a half with three teams from south of Hlangwane. Thirteen of his 22 horses and half his drivers were hit and the attempt had to be abandoned. For two hours Buller stood under shellfire, a fragment of which struck him in the side, watching with growing anxiety the desperate attempts to save the guns. At 11 a.m., shocked by the hopeless sacrifice and dismayed at the collapse of his plan, he ordered the guns to be left and a general retreat by the whole force.[28]

To withdraw in broad daylight over open ground in full view of an intact and mobile enemy is not an easy operation. Fortunately the Boers refrained from following up this retirement, either deterred by the long-range 4.7-inch Naval guns or perhaps from their

2nd Queen's of Hildyard's brigade fighting in Colenso village under fire from the kopje in the previous picture.

Photograph taken after the battle of spot where ten guns of 14th and 66th Batteries RFA were lost. This gun position was 990 yards from kopje shown on page 86.

An impression by Sidney Paget of the attempt to save the guns at Colenso, showing Lieutenant Roberts (left) and Corporal Nurse hooking in a limber to one of the volunteer teams.

reluctance to kill other white men unless absolutely necessary. Thus the more closely engaged forward troops were able to break contact more easily than might have been the case, but even so some detachments were left behind, either through not receiving the orders or a reluctance to abandon positions where they felt secure. On the left Lyttleton's Rifles and Light Infantry had covered the withdrawal of Hart's shattered but still pugnacious Irish by 11 a.m., though a party of Inniskillings who remained close to the bank found themselves surrounded by Boers at 5 p.m. Their quick-thinking colonel managed to talk them out of being captured. In the centre some of the Devons held on too long near the abandoned 15-pounders and were made prisoners in the afternoon, enabling the Boers to carry off the remaining 10 guns. The most difficult disengagement was for the MI on Hlangwane and not until the lethargic Barton was induced to push forward 2nd Royal Fusiliers in support could they get

clear, losing as heavily in the process as they had in their attack.

The following day Buller took the whole force back to Frere and Chievely. In an attack that had inflicted no more than 40 casualties on the Boers, and can scarcely be called an attack at all, 145 had been killed, 762 wounded and 220 were missing or prisoners. The hardest hit had been the Irish Brigade with 523 casualties, of which just under half were Dublin Fusiliers. Long's two batteries lost 84, more than half of whom were missing. Poor maps, inadequate reconnaissance, underestimation of the enemy, defects in the Army's training and organization, Hart's and Long's impetuousity—all had contributed to the disaster; though Botha later claimed that by inducing the Boers to open fire prematurely, Long had saved Buller from a far worse slaughter. It is difficult to see how an attack in daylight across a river obstacle against an alerted enemy holding unknown positions in natural defensive country could have succeeded. As for the speed with which Buller cancelled the operation—when only one brigade had been fully committed—either he must be credited with stopping something before it got worse, or the lack of self-confidence he had expressed before leaving England had manifested itself in a lack of faith in his own plan. All plans are subject to upsets but Buller did not possess the flexibility of the Duke of Wellington who, likening his plans to a rope, said, 'If anything went wrong, I tied a knot and went on'. Buller had great physical courage and a devotion to his men who, unaware of strategy and tactics, repaid it with total confidence, even after Colenso, but underneath his phlegmatic exterior he seethed with self-doubt and he knew now, if he had not known before, that handling a large force under modern conditions required qualities different from those he had displayed to such perfection 20 years before with a regiment of irregular horse against Zulus. So downcast was he in the aftermath of Colenso that he signalled to White in Ladysmith that it would take a month to get there and that if White could not hold out that long, he should give Buller time to fortify himself on the Tugela after which 'I suggest your firing away as much ammunition as you can, and making the best terms you can'. White's poor generalship may have been the cause of Buller's difficulties, but he was not prepared tamely to surrender his garrison.

Rifle Brigade (left foreground), Irish Fusiliers, sailors with a 12-pounder, and others watching the attack at Colenso. The naval gun-crews can be seen under the muzzle, wearing Sennet straw hats.

Coming on top of Magersfontein and Stormberg, Colenso, with its puncturing of Buller's reputation, was the signal for changes in the prosecution of the war. Britain now realized it was facing more than a colonial punitive expedition and, after a week of total dejection, a patriotic sense of purpose and determination gripped the country and the Empire. The 5th and 6th Divisions were already on their way to South Africa and two more were to be mobilized. Australia, Canada and New Zealand pledged further contingents. At home, following a suggestion by Buller, a force of 10,500 Imperial Yeomanry to act as MI companies was to be raised for a year's service from the existing Yeomanry and civilian volunteers; except for weapons and ammunition provided by the War Office the cost was to be borne by charitable contributions. The City of London raised and paid for a 1,700-strong force of all arms drawn from 49 different Volunteer units in London, Middlesex, Essex and Surrey—the City Imperial Volunteers or CIVs. Companies of Volunteer infantry battalions were to be attached to their parent Regular battalions to replace Regular companies converted to MI. Militia battalions were to be embodied either to replace

Field-Marshal Lord Roberts of Kandahar VC.

General Lord Kitchener of Khartoum.

Regulars in colonial garrisons or to go to South Africa as line-of-communications troops. All these non-Regulars volunteered for active service and, according to *The Times History*, the numbers who came forward represented: one man in five of the Militia and Yeomanry; one in 15 of the Volunteers; and one in every thousand of the remaining civil population of military age. Most came from middle or lower middle class backgrounds, instead of the working class from which most Regular soldiers originated. Consequently it was hoped that their lack of military training would be redressed by higher education and intelligence. That the first of the Volunteers left England within a month of Colenso reflects highly on those outside the War Office who were chiefly responsible for their raising and equipping.

The events of Black Week convinced the authorities that a change in the command structure in South Africa was essential. Though Buller was to remain in command in Natal, he was to be supersed-

ed as commander-in-chief by Field Marshal Lord Roberts of Kandahar, aged 67 but still alert and vigorous, who was to be accompanied, as chief of staff, by the 49-year-old Lord Kitchener of Khartoum, the conqueror of the Sudan the year before. The appointment of these two saw the end of the long dominance of military affairs by Wolseley and his Ring and, though neither had experience of South Africa and the Boers, there was no-one whose miltary prestige stood higher and neither had had much hand in the organization of the home Army, whose unreadiness for war had already been demonstrated. Roberts had just learned that his son had been awarded the Victoria Cross, which he himself had won 42 years before in the Indian Mutiny, but then, on the evening of his appointment, that he had died from his wounds. Two days before Christmas, accompanied by the towering, sombre figure of Kitchener, the little Field-Marshal, in deep mourning, embarked for South Africa.

8. THE DUG-OUT POLICEMAN

White had been unable to make any diversion to assist the attack at Colenso for the simple reason that Buller had not informed him of its date or direction. The realization of its failure lowered his garrison's morale which, exacerbated by shortages and disease, had not been improved by White's largely passive defence against an investing force whose numbers steadily decreased from desertion or from joining Botha on the Tugela until its strength was less than the garrison's. Fortunately for White, Joubert's prosecution of the siege had been less than aggressive, but after Colenso Joubert was pressured by Kruger into taking offensive action. On the night of 6 January 1900, 5,000 Boers attacked the Platrand ridge south of Ladysmith, known to the British as Wagon Hill on the western end and Caesar's Camp on the eastern. This was supported by diversions from the north-west and north-east. These were thrown back, but the fighting on the Platrand lasted well into the next day. Thanks to a stubborn resistance by the ILH, Manchesters and Gordons, and a costly counter-attack by 2nd Rifle Brigade, the Boer attacks were held but they still retained positions along the crestline. As dusk approached a storm broke and three companies of 1st Devons made a most gallant charge[29] across Wagon Hill to clear the crest. The day's fierce fighting had cost 400 casualties and, viewing the carnage on Wagon Hill, Colonel Rawlinson of White's staff, who had fought in the Sudan, was moved to record: 'White corpses are far more repulsive than black'. (Sixteen years later 19,240 men under his command were to lose their lives in a single day's fighting.) White had sent frantic signals to Buller demanding assistance and after the battle sent another saying he could no longer be expected to make any diversion to assist the relief force.

Having remained inactive for three weeks after Colenso, but now reinforced to a strength of 30,000 by the arrival of Sir Charles Warren's 5th Division (10th and 11th Brigades), Buller decided to try and reach Ladysmith by way of Potgieter's Drift to the west. Leaving Barton's brigade facing Colenso he set off on 10 January with Dundonald's mounted brigade, five infantry brigades, eight batteries, ten naval guns and 650 transport wagons. From the heights on the north bank the Boers watched the slow progress of the 17-mile-long column as it toiled through the heavy mud of the sodden track. Riding ahead, Dundonald occupied Mount Alice overlooking Potgieter's and the following morning the South African Light Horse seized its pontoon ferry.

Across the river the road ran over the low Brakfontein ridge to Ladysmith, 18 miles away to the north-east, but to west and east the ridge rose to the dominating heights of Spion Kop and Vaal Krantz. Westwards from Spion Kop ran the three-mile range of Tabanyama, culminating in the prominent Bastion Hill, after which the high ground fell away down to Acton Homes on the Free State-Ladysmith road. The Boers, alerted by Buller's march, were already preparing to dispute any attack through Potgieter's from the Brakfontein ridge. Buller conceived the plan of throwing two-thirds of his force across the river five miles upstream at Trichardt's Drift to turn the lightly-held Boer western flank and then threaten the enemy rear from the Free State road; the remainder of the force, having demonstrated against Brakfontein, would then attack to link up with the left-flanking force. Brakfontein was allotted to Lyttleton, with his own 4th Brigade, Coke's 10th Brigade, two batteries and the Naval guns. The flanking force would consist of Clery's 2nd Division (2nd and 5th Brigades), Woodgate's 11th (Lancastrian) Brigade, Dundonald and eight batteries, all under the command of Sir Charles Warren.

The plan, which would involve operations over some seven miles of front, would fully extend the

The Wagon Hill picquet on the west end of the Platrand.

greatly outnumbered 7,000 defenders but would require speed of execution if the Boers' advantages of superior observation and mobility were to be overcome; much would therefore depend on the drive and determination of its commander. Warren, an irascible, opinionated but conscientious ex-sapper of 58, had been called out of retirement after a curious career which, apart from earlier soldiering in South Africa 20 years before and more recently as GOC Singapore and then the Thames District, had been singular for his having been a parliamentary candidate, an enthusiastic Freemason, and an eccentric Chief Commissioner of the Metropolitan Police. His arrival, and opinions on the conduct of the war, had not endeared him to Buller, who was further irritated by the knowledge that Warren held a dormant commission, nominating him as Buller's successor in the event of the latter's death or disablement. Taking their tune from their master, Buller's staff soon dubbed the newcomer 'the dug-out ex-policeman'. Thus it is surprising that Buller should have entirely handed over the important turning movement to Warren, unless he shrank from controlling it himself or, as he later claimed, it was less testing than Lyttleton's role.

Within days of issuing his orders on 15 January, Buller experienced misgivings about his new subordinate. Lyttleton energetically seized a bridgehead at Potgieter's on the 16th, which led the Boers to reinforce Brakfontein, but not until the following morning did Warren begin to cross at Trichardt's. The crossing was unopposed but then, having instructed his brigadiers to rehearse their forthcoming assault, he devoted the next two days to supervising personally the construction of a pontoon bridge and the passage of each of his baggage wagons. The only operational command he issued in this time was to order Dundonald, who on his own initiative had ridden on towards Acton Homes, to return the Royal Dragoons to camp 'to prevent the oxen from being swept away'. Reluctantly Dundonald obeyed but pressed on with the rest of his brigade. Having successfully ambushed a Boer force, he established himself in a commanding position near Acton Homes, sending back for guns and reinforcements. Far from exploiting this advantage on the extremity of the Boer flank, Warren was furious, ordering Dundonald to return with all his men to guard the infantry's left and the baggage.

However dogmatic Warren was about the use, or misuse, of cavalry, he was less certain how to proceed himself. He considered, and abandoned, a night attack; he marched Hildyard's brigade westwards and back again; and finally decided on a frontal

Maxim of 1st Devons in action at Ladysmith. These men have the Indian pattern water bottle, having been one of the battalions from India.

Lieutenant-General Sir Charles Warren.

attack against Tabanyama to secure the Fairview Farm track that ran across it to the Ladysmith road. The attack was to be deliberate and methodical, each stage covered by an artillery bombardment, which he calculated would take three days (to cover eight miles); once the crest was taken he intended to return all his wagons back across the Tugela, since he considered they would be vulnerable on the Fairview track to fire from Spion Kop. In the same way that Buller had delegated to him, he now entrusted the attack to Clery, a 61-year-old veteran of the Zulu War, whose reputation as a fighting general was somewhat belied by his blue-dyed whiskers and varicose veins.

For the next two days Hart's Irishmen and Woodgate's Lancastrians doggedly fought their way up to the crest, only to find that it was not in fact the true crest, and to be halted by well-dug-in Boers, whom the energetic Botha had moved across during the days wasted by Warren. Due to Clery's maladroit arrangements, the two brigades became intermingled so that some of Hart's men found themselves under Woodgate and some of Woodgate's under Hart, which was hardly conducive to mutual confidence.

Only on the left was any dash shown. Here Dundonald, again acting on his own initiative, sent forward the SALH, whose four squadrons supported each other in a masterly demonstration of dismounted fire and movement to seize the important Bastion Hill. Hildyard sent up some infantry in support but despite this position being able to enfilade the flank and rear of the Boer trenches and a plan concocted by Hart and Walter Kitchener[30] to attack from it, Clery halted the whole operation.

Lieutenant-General Sir Francis Clery.

Spion Kop from the Boer side on Tabanyama. Tugela in the right distance. Photograph by Horace Nicholls.

In the week that had elapsed since he had issued his orders, Buller had watched with growing impatience Warren's ponderous and ineffective movements. He had not, however, given any orders to expedite the faltering offensive, contenting himself with offering suggestions or comments—behaving, as *The Times History* put it, like 'an umpire at manoeuvres'. On the evening of the 22nd he exasperatedly told Warren he must either get on, withdraw completely or capture Spion Kop. This last was almost an afterthought, stemming from Warren's observation on the vulnerability of the Fairview Road from the Kop. The next day, having slept on it, he ordered Warren to seize Spion Kop at once or retire across the river.

From hereon the thoughts of all commanders concerned became concentrated on one object and one alone: the occupation and holding of this near-precipitous hill, 1,470 feet above the Tugela. What was to happen afterwards, how the rest of the 21,000 men and 58 guns strewn along the river banks were to be employed, was not explained. When Buller was asked by a staff officer what the assault force was to do once it was on top, he replied, 'It has got to stay there'. No-one had any idea what the summit was like, how strongly it was held or what lay beyond. Anyone present with memories of the earlier war must surely have been struck by the scheme's sinister similarity to Majuba.

Warren gave the task to Coke, promoted for the occasion from command of 10th Brigade, though hardly the most suitable choice for hill climbing since he was still hobbling from a recently-broken leg. The actual assault was to be made by Woodgate, who nominated his 2nd Lancashire Fusiliers, six companies 2nd King's Own Royal Lancaster and two of 1st South Lancashire; to these were added 200 men of Thorneycroft's MI (dismounted) and half of 17th Company, Royal Engineers, 1,700 men in all. In reserve was 10th Brigade, now temporarily commanded by Colonel Hill of 2nd Middlesex. No guns could be taken but an artillery officer with signallers was to accompany Woodgate and a mountain battery was summoned; unknown to Warren it was still 25 miles away. The track was to be improved for artillery by the rest of the RE company. Although a quantity of telegraph cable was available, no-one thought to take any, so that communications would be restricted to the heliograph by day and oil-fed lamp by night.

At 11 p.m. on the 23rd the steep climb began, led by the gigantic Thorneycroft, who had spent the afternoon memorizing the twists and turns of the narrow track leading up from Trichardt's. So dark and drizzling was the night that it was 4 a.m. by the time the summit was reached. A Boer picquet challenged, Thorneycroft's colonials charged, and the hill-top was theirs. A thick mist prevented any signal being made, so the troops gave three cheers to announce their arrival to those below.

Work was hurriedly started on a 300-yard-long trench in the shape of a flat inverted V facing north-west and north, but so ineffective were the men's entrenching tools on the rocky surface that a parapet had to be built up with boulders. A few sangars were constructed at either end. When the mist cleared at about 8 a.m. Woodgate saw that the trench lay across the middle of a plateau whose northern rim, the true crest, was only between 50–150 yards away; beyond it was dead ground from the trench. Furthermore, from the right end of the trench the plateau narrowed into a saddle terminating in a rise known as Aloe Knoll, only 300 yards away, which had been invisible in the mist. It was too late to do more than double some men forward to the true crest.

As the sun emerged to herald a blazing hot day and illuminate the ominous features of the terrain, so the Boers responded to this intrusion on to their

Colonel Thorneycroft, right, with 'TMI' on his helmet, with Colonel Rawlinson, who was in Ladysmith during Spion Kop and was later a successful column commander.

heights. Aroused by the picquet from the Kop, Botha had summoned Opperman's Pretoria and Henrik Prinsloo's Carolina Commandos to eliminate this handhold on the key to their position. From the north-west round to the east six guns and two pom-poms began to shell Woodgate's packed and shallow trench, while riflemen clambered up to fire at close range from the northern rim. Against the latter the infantry kept up a heavy musketry, but there was no protection from the shell-fire. Worst of all, for the Lancashire Fusiliers on the right, was the enfilade fire straight down the trench from

Boer snipers in action at Spion Kop.

Aloe Knoll, cleverly occupied by the Carolina Commando. So began an ordeal for both sides that was to last until nightfall: fire-fight, attack, counter-attack, then the fire-fight resumed—while all the while casualties mounted and men grew exhausted from heat, thirst and fear.

At 8.30 a.m. Woodgate was mortally wounded and the next senior, Crofton of the King's Own, sent an alarmist signal back to Warren, beseeching reinforcements. Warren, who was out of sight of Spion Kop and had no idea of the configuration of the summit nor the exact position of his troops, had hitherto been unconcerned by the sound of firing but, on receipt of Crofton's message, he told Coke to send up the Imperial Light Infantry,[31] 2nd Middlesex and 2nd Dorsets and at the same time requested help from Lyttleton at Potgieter's. Any idea of relieving pressure on Spion Kop by a diversion across Tabanyama, its defences now reduced, apparently did not occur to him, any more than it did to Clery, whose two brigades remained inactive and unused all day. Lyttleton, on the other hand, had been active since dawn,

engaging the Boers on Brakfontein, as he had during Warren's earlier ventures, and he now responded at once, sending 2nd Scottish Rifles (Cameronians) towards Spion Kop and 3rd 60th Rifles against the feature known as Twin Peaks, two miles east of, and overlooking, Spion Kop, behind which was one of the guns enfilading the Kop. The Naval guns at Potgieter's and Mount Alice began to shell the eastern flanks of Spion Kop and Aloe Knoll, but soon had to desist in response to an agitated signal from Warren, again betraying his ignorance of the situation on the summit, claiming that the sailors were firing on his men. Buller, too, took a hand as, alarmed at the tone of Crofton's message, which had been relayed to him, he suggested to Warren that Thorneycroft, 'a good hard fighting man', be put in command to save the hill being lost. Warren concurred but did not inform Coke, who was now stumbling up the hill.

Amid the morning's blood-bath on the Kop, Thorneycroft had indeed been outstanding, rallying the men here, leading a charge there. Shortly after midday, on being told he was in command, he rushed over to the right to try and prevent the capture of some Fusiliers who, driven beyond endurance, were surrendering. He bellowed at the Boers to clear off

and then, as the first of the Middlesex appeared, led another charge to restore the right flank, while Crofton, recovered from his earlier panic, rallied the left flank, again menaced from in front. The leading companies of Middlesex and ILI plugged the gaps in the trench, now overflowing with dead and wounded, and at 2.30 Thorneycroft found time to write a report for Warren. Having listed his heavy casualties and his men's desperate need for water, he urged that the enemy guns must be attacked if the hill was to be held.

Coke, still making his laborious way up, saw and endorsed this message but, deeming there were sufficient troops on the summit, halted the Dorsets and the approaching Cameronians. However for some time the Boers from the Aloe Knoll direction had again been pressing the summit's right, now held by Colonel Hill and the Middlesex, and were attempting to take up new positions on the southern rim in Hill's rear. In the nick of time Colonel Cooke led some of his Cameronians in a counter-attack and sent others to the left, which was also weakening. Their timely intervention, notwithstanding the fierce fighting that ensued, stabilized the situation and by 4.30 the Boers withdrew out of close range, although they continued to pound the summit with their guns.

This struggle had received valuable indirect support from the east, where all afternoon 3rd 60th, with regimental scores from the earlier war to settle, had been fighting their way up Twin Peaks. So determined was their advance that the Boer commander, Schalk Burger, begged Botha for reinforcements from Spion Kop, to which Botha, aware of how vital the Peaks were to the Boer line, had to accede. Across the river Buller, pessimistic of the Rifles' success, repeatedly ordered Lyttleton to recall them, but each signal was ignored by the 60th colonel, Buchanan-Riddell, a veteran of 1881. At 5 p.m. his men crowned the heights to drive away Burger, his reinforcements and his guns. More concerned at the disobedience to his orders than the possibilities opened up by the seizure of this tactically important objective, Buller insisted on recalling the Riflemen, who withdrew after dark, leaving their spirited colonel dead behind them.

Meanwhile Coke had at last reached the summit and, unaware of Thorneycroft's appointment, conferred with Hill, whom he assumed, as did Hill, was in

British dead piled in the main trench on the summit of Spion Kop. The nature of the trench shows how vulnerable were men firing from it, particularly to enfilade fire. Photograph taken by a Boer two days later.

command. From what he learned he sent a message down to Warren, reporting the situation as extremely critical, stating flatly that the men would not stand another day's shelling and mentioning the possibility of an evacuation. Without contacting Thorneycroft he returned to his headquarters on the track. Informed by Cooke of the Cameronians about the command confusion, Thorneycroft tried to resolve it with Hill but was unable to locate him. Confident of his own position he sent off another messenger to Warren at 6.30, emphasizing the exhaustion of his men, their need for stretchers, water and ammunition, the impossibility of holding the hill unless the enemy guns were dealt with, and asking for orders. It was now growing dark and the firing died down.

Throughout the day Warren had left the savage battle to Coke and Thorneycroft, busying himself with administrative matters within the capability of a good staff officer, though without displaying any urgency. His knowledge of what was happening came largely from messages relayed by Buller's headquarters, his own being out of heliograph contact with the summit, or latterly from written messages which took over an hour to reach him. Nothing he learned induced him to make use of Clery's 10,000 idle men, nor did he reply to the reports he received. Not until 8 p.m., when he received Coke's gloomy report, followed by a graphic eyewitness description of conditions on the summit from Winston Churchill,[32] did he stir himself to assemble a convoy of much-needed stores and prepare the way for a naval gun. Churchill volunteered to return and tell Thorneycroft what was being done and to hold fast. Finally Warren ordered Coke to report to him. Without oil in his signal lamp to demur, Coke had no choice but to limp down the hill again.

Meanwhile Thorneycroft had come to the end of his tether. All day under terrible conditions he had valiantly sustained the defence. His casualties lay thick around him, his men were spent and waterless, he had heard nothing from Warren, Coke or Hill, and his recommendations had been ignored. Rather than see his surviving men slaughtered the next day, he decided to abandon the position. At 8.15 he began to thin out his troops. Hill suddenly appeared, remonstrating against the decision, as did a staff officer of Coke's, but Thorneycroft would have none of it. Some time later, after climbing upwards against men straggling down with wounded, Churchill found him still at the top, 'sitting on the ground surrounded by the remnants of the regiment he had raised, who had fought for him like lions and followed him like dogs'. Churchill told him what Warren was sending up and pressed him to stay but Thorneycroft, disillusioned with his superiors, replied, 'Better six good battalions safely down the hill than a mop-up in the morning'. The bitter irony of it all was that, unknown to anyone, the Boers, appalled by their own casualties and exhausted by their efforts, had also departed and crept silently away. Soon only the dead occupied Spion Kop.

This dreadful day of bloodshed and wasted sacrifice had cost some 1,200 British casualties, of whom over 300 were killed; Thorneycroft's MI and the Lancashire Fusiliers lost well over half their officers. The Boers suffered about 300 casualties, the heaviest, 62 per cent, being borne by the Carolina Commando on Aloe Knoll.

By the time news of Thorneycroft's decision reached Warren at 2 a.m. it might still have been possible to retrieve matters, but neither Warren nor Buller had the will to continue. In contrast, as soon as he learned of his men's retreat, Botha bullied and cajoled them to return. Thus it was that when day dawned the Boers again held Spion Kop, the look-out from which years before their trekker forefathers had first sighted Natal. Discarding his passive role Buller reduced Warren to command of the 5th Division, and personally organized the withdrawal of the entire force across the river. By 27 January this had been accomplished without loss.

Though advised by Roberts, who had reached the Cape, to stay on the defensive, Buller felt compelled to try again to relieve Ladysmith. Believing he had been let down by the gunner, Long, at Colenso and now by the sapper-policeman, Warren, he entrusted his third attempt to his fellow-Rifleman, Lyttleton, who was to capture Vaal Krantz on 4 February. The attack was to be preceded by a complicated deception plan against Brakfontein. Alerted, but not deceived, by the over-long preparations, the Boers reinforced the threatened point. Though Lyttleton and his men[33] did all that could be expected of them, Buller's resolve was weakened by the resistance, he procrastinated, and, after three day's fighting, ordered Lyttleton to withdraw. Another 400 men had been lost to no avail and by 10 February the Ladysmith relief force was back at Chievely, whence it had set out a month before.

The operations had been characterized, on the Boer side, by quick reaction, determination, skill in the use of ground and weapons, all backed by courage and endurance. The last two qualities had been fully displayed by the British and Colonial regimental officers and men, but had been squandered by lack-lustre commanders with untutored staffs who, though possessed of a superiority of force, had been incapable of concerting its several components to achieve decisive victory. Only Dundonald and Lyttleton had shown any tactical insight.

The Ladysmith garrison, hungrier and sicker than before, remained unrelieved. The only hope was that their besiegers would soon be drawn off, if not by Buller, by the great offensive being planned by Roberts in the west.

9. WHITE FLAG ON THE MODDER

ORANGE FREE STATE, FEBRUARY–MARCH 1900

Roberts's strategy to end the war was to strike at Bloemfontein and subsequently Pretoria, thereby not only capturing both Republics' seats of government but, by so doing, compelling the Boers to abandon their sieges of Ladysmith, Kimberley and Mafeking and their attempts to foment rebellion in Cape Colony. While Buller held on in Natal, Roberts planned to bring up French's Cavalry Division from the Colesberg area to Modder River, leaving Gatacre to look after Cape Colony assisted by Clements' 12th Brigade and the Colonial Division to be formed at Cape Town by Brabant. Then, while Methuen's 1st Division demonstrated against the now-strengthened Magersfontein position, Roberts, having concentrated around Graspan and Enslin stations, would forsake the western railway communications and strike east across the veldt to the midland, Cape-Bloemfontein, line, prior to advancing on the capital.

His forces included French's cavalry, the recently-arrived 6th and 7th Divisions (13th and 18th, 14th and 15th Brigades), the newly-formed 9th Division (3rd (Highland) and 19th Brigades), and a division's worth of Mounted Infantry. Roberts had raised the latter by withdrawing companies from infantry battalions to form eight battalions of Regular MI, each about 450 strong, to which were added Rimington's Guides, 600 Australians and New Zealanders,[34] three regiments raised in Cape Colony (Roberts's, Kitchener's and Nesbitt's Horse) and the CIV's MI. These troops, together with eight Regular Cavalry regiments and seven RHA batteries, would provide what had hitherto been badly lacking, a mounted force of nearly 11,500 men, though some of the cavalry horses were out of condition after the voyage and many of the Regular MI would have to learn to ride as they went along. With his three infantry divisions, each about 6,600 strong, nine field batteries, one howitzer battery and six Naval guns,

Roberts would have a total strength of 37,000 and 64 guns (excluding Methuen's division).

To supply this large force away from the railway Kitchener completely reorganized the existing transport system. Hitherto, each unit and formation had its own transport and drew its supplies from the next higher headquarters. Kitchener now centralized the whole, except for unit water and ammunition vehicles, to provide a transport column of 21 mule-drawn and 6 ox-drawn wagon companies, totalling 1,734 wagons, 20,600 animals and 4,020 drivers. Kitchener conceived this arrangement to be more economical, but it was inflexible, contrary to familiar practice, and suffered from a shortage of officers with transport experience. He forced it through in a fortnight but its shortcomings would soon become apparent.

Roberts concealed his intentions from all but a few selected officers while deception plans were effected to suggest an offensive towards Norval's Pont, north of Colesberg, or a flanking move to the west of Magersfontein. Despite Milner's strongly-expressed fears about the threat to Cape Colony from the 7,000 Boers around Colesberg, Roberts stuck to his plan until the second week in February. He then learned of Buller's failures on the Tugela and, more worrying, that the antipathy between Kekewich and Rhodes at Kimberley had exploded into the latter's threat to surrender the town. Faced with the possibility of both Ladysmith and Kimberley falling to the Boers, Roberts decided he must alter his plan so as to relieve Kimberley first. He would march east from the railway to the Riet River but then send the Cavalry Division riding north-east to the Modder, 15 miles east of Magersfontein, thereafter swinging north-west to Kimberley while the infantry divisions followed. By this means he hoped to leave Cronje uncertain whether he was heading for Bloemfontein,

Lieutenant-General French, Cavalry Division.

Lieutenant-General Kelly-Kenny, 6th Division.

Lieutenant-General Tucker, 7th Division.

Major-General Smith-Dorrien, 19th Brigade.

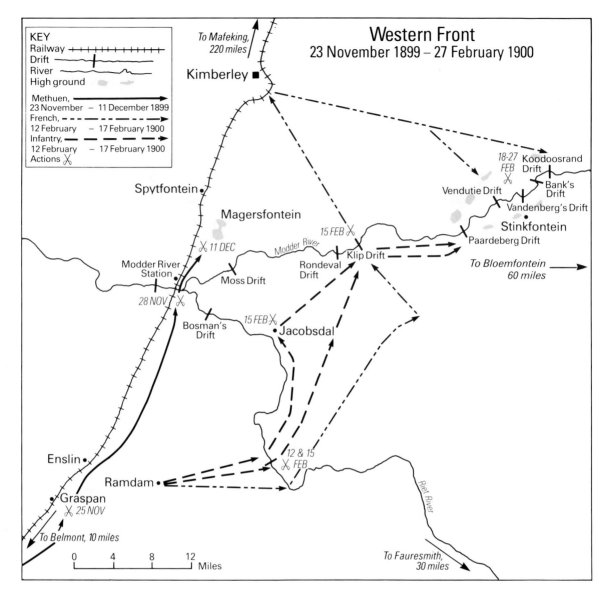

Western Front
23 November 1899 – 27 February 1900

To Mafeking,
220 miles

Kimberley ■

18-27
FEB ✕ Koodoosrand
Drift

Vendutie Drift   Bank's
Drift

Spytfontein •   Vandenberg's Drift

Magersfontein   • Stinkfontein
Paardeberg Drift

15 FEB ✕
✕ 11 DEC   Modder River
Modder River   Klip Drift   To Bloemfontein
Station   Rondeval   60 miles
Moss Drift   Drift

28 NOV ✕

Bosman's   15 FEB ✕
Drift   • Jacobsdal

Enslin •
12 & 15
Ramdam •◄   ✕ FEB

• Graspan
✕ 25 NOV

Riet River

To Belmont, 10 miles

0   4   8   12
|⎯⎯⎯|⎯⎯⎯|⎯⎯⎯| Miles

To Fauresmith,
30 miles

attacking Magersfontein from the rear or aiming for Kimberley.

Before dawn on 11 February, leaving their bivouacs standing at Modder River Station, French's cavalrymen rode south for 20 miles to the flank march's start-point at Ramdam Wells, eight miles due east of Enslin Station, where Tucker's 7th Division had arrived. Only one MI brigade under Alderson had reached Ramdam, the others having been delayed further south, but French decided to push on the 15 miles to the Riet with Alderson and the three cavalry brigades in the early hours of the 12th.

Meanwhile Cronje at Magersfontein had not learned of French's departure from the Modder until midday on the 11th but, still confronted by Methuen and convinced that the main British thrust would stick to the railway, he reckoned that French must be about to raid Fauresmith to the south-east and sent Christian De Wet with 450 men to halt French on the Riet. As French's patrols approached the river De Wet opened fire but, using one brigade to distract the enemy, French seized another drift upstream and passed his division across, whereupon De Wet made off further upstream, still convinced that French's

objective was Fauresmith. French now halted on the Riet to rest his men and horses, who were suffering from the intense heat, and to await the 7th Division.

On the 13th he rode on north-east to cover the 25 miles of waterless veldt to the Modder. By 5 p.m., having deluded a small Boer force as to his line of advance, he suddenly wheeled north-west and seized the crossings at Rondeval and Klip Drifts. He was now within 20 miles of Kimberley, but 500 of the heavily-laden cavalry horses were incapacitated from heat, dust and lack of water. In any case he had to wait for the infantry to come up and hold the crossings.

Meanwhile the 7th and Kelly-Kenny's 6th Division, plus the missing MI under Colonel Hannay, had reached the Riet and the 9th Division was at Ramdam. Concerned at French's vulnerability without infantry support, Roberts ordered Kelly-Kenny to continue onwards at best speed. Despite the terrible marching conditions and the men's lack of acclimatization the 6th Division, many of them Reservists, linked up with French at 1 a.m. on the 15th, having averaged one mile per hour.

Reports of these movements had persuaded Cronje that he had been wrong about Fauresmith but, reluctant to abandon his strong position at Magersfontein and encumbered by his wagon train full of women and children, he told himself that

Charge of the 9th and 16th Lancers at Klip Drift, 15 February 1900. By W.S. Small, after an eyewitness sketch by G.D. Giles.

Roberts was trying to lure him away, prior to attacking up the railway. He decided to sit tight with his main force, though withdrawing his wagon laager to greater safety and sending 800 men to block any further advance by French.

With the Modder drifts secured by the 6th Division, French launched his dash for Kimberley from Klip Drift. The most direct route ran up a broad valley between two miles of kopjes, on which the Boers sent by Cronje were waiting. At 8.30 a.m. on the 15th, covered by seven RHA batteries, the 9th and 16th Lancers of Gordon's 3rd Cavalry Brigade charged at a gallop in open order up the valley, followed by the rest of the division. Hammered by the artillery and unsighted by the vast dust cloud rising from the massed horses' hooves, the Boers' marksmanship availed them nothing. At the end of the valley more Boers lay in wait along a low ridge but, as the thunderous charge and glittering lance-points drew ever closer, their nerve broke and everywhere they fled to carry the news that the cavalry had broken through. Speed and dispersion had overcome the last Boer position before Kimberley for a loss of only two killed and 17 wounded and the

French's cavalry and RHA surprising Cronje's convoy at Vendutie Drift from the north bank of the Modder on 17 February. Beyond the river is Kitchener's Kopje, with Stinkfontein Farm amid trees to the left, and the ground where Kitchener attacked the next day. Gun Hill and Paardeberg Drift are off the picture's right edge. Painting by G.D. Giles.

morale effect of French's ride undermined the whole Boer position on this front. The besiegers of Kimberley melted away to the north-east and at 4 p.m. the first cavalry patrols rode into the town. After 124 days' siege Kimberley was relieved, much to the satisfaction of Rhodes, who wasted no time in poisoning French's mind against Kekewich, on whom the burden of its successful defence had rested.

All day Cronje had been distracted by a bombardment of Magersfontein from Methuen's guns and reports of an attack to his south on Jacobsdal. Here the City Imperial Volunteers had undergone their baptism of fire, going into action with Wavell's 15th Brigade of 7th Division, despatched by Roberts to divert attention from French and to secure a forward base within reach of the railway. When Cronje learned, later in the day, that French was now behind him, the realization that he had completely misjudged the British intentions came as an acute shock to him and his burghers. Pressed by his men to escape before they were trapped, he resolved to make a break for Bloemfontein, 90 miles due east. A risky move, since he would have to cross Roberts' line of advance at right angles, and necessarily slow, as he

refused to abandon his wagons and his burghers' families, but he hoped President Steyn would send out help from Bloemfontein and that Ferreira's men from Kimberley would protect his left, or north, flank, while De Wet should be in a position to threaten the British rear from the south.

De Wet was indeed still at large, having been lurking with a thousand men upstream of the British crossings of the Riet, and had that very day, the 15th, secured the only Boer success. Unseen and forgotten by the British columns intent on their advance northwards, he had been watching the ponderous and time-consuming passage of Kitchener's unwieldy wagon train across the Riet. The oxen had been so gravely overworked assisting the mule-drawn wagons that it had been decided to rest them on the 15th, leaving them a small escort, while the last of the fighting troops, 9th Division, pushed on. As soon as the 9th's rearguard was out of sight, De Wet pounced, surprising the escort and stampeding the oxen. By this coup he deprived Roberts of 1,600 oxen, 170 wagons and four days' supplies. Reinforcements hurriedly sent back were unable to dislodge De Wet so Roberts, unwilling to be deflected from catching Cronje, abandoned the convoy even though this meant his troops would have to subsist on half-rations until the huge loss could be made good. On the other hand De Wet was precluded from giving immediate aid to Cronje as he spent the next two days carrying off his loot.

Through the night of 15th-16th Cronje's 5,000 men

and 400 wagons moved silently eastwards, keeping parallel to and some four miles north of the Modder. Neither Methuen before Magersfontein, French around Kimberley, nor Kelly-Kenny and Hannay's MI at Klip Drift were aware of their passing. Just after dawn Hannay's Regulars and Colonials were riding north to link up with French when they spotted a huge dust cloud two and a half miles to the north-east. Sending off a report Hannay gave chase. At Klip Drift 6th Division had been preparing to follow Hannay but was now ordered by Kitchener, who had joined Kelly-Kenny, to make for the Boer convoy; Knox's 13th Brigade had already wheeled right in pursuit. However Hannay's men were still learning their trade and were thrown into confusion by the skilfully handled Boer rearguard, which then successfully resisted all efforts by Knox's battalions,[35] thus allowing Cronje's main body to draw further away and entrench in a laager on the river bank.

Though Kitchener had confidently signalled that he had all Cronje's army in his sights, urging a concentration upon him, Roberts, then at Jacobsdal with 9th Division, was as yet unconvinced. He telegraphed French to cut in ahead of the retreating Boers, but unknown to him the line to Kimberley had been damaged. Methuen had not bestirred himself until midday on the 16th to report that Magersfontein had indeed been completely evacuated, though Roberts feared Cronje might have split his force and could even now be threatening Kimberley following, as he believed, French's departure. Not until 6 p.m., on receipt of another pressing message from Kitchener, did he send off 9th Division and repeat his earlier order to French, who at the same time had received orders from Kitchener to make for Koodoosrand Drift, 18 miles east of where Cronje had halted and 30 from Kimberley.

French had spent the 16th in a fruitless attempt to round up Ferreira's men. His brigades were scattered and after six days' continuous riding in intense heat his horses were exhausted. Nevertheless at 3 a.m. on the 17th he rode out with Broadwood's 2nd Brigade,[36] leaving orders for Gordon to follow on the 18th. His advance was observed by Ferreira who, instead of joining Cronje, dispersed to the north-east. By 10.15 a.m. French was four miles west of his objective when Cronje's column was spotted an equivalent distance due south about to cross the Modder at Vendutie

2nd Royal Canadians of Smith-Dorrien's brigade crossing the Modder by lifeline at Paardeberg Drift. In the water close to the near bank are two MI and some of 82nd Field Battery, most of which is on the skyline.

Drift. French was in the nick of time; in another hour or so Cronje would have had the river between him and his pursuers with a clear run east to Bloemfontein. Sending the 12th Lancers to contain Cronje's flank guard, which was in position above Koodoosrand Drift, French swung south to engage the main body with his two RHA batteries, protected by the 10th Hussars.

The previous night Cronje had slipped away in the darkness and it had not been until the early hours of the 17th that 6th Division had set off in pursuit along the south bank, followed after an inexcusably late start by Hannay's MI. Despite Kitchener's goading, it was to take the tired and hungry infantry until dark to cover the 14 miles to Paardeberg Drift, where Cronje's rearguard had again halted Hannay, who had overtaken the infantry and occupied some rising

Sergeant Bowles' gun of 82nd Field Battery supporting 19th Brigade at Paardeberg.

ground on the south bank, four miles from the Boer main body at Vendutie. Thus it had been left to French's greatly outnumbered cavalrymen from the north to engage the enemy all day on their own, praying for the arrival of other troops on the south bank to prevent the Boers escaping. This Cronje could have done, either in the afternoon or during the night, but, burdened with his wagons and families, he decided to laager on the north bank, dig in and fight it out.

Luck had therefore smiled on Kitchener and, with Roberts suddenly taken ill at Jacobsdal, he now assumed command despite being several years junior to Kelly-Kenny, who stiffly accepted the situation. With Colvile's 9th Division reaching Paardeberg during the night after an arduous forced march, Kitchener determined to finish Cronje off the next day at all costs.

The area where Kitchener expected a quick decision was roughly a tilted, elongated oval, bisected by the Modder which flowed for 11 miles from Koodoosrand Drift at the north-east end, through Bank's, Vandenburg's and Vendutie Drifts to Paardeberg in the south-west. The river ran between high, steep, bush-covered banks about 200–300 yards

apart from which open ground sloped gradually upwards for between 1–3 miles to low ridges forming the rim of the oval. From Koodoosrand the ridges on the south bank ran through Stinkfontein, a hill known as Kitchener's Kopje, 2 miles from the river, to Signal Hill, close to Paardeberg Drift. From the latter the high ground on the north bank ran to Gun Hill, due north of Signal Hill, then out in a wider arc, where French had been holding since the 17th, back to Koodoosrand. Between Gun and Signal Hills the river made an elbow-shaped bend from which a deep donga ran out towards the former.

From this bend upstream for two miles to the wagon laager at Vendutie, the Boers had dug themselves into the high banks on either side. Beyond the laager only the north bank was held, and that more lightly, but the men on the Koodoosrand ridge remained in position. All the trenches were well hidden and had good fields of fire.

Kitchener had made his name 17 months earlier crushing the Dervishes at Omdurman. There he had commanded 10,000 more men than the 15,000 he now had at Paardeberg, but the close-order formations he

The moment of cease-fire for the Royal Canadians at Paardeberg, as depicted by R. Caton Woodville. Their maple-leaf badge can be seen on the helmets. Artistic licence shows the Modder between the Canadians and the laager, which was not the case.

had adopted against the Dervishes had allowed him to exercise a tight, personal control over his whole force. Even so his handling of the battle had left something to be desired, and its successful outcome had owed much to the presence of mind of one of his brigadiers, now the new commander of the Highland Brigade (9th Division), Hector MacDonald, the onetime ranker-subaltern of the 92nd on Majuba Hill. Kitchener's plan for Paardeberg, a frontal attack against the south bank in conjunction with a pincer movement against the laager on the north bank, would spread his formations over a much wider area than Omdurman, which would make his preference for personal control more difficult and would require good communications, careful co-ordination (for which he did not have the staff) and a clear understanding of his intentions by, and mutual co-operation between, his subordinate commanders. Unfortunately Kitchener found it hard to delegate and these requirements would not be met in the coming battle.

Before dawn on the 18th Hannay was sent off up the south bank with four battalions of MI[37] to seize Bank's and Vandenburg's Drifts, supported by 1st Welch and 1st Essex of Stephenson's 18th Brigade (6th Division), prior to forming the eastern pincer. At 6.30 a.m. 76th and 81st Batteries RFA opened fire, causing much damage to the laager, and half an hour later Knox's 13th Brigade and Stephenson's third battalion, 1st Green Howards,[38] went forward against the south bank between the elbow bend and Vendutie. At the same time Kitchener told Colvile to send in the Highland Brigade on 13th Brigade's left. MacDonald advanced at 7.45 but after three-quarters of an hour Kitchener realized that he had underestimated the Boer resistance and that the whole frontal attack was slowing down. He therefore sent orders to Smith-Dorrien, commanding 19th Brigade of Colvile's division, to cross the river at Paardeberg Drift and establish himself on the north bank. Before this could take effect, elements of the Green Howards and 13th Brigade, including all the Duke of Wellington's, had reached the bank, driving away the defenders, but were unable to suppress the fire from the far bank. At 9.30 Knox was wounded and shortly afterwards Kelly-Kenny, who had favoured surrounding the Boers and starving them into submission, halted the frontal attack. Half an hour earlier the Boers had stopped the Highland

Brigade's advance, but some of the Black Watch and Seaforth managed to ford the river and link up with the 7th MI who had crossed earlier. They advanced towards the deep donga at the elbow bend but were then halted to avoid masking 6th Division's fire. At 10 a.m. MacDonald was also wounded and the Highland effort was spent.

Kitchener had not vouchsafed to his divisional commanders his concept of the battle, so their subordinates had little notion of what the orders they received, from their superiors or directly from Kitchener himself, were intended to achieve. By 10.15 19th Brigade, which incidentally contained Canada's first contribution to the war, the 2nd Royal Canadian Regiment, had reached the north bank, but Smith-Dorrien, without any clear idea of what he was to do next and ignorant of the Highland Brigade's dispositions on his right, decided to encircle the Boer right by seizing Gun Hill. The Canadians, nearest the river, came under heavy fire from the deep donga while crossing open ground, but by 11 a.m. Smith-Dorrien was on Gun Hill with 2nd KSLI, 1st Gordons and 82nd Battery.[39] Here he took up a defensive position and made contact with French's outposts around the northern rim.

With everything at the western end of the battle at a standstill, Kitchener turned his attention to the east, where his plan had gone badly adrift. The 6th MI had successfully seized Bank's and Vandenburg's Drifts by 8.30 and linked up on the north bank with the 12th Lancers, sent by French who had undertaken to watch the approaches from the north-east. However Hannay's advance had not only drawn fire from the Modder, but increasingly from the ridges to his right beyond Stinkfontein, where Boer reinforcements led by President Steyn himself were arriving from Bloemfontein. At 9 a.m. Hannay turned to meet this threat and Stephenson, who knew only that he was to support Hannay, wheeled the Welch and Essex likewise. For the next two hours, instead of developing the pincer movement on the far bank, both Hannay and Stephenson were containing this attack from the east. At 11 a.m. Kitchener arrived and ordered them to attack the laager immediately. Leaving the New South Wales MR and Kitchener's Horse with 81st Battery to occupy Steyn, Hannay crossed at Vandenburg's to attack down the north bank, while Stephenson advanced down the south, supported by 76th Battery. However this attempt

'You have made a gallant defence, sir'. Roberts meeting Cronje after the surrender. The tall wagon in background was Roberts' mobile headquarters.

fared no better than those in the west and by 2 p.m. both MI and infantry had been brought to a standstill between 700–1,000 yards of the laager.

Despite his casualties and the failure of his plan, Kitchener remained determined to take the laager. Galloping back westwards he insisted that Kelly-Kenny and Colvile resume the attack. The former flatly refused to hazard 13th Brigade any further but agreed to extricate Stephenson, prior to sending him round via Vandenburg's to assist Hannay. Colvile's only uncommitted troops were the half of 2nd DCLI on baggage guard; this he ordered across the river to attack the deep donga. Finally Kitchener signalled to Hannay to 'gallop up and fire into the laager'.

By now the stress of the day's fighting, following the difficulties and setbacks of the past week with his barely-trained MI, had brought Hannay close to desperation. Kitchener's brief order, with no timings and only vague references to other troops, seemed to him like a death warrant for his unfortunate men. Dispersing his headquarters, he raced for the laager, followed only by a handful whom he quickly outdistanced. He fell, riddled with bullets, within the Boer trenches, making his own sacrifice in protest against Kitchener's indifference to casualties.

Two hours later, at 5.30, Stephenson, now on the north bank, sent forward the Welch and Essex to join up with the 4th MI, still lying out on the veldt where Hannay had left them, and then to charge the laager.

The two battalions, which had been constantly in action all day, had over a mile to go across open country under heavy fire. They got to within 600 yards of the laager but the final stretch proved impossible to cross. At 6.30 they withdrew.

This attack had almost achieved, by chance, the simultaneous pincer movement Kitchener had been seeking all day but had failed to accomplish. At 5.15 Smith-Dorrien, who had neither received, sought, nor issued any further orders since occupying Gun Hill at 11 a.m., suddenly saw his Canadians rise from cover and charge forward with other troops attacking up the north bank towards the deep donga, from which the Highland Brigade had suffered severely earlier. This attack, most gallantly made, was led by the half-battalion of DCLI, and the Canadians and Highlanders had spontaneously joined in. But, cut down by musketry, their colonel, Aldworth, killed, and exhausted by their furious charge, the Cornwalls went to ground 300 yards from the donga, waiting for supports that never came. Smith-Dorrien, who had seen it all, later excused his inactivity by claiming that the attack, of which he had not been warned, had failed before he could organize support.

Some of the 4,105 Boer prisoners taken at Paardeberg under guard.

While this was going on a dramatic intervention crowned the misfortunes of the day. Up from the south rode De Wet with 600 men. Seizing Kitchener's Kopje he opened fire at the rear of the batteries firing across the river. By 6 p.m. the ridges from the kopje to Koodoosrand were in Boer hands. A hurried counter-attack was mounted by 2nd Buffs and 2nd Gloucesters but, when darkness fell, they had got no further than the base of De Wet's position and they were ordered to dig in.

Kitchener's handling of the battle had resulted in uncoordinated attacks which had withered under intense fire from strong positions and cost 320 dead and 942 wounded. His troops were spent after the day's fighting and hard marching on short rations in the previous week. Cronje's unpromising position at dawn had been transformed by De Wet's arrival, but his men too were exhausted by the shellfire, his horses were decimated, his laager was a shambles and only a few were prepared to make a run for De Wet under cover of darkness through the British outposts.

The majority pulled back from their most distant positions towards the laager, to hold only some two miles of river.

When Roberts arrived next day he at first inclined to Kitchener's pleas for a renewed assault. Knowing that 14th Brigade of 7th Division would arrive that day and that the Guards Brigade from Methuen was on its way, he denied Cronje's appeal for an armistice to bury his dead. But then, concerned at the troops' fatigue, the casualties incurred by Kitchener, and the divisional commanders' reluctance to suffer more when medical facilities were already overstretched, he hesitated. Kelly-Kenny remained in favour of shelling and starving Cronje into submission, but any delay would disrupt Roberts' strategic aim, allowing other Boer forces to concentrate against him, rescue Cronje and cut off Roberts from his communications with the Cape. Indeed 2,000 Boers were marching from Natal to join those at Bloemfontein. Moreover Milner's despatches spoke of commandos fomenting rebellion in the Western Cape, while Clements with only one strong brigade and 600 Australians was under pressure from superior forces under De la Rey at Colesberg. If Clements broke, De la Rey would be free to seize Naauwpoort and De Aar junctions, or turn north and attack Roberts' rear. Most immediate of all was the menace of De Wet. During the 19th and

Infantry, including some Canadians on right, halted during the march on Bloemfontein. This shows the infantryman's load of rolled blanket and greatcoat, with mess-tin above, strapped to the back of the waistbelt and balancing the pouches in front. The haversack was increasingly carried on the back, instead of over the right shoulder balancing the water bottle over the left. Canadian pouches were of a different pattern.

20th attempts were made to dislodge him but though the Gloucesters got up on to one end of his position, Roberts recalled them, having decided to drive De Wet off his feature with French's cavalry from the south and east[40] on to the infantry waiting between De Wet and the river. If this failed Roberts believed he would have to withdraw and reorganize.

When the attack went in on the 21st, it did not exactly fail but De Wet, realizing the game was up, spotted a gap between French's troops and galloped through it with most of his force and got clear away. With that threat removed, Roberts settled down to tighten the noose round Cronje.

Now completely invested by an inner ring of infantry and an outer of mounted troops, conditions within the laager were rapidly deteriorating. Under constant bombardment, harassed by infantry, surrounded by rotting corpses of men and animals, short of food and medical supplies, and beset by heat and stench, only Cronje's iron will kept his men together. On the 23rd it began to rain continuously, which swept away the corpses, but flooded the rifle pits and shelters dug in the banks. By the 26th many Boers were urging surrender but, since the morrow was the anniversary of Majuba, Cronje refused to countenance it.

The significance of the date was not lost on the British either, particularly Hector MacDonald, who with more reason than most to avenge that day, suggested to Colvile an attack up the north bank. Roberts agreed. Before dawn Colonel Otter's Royal Canadians tried to rush the nearest Boer trenches. The Boers were not surprised but the Canadians dug in and a heavy fire-fight ensued. At 6 a.m. a white flag went up in the Boer trench and Roberts received a message that Cronje was prepared to surrender. At 7 a.m. the opposing commanders met. 'I am glad to see you' said Roberts,' you have made a gallant defence, sir'.

Into captivity passed 4,105 Boers, about a third of them Free Staters, the rest from the Western Transvaal. Cronje and his wife were transported to St Helena. Paardeberg was the first major British tactical victory of the war and strategically it had an adverse effect on the Boer cause. Their western effort was finished except for the continuing siege of Mafeking.

111

At Colesberg Clements had held, chiefly due to two splendid stands by 2nd Worcesters and some Australians (Victorians and South Australians). President Steyn, alarmed by Roberts's offensive, had first halted De la Rey, then ordered him to retire to Bloemfontein, enabling Clements to recapture Colesberg. Eastwards, further Boer withdrawals permitted Gatacre and Brabant to advance, the former eventually occupying the scene of his earlier defeat, Stormberg, on 5 March. In Natal the Boers holding the Tugela, weakened by the loss of the 2,000 sent westwards, had also had no cause to celebrate Majuba Day, as will shortly be seen. Only the rebellion in the Western Cape was still causing concern and a force, largely of Colonials and Yeomanry, was assembled to deal with it.

Seriously worried by the possible repercussions on Boer, especially Free State, morale if Bloemfontein fell, Steyn and Kruger determined to halt Roberts at all costs and ordered all available men to concentrate at Poplar Grove, 45 miles west of the capital and 20 east of Paardeberg, where De Wet was already in position. By 5 March 6,000 burghers, with twice as many expected within a week, were spread along a 25-mile line of kopjes astride the Modder, well sited to block a frontal assault but open on the flanks, particularly the south.

But the Boers were not to have a week's respite. After a pause at Paardeberg to bring up reinforcements and reorganize the MI more effectively in four brigades,[41] Roberts advanced on 7 March. His plan was for French's cavalry and two MI brigades to sweep wide round the Boers' left to cut their line of retreat to Bloemfontein, while the 6th Division and Guards Brigade were to roll up the Boer left towards the Modder as the 7th Division drove up its south bank and the 9th up its north; the object being to drive this Boer force into the Modder and surround them as at Paardeberg.

In the event French, who was having an off day, did not move fast enough, Kelly-Kenny was late starting, and the Boers, seeing this large force coming against them, proved reluctant to meet it and reverted to their old practice of riding away to fight another day. They had been forced out of a well-prepared position at little cost, but a great opportunity had been lost through excessive caution and delay.

It was perhaps as well for Roberts that he had not known he had missed the chance of capturing Kruger himself. The old President had come to Poplar Grove to exhort his men but in the event found himself trying to prevent a retreat becoming a rout, assisted only by De la Rey and some 1,500 policemen. Despite his impassioned pleas and threats only a few volunteered to stand with De la Rey, though most of the others were rallied by Steyn and De Wet for the defence of Bloemfontein.

On 10 March Roberts advanced again with each of the three infantry divisions ten miles apart and the mounted troops divided among each column with the aim of cutting the railway south of the capital. The centre column he commanded himself, French the left and Tucker the right. French was the first to make contact with De la Rey near Dreifontein. He tried to bypass the position to the south but De la Rey side-stepped to halt him. The cavalry and MI were unable to make headway and Stephenson's 18th Brigade was ordered to attack at 12.30 p.m. Though reinforced by half 13th Brigade, such was the heroic resistance put up by the Johannesburg and Pretoria Police that it was not until 6 p.m., when a fine assault by 1st Essex threatened their horse-lines, that the remnants abandoned their position.

The day's action had cost over 400 British casualties, including 82 dead, amongst the latter being Lieutenant Parsons of the Essex who had been recommended for the Victoria Cross at Paardeberg and was again prominent in his regiment's final charge. The Boers had lost 100 killed and the heart went out of the burghers preparing to defend Bloemfontein. The machinery of the Free State Government had already been sent north and the burghers followed, evacuating the town. On the 13th Roberts and the cavalry rode into the Free State capital. With its capture and the flight of its defenders, coming on top of good news from Natal, many British thought the war was as good as over.

10. MY BRAVE IRISH

Throughout late January and into February the rumble of Buller's guns and the distant movements of the Boers above the Tugela had alternately lifted and dashed the spirits of Ladysmith's defenders, daily grower weaker for want of food. The chronic shortage of meat had been slightly alleviated from 1 February by White's decision to slaughter the cavalry horses—much to their riders' outrage—but enteric fever was rife and by 27 February the garrison's bread ration was halved. Enfeebled though they were, their hopes surged anew the following day when the outposts spotted hundreds of wagons and thousands of riders trekking north, away from the Tugela, away from Ladysmith. Had Buller done it at last?

After the failures at Spion Kop and Vaal Krantz Roberts had refused Buller's request for reinforcements, insisting that he remained on the defensive until his own offensive could take effect. However Buller, fearing that White could not hold out much longer, determined to try again in the Colenso area which, if he could but break through, offered the shortest route to Ladysmith. Having by now gauged the quality of his enemy and the nature of modern warfare, he appreciated that only by crumbling up the Boer positions one by one with a judicious combination of infantry and artillery could he open the way for his two mounted brigades.

To confront Buller, Botha had mustered between 5,000—6,000 men of whom he posted about half, with five guns, on the high ground south of the river east of Colenso. At the first battle, on 15 December, the Boers had only held part of this ground, on Hlangwane, but their positions now stretched two miles eastwards to Green Hill before running back north-east to the southern end of the Monte Cristo ridge, whose northern peak dropped steeply down to the Tugela. A mile and a half forward of this north-east section rose Cingolo Hill, held by 300 men. On the far bank, due north of Colenso, the Boers held the low kopjes in the angle formed by the river as it turned north, from where they had resisted the main attack on 15 December.

Buller intended first to roll up the Boer positions on the south bank from the east. Despite his anxiety about Ladysmith and although he had signalled White to expect him on 13 February, the operations began sluggishly, because of his concern about the effects of the heat on his men. Not until the 17th did he order Lyttleton, now commanding 2nd Division (2nd and 4th Brigades), to move against the Green Hill-Monte Cristo line, supported on his right by Dundonald's 2nd Mounted Brigade and on his left by Warren's 5th Division (6th, 10th and 11th Brigades).

Lyttleton planned to seize Cingolo first but was forestalled by Dundonald who, finding a covered approach round the south-east, pushed his Colonials to the top, capturing this important outpost before Lyttleton's infantry could reach it. This secured the right of a start-line for a three-brigade attack the following day. By the evening of the 18th the whole enemy position from Green Hill to the north end of Monte Cristo had been captured by 6th Brigade and 2nd Division and all the Boers, except those on Hlangwane, had made off to the north bank. These attacks had been well handled by Lyttleton and his brigadiers, brigades and battalions supporting each other forward with all movement properly covered by artillery, Maxim and long-range rifle fire against known enemy positions, instead of the wasteful area bombardments which ceased as soon as the infantry advanced. Unfortunately the rest of the force remained unused, leaving Hlangwane undisturbed and enabling the retreating Boers to reach the far bank unmolested. Nevertheless the enemy were considerably demoralized and the defenders of Hlangwane, anxious to put the river between them and the British, abandoned their position during the

11th Brigade's attack on Railway Hill, 27 February. The railway running between Railway and Pieter's Hills is marked at right. The infantry are attacking left to right towards the Boer breastworks on the skyline.

night of the 19th. Buller closed up to the river but, despite the sight of the wagon laagers on the far side moving off northwards, declined to pursue, thus giving Botha time to rally his burghers and take up fresh positions along the tangle of hills, running from the loop where the Irish Brigade had suffered on 15 December to Pieter's Hill, east of the Ladysmith railway at the apex of the great northerly bend downstream from Colenso.

These positions overlooked the triangular-shaped low ground around the Colenso kopjes on the left bank west of Hlangwane. Yet it was into this confined area that Buller began pushing Warren's 5th Division, followed by 2nd Division, over the 21st and 22nd. From its northern end a series of steep-sided hills rose north-east close to the Tugela, between which the road and railway to Ladysmith ran along the left bank. These heights came to be known as Wynn's, Hart's (or Inniskilling) and Railway Hills; between the last-named and Pieter's the railway went through a pass before running due north across the plain to Ladysmith. Not until the Boers were driven from this chain of hills could Buller break through to the beleaguered town.

On the 22nd Wynn's 11th Brigade attacked the hill

named after him but, though reinforced by parts of 2nd and 4th Brigades, was unable to secure more than a lodgement on the lower slopes and fighting continued into the next day. Wynn was wounded and his brigade was given to Walter Kitchener, lately commanding 2nd West Yorkshire. Having lost over 500 casualties it was withdrawn and replaced by Hildyard's 2nd Brigade. In an attempt to outflank Wynn's Hill, Buller ordered 5th (Irish) Brigade to advance along the river bank below Wynn's and attack Hart's Hill on the afternoon of the 23rd, reinforced by half of Norcott's 4th Brigade.

Much of the approach march was in dead ground except for an exposed section across a railway bridge swept by pom-pom and rifle fire. Here numbers of men fell. At 4 p.m. Hart ordered the advance up the steep convex slopes of the objective. The sun was beginning to set when the leading companies of the Inniskilling Fusiliers reached the false crest and the Boer trenches were seen 400 yards away. Then began the terrible drum roll of Boer musketry, from in front and in enfilade from Wynn's and Railway Hills. The Inniskillings dashed forward into the hail of fire, followed by the Connaughts and Dublins, as Hart, well to the front, ordered his bugler to sound the 'Charge' repeatedly. The British guns across the river were firing overhead, but the Boer riflemen never faltered in their murderous fusillade. Colonel Thackeray of the Inniskillings was killed and scores of his officers and men went down. The attack withered but, as the Connaughts and Dublins came

4th Brigade attacking up the slopes from the Tugela against Hart's Hill, at top, 27 February. Boer trenches and breastworks are marked in white on the hill. This scene occurred to the south, or left, of the previous picture.

up, again the lines struggled forward. With the light failing the British gunners had to cease fire and without support the gallant Irish simply could not prevail. The survivors fell back some way down the slope and began to construct protective sangars under cover of darkness. The Inniskillings had lost half their strength and 30 per cent of the other attacking companies were casualties.

During the night elements of 2nd and 4th Brigades, not already committed to Wynn's Hill, were sent forward to Hart but when day dawned, so heavy was the continuing enfilade fire, that Buller was persuaded against renewing the attack. In any case the divisional and brigade structure had broken down, with parts of brigades, even battalions, inter-mingled with others. The situation of Buller's force along the Tugela, on or below Botha's dominating positions, was akin to climbers clinging to a rockface but prevented by an overhang from reaching the summit and unable to help each other. It was time for a new plan, but so desperate was the plight of the

wounded still lying in no-man's-land, that an armistice was agreed on the 25th to recover them.

Though disposing of six infantry brigades, Buller had hitherto committed only one at a time, reinforcing each with parts of others when the attacks faltered. He had lost 1,300 men to no end when light began to dawn on this, the eighth day of operations. Rather than trying to dig out the defenders successively from the south, he would lever them away from the hills at the north-east end of their line, going first for Pieter's Hill then, in quick succession, Railway and Hart's Hills, thus outflanking and enfilading each position in turn. By withdrawing most of the artillery to the right bank, he planned to support the attacks with 70 guns and long-range Maxim and rifle fire from two battalions. Lyttleton was to guard the left flank with 10th Brigade and the mixed-up battalions on Wynn's Hill.[42] Rather than try to reconstitute the original brigades, which would have involved excessive and probably costly movement, it was decided to leave those in forward positions where they were, and to use the less exposed to reinforce the assault brigades under Warren. Pieter's was to be attacked by Barton's 6th (Fusilier) Brigade, whose two detached battalions would be replaced by the Dublins from 5th Brigade. Kitchener's Lancashire battalions of 11th Brigade, reinforced by 2nd West Yorkshire from 2nd Brigade, would take Railway Hill, and Norcott's 4th Brigade, with 2nd East Surreys, Hart's Hill. The remains of the Irish Brigade would be in reserve. 11th Brigade was moved to the right bank on the 25th, as were Barton's 2nd Royal Irish Fusiliers to rejoin his Royal Scots Fusiliers which had never crossed. Other battalions for the attack were to remain in the gorge on the left bank to join their new brigades just before the assault. The old bridge opposite Hlangwane was dismantled after dark and its pontoons moved north to a new site below Hart's Hill before dawn on the 27th. Here, as in the west, Majuba Day was to be one of decision. Just as the advance began the news of Cronje's surrender was received by telegraph and was immediately passed on to the men.

By 10 a.m. the new pontoon bridge was complete, the massed guns opened fire and Barton's Fusiliers crossed, picking up the Dublins on the far side and advancing in single file to the right under the steep bank until they were below the cliff-like slopes of Pieter's. At 12 noon the climb began. The summit, held by the Heidelberg Commando, consisted of three peaks echeloned back one behind the other over the space of a mile. As the Irish Fusiliers came in sight of the nearest they drew a brisk fire from Railway Hill to their left but raced forward undeterred and quickly captured the peak from the surprised Heidelbergers. From here they returned the fire from Railway Hill and opened up on the next peak to help the Scots Fusiliers forward. However the Heidelbergers quickly recovered and, aided by the Standerton men to their left, brought a heavy and costly fire to bear on the Scottish battalion which was directed on to the central and furthest peaks. Most of the supporting artillery fire was falling on Railway and Hart's Hills, Barton having only the Naval guns from Monte Cristo. Nevertheless, by 2.30, the Scots Fusiliers had taken the central peak and linked up with the Irish Fusiliers but, though reinforced by the Dublins, they were halted 300 yards from the final objective.

Meanwhile Kitchener's battalions had assembled below Railway Hill and at 3 p.m. started their ascent. On the right the West Yorkshires climbed unobserved up the re-entrant between Railway and Pieter's Hills to just below the Boer left, helped by the bombardment and the Irish Fusiliers on Pieter's. When they were in position, Kitchener launched the South Lancashires against the centre and the King's Own at the Boer right. The three battalions made a fine charge, driving the Johannesburgers from their trenches, but the King's Own, with further to go, were held up by fire from Hart's Hill. Turning to face this they charged across the intervening ground and gained a foothold on the extreme end of Hart's, just as Norcott's attack from below was developing.

With this help the East Surreys swarmed up and on to the crest. On their left 1st Rifle Brigade's leading companies were halted by fire from in front and from Wynn's Hill. However their supports came up and, with 2nd Devons, left behind on Wynn's, subduing the enfilade fire, the Riflemen went forward again. The Boers now evacuated Hart's Hill though keeping up a continual musketry upon it until after dark.

With Hart's and Railway Hills in British hands, only the last peak on Pieter's remained untaken. His left now secured, Barton withdrew three companies of Irish Fusiliers and ordered them to attack. As the day drew to a close the Northern Irish went forward again, covered by the rifle fire of their Southern countrymen, the Dublins. Determined though they were, the last Heidelbergers were equally so. The Mausers cut a swathe through the Irish ranks, men falling all round, but eventually two-thirds of them clambered on to the southern end of the objective. Still the Heidelbergers fought on from the far end and the Fusiliers, exhausted and with all their officers killed or wounded, could do no more. With darkness falling they took cover among the rocks they had reached. Later that night the Heidelbergers crept silently away.

From Pieter's Hill to Colenso the Tugela heights were at last in Buller's hands. The day's fighting had cost some 500 casualties, nearly half sustained by Barton's Fusiliers. Over the past fortnight 26 officers

4.7-inch Naval guns on Monte Cristo supporting the Fusilier Brigade's attack on Pieter's Hill, 27 February.

and 347 men had been killed or died of wounds, and 99 officers and 1,710 men wounded. When the reports reached Queen Victoria, she was particularly moved by the casualties of the Irish regiments, telegraphing to Buller: 'I have heard with the deepest concern of the heavy losses sustained by my brave Irish soldiers'. Later she ordered the formation of the Irish Guards to commemorate their gallantry and devotion on the Tugela.

The Boers had lost about 500 men during this last offensive, the hardest hit being the Krugersdorpers and Johannesburgers holding Hart's and Railway Hills. For over two months Botha's powerful leadership and tactical skill had held them to the defence of the Tugela line, but now the lack of discipline inherent in all Boer forces surfaced; the burghers had had enough. With Buller's successful assault on the 27th, coming on top of the demoralization of the 19th and the disheartening news of Cronje's surrender, it struck young Deneys Reitz, whose entire corporalship had perished on Pieter's, 'that the whole universe seemed to be toppling about our ears. Wherever we looked Boer horsemen, wagons and guns went streaming to the rear in headlong retreat'. Deaf to all Botha's appeals, the majority had but one idea—to get home, every

man for himself. Arriving at Joubert's headquarters outside Ladysmith, Botha found the same story. There was nothing for it but to hope he could rally them later.

To the defenders of Ladysmith, buoyed up by the sounds of battle on the 27th, the sight of the fleeing Boers the next day brought exhilaration at the thought that their trials were nearly over, mingled with frustration that they were powerless to intervene. All day the eyes of the outposts strained to the south for the first sight of the relief column, but no-one came. Then, just before 6 p.m., khaki-clad horsemen in slouch hats were spotted riding towards the town from the south-east 'in a formation which never yet have Boers made'. Some of the Natal Carbineers rode out on a few of the remaining horses to meet them and found, amid scenes of great emotion, they were men of their own regiment from Dundonald's brigade.

The latter's reconnaissance had been led by Major Hubert Gough's Composite Regiment. After a few skirmishes with retreating Boers, Gough had arrived

117

'My Brave Irish'. R. Caton Woodville's painting of the last charge on Pieter's Hill by 2nd Royal Irish Fusiliers, assisted by 2nd Royal Dublin Fusiliers.

within three miles and sight of Ladysmith when he received an order from Dundonald to retire. Ignoring this, he rode on, sending back a message that the way into Ladysmith was clear. At 6.15, with a squadron each of Natal Carbineers and Imperial Light Horse riding abreast, he entered Ladysmith to be greeted by White and his staff. Visibly worn down by the responsibility of the past 119 days, White welcomed Gough unemotionally: 'Hallo, Hubert, how are you?' Shortly afterwards, moved by the ovation given him by his soldiers and townsfolk, he made a short speech, acknowledging all their support, and ending, 'Thank God we have kept the flag flying'.

Aware that Buller was doing nothing to pursue the Boers, White next day sent out a column northwards to try and deny the use of the railway to the enemy for their retreat. Only 2,000 men were found fit enough to march. It was a brave attempt but, after firing at Modder Spruit Station without being able to prevent the last train leaving, the men were too weak to do more than march back to Ladysmith.

Meanwhile, appraised of affairs in Ladysmith by Dundonald who, unwilling to be outdone by Gough, had followed him into the town on the 28th, Buller had unhurriedly begun to set his army in motion accompanied by 75 wagons of food and medical supplies for the garrison. He visited White on 1 March and two days later made his formal entry into the town at the head of his troops, led by the Dublin Fusiliers. A Ladysmith chaplain wrote: 'The contrast between the robust and bearded veterans of a dozen battles, and the pale, emaciated defenders of Ladysmith was great—till then we had not realised how wasted and weak we were'. The general mood was of quiet contentment and satisfaction as Buller's men swung past, the only emotion being shown when men of regiments like the Devons, Irish Fusiliers, 60th and Rifle Brigade recognized friends in their sister battalions who had endured the siege.

So Ladysmith was at long last relieved, uniting, as Buller wrote in an Order of the Day, 'two forces both of which have, during the last four months, striven with conspicuous gallantry and splendid determination to maintain the honour of their Queen and country'. Sir George White was invalided home, leaving in his wake a whispering campaign against Buller orchestrated chiefly by Ian Hamilton[43] with some support from Buller's own generals.

Buller was no military genius, not that he ever claimed to be one, and his critics could fairly point to his missed opportunities, his bouts of lassitude, pessimism and indecision, his delegation of authority verging at times on abdication, his self-confidence ranging from one extreme to the other. On the other hand he had been faced in Natal by a situation brought about by White's ignoring his strategic advice; by a formidable and well-armed enemy possessing all the advantages of terrain; and by a form of warfare for which the Army and its generals were unprepared by experience and training, and in which an attacker needed a 3:1 superiority for success, a proportion by no means available to Buller at his first attempt. By Spion Kop he had a sufficiency of force which he failed to concentrate, but from then on he began to learn from his mistakes and ultimately, on 27 February, proved that he had graduated with some honour, even if this success was marred by his failure to exploit it. The most remarkable thing about Buller was that, notwithstanding the hardships and sacrifices he inflicted

2nd Gordon Highlanders, of the Ladysmith garrison, presenting arms as Buller's army enters the town.

upon his men, he never lost their affection, trust and esteem. To claim, as Churchill did, that this derived solely from 'the serious attention' he paid to their feeding seems too facile and condescending to the ordinary soldier; as Kipling rightly observed: 'An' Tommy ain't a blooming fool—you bet that Tommy sees!' Buller's Tommies on the Tugela certainly saw much in their commander that was deserving of their loyalty and tenacity.

With the capture of the Free State capital Roberts hoped that the smaller Republic was virtually out of the war. In response to his offer of an amnesty to all burghers except their leaders, many were going home and handing in their arms—though these were frequently obsolete weapons, not the precious Mausers, which were buried secretly. Against this there were still bodies of Boers in the field: 13,000 in Natal holding the Biggarsberg, north of Ladysmith, and Van Reenan's Pass in the Drakensberg; a thousand fomenting rebellion in the north of Cape Colony and twice as many around Mafeking; about 6,000 under De Wet and De la Rey north of Bloemfontein; 2,000 in the west blocking the approaches to Mafeking and the Transvaal under Andries Cronje and Du Toit; and Olivier was retreating from the Colesberg-Stormberg area into the Eastern Free State with 6,000. By late March Olivier had successfully evaded a force sent too late to halt him at Thaba 'Nchu, east of Bloemfontein.

Roberts had entered Bloemfontein with 34,000 men. In addition there was Buller's army in Natal, now 55,000 strong after the relief of Ladysmith. Notwithstanding the forces still ranged against him and the vulnerability of his 350-mile, single-line track of railway communications to the Cape ports, Roberts believed that, after a period of rest for re-equipping and reorganizing his troops, a converging advance of all British forces upon Pretoria, together with a policy of clemency in the conquered territory, would speedily bring the war to a close. He thought that the Boers' will to fight on could be broken more quickly by occupying their seats of government than by destroying their armies—a theory that failed to take into account how little such places counted in the Boer mentality. Buller, who knew the Boers better, foresaw endless conflict unless the commandos roaming the Free State were first vanquished.

Events were soon to give a foretaste of how right he was.

On 17 March Presidents Kruger and Steyn held a council of war at Kroonstadt. Many Boers were losing heart, Kruger was ailing and Piet Joubert was near to death,[44] but all the leaders agreed the fight must continue. Kruger made an impassioned speech in Biblical terms, reminding the burghers of their sacred mission as God's chosen people. The younger Steyn was more down to earth, predicting trouble for Britain in India from Russia, and proposing the despatch of a mission to gain moral and practical support from sympathizers in Europe. The most realistic contribution came from the dedicated and ruthless De Wet, now appointed Commandant-General of the Free State Forces. First he suggested that all burghers should be allowed to go to their homes for ten days, after which the best men would return refreshed and eager to fight on, while the less resolute would be weeded out. The ponderous wagon trains loaded with families, which had so weakened Cronje at Paardeberg, should be abolished, leaving the commandos with much greater mobility. De Wet insisted that the Boers must exploit the vulnerability of the long British supply lines and rear areas by frequent raids against them. Supported by De la Rey, he urged a change-over from the conventional de-fensive tactics employed hitherto to guerilla war-fare. While reluctant to forsake completely attempts to block Roberts' advance, the Presidents agreed to De Wet's first project: a raid on the Bloemfontein Waterworks near Sannah's Post, which lay between the former capital and Thaba 'Nchu. This would not only seriously imperil Roberts' water supply but would also worsen the epidemic of enteric fever then rife in the British camps. Unknown to De Wet, an added bonus was about to fall into his lap.

After the failure to halt Olivier's commando, a

General Christian De Wet, third from right, and staff: from right, Commandant Von Grahn, Commandant Nell, De Wet's secretary, Field-Cornets Francis and Colson, Jones (a scout), Nell's son.

1,700-strong column under Broadwood, consisting of his own understrength 2nd Cavalry Brigade, Alderson's MI brigade, and Q and U Batteries RHA, had been operating in the Thaba 'Nchu area. Learning that Olivier's superior force had turned back towards him, Broadwood retreated towards Bloemfontein, taking with him a convoy of 92 wagons containing stores and civilian refugees. Arriving at Sannah's Post on 30 March and confident he had outstripped Olivier, he bivouacked beside the Modder. Next morning the bivouac was fired on from across the river. Despatching a messenger to Bloemfontein and hastily deploying his MI to cover his retreat, Broadwood sent off the wagons followed by U and Q Batteries. As the wagons and U Battery were crossing the Koorn Spruit, a tributary of the Modder, they suddenly found themselves surrounded by a mass of Boers concealed under the banks: De Wet's men. All were silently taken prisoner. Alerted just in time, Major Phipps-Hornby got his Q Battery into action and, well-supported by the Regular MI and New Zealand Mounted Rifles, managed with great gallantry but suffering heavy casualties to save five of the two batteries' 12 guns from the trap; the severity of this encounter was later recognized by the award of four VCs to Q Battery, including one to Phipps-Hornby himself. Broadwood eventually extricated the rest of his force and troops came out from Bloemfontein, but they were unable to catch De Wet, who got away with seven guns, the wagons and 400 prisoners.

Sending off his prizes northwards, De Wet rode south and attacked a garrison of 600 men of the Royal Irish Rifles, forcing their surrender after a 24-hour fight, at Reddersburg. Turning east, he struck at Wepener, held by 1,900 of Brabant's Cape Colonials under Colonel Dalgety.[45] By now his operations had stirred Roberts' headquarters into a frenzy of activity. Gatacre was sacked from 3rd Division and sent home for failing to rescue the Reddersburg garrison, and two columns, including Rundle's newly arrived 8th Division (16th and 17th Brigades), were sent to advance on Wepener from west and south. Despite outnumbering the Wepener men by four to one, De Wet was unable to overcome their stout resistance. After sixteen days' siege and aware of the approaching columns, he broke off his attacks and got clear away to the north, defying the combined efforts of Brabant, Rundle, French and Pole-Carew to catch him. His four weeks' marauding had shown that the Boers were far from beaten and had raised Boer morale everywhere, but he had not cut the railway and the waterworks had been recaptured.

121

Alderson's MI covering the retirement at Sannah's Post, 31 March. The Waterworks pumping station on the Modder extreme right, Sannah's Post extreme left. The ambush of the RHA occurred further left. Note the horse-holders, normally one in four. By C.M. Sheldon after a sketch by Captain St Leger.

This fighting south-east of Bloemfontein and the enteric epidemic, which had caused 4,500 sick due to defective medical arrangements, plus the need to bring up reinforcements of both men and horses, had delayed but not altered Roberts' plan to advance on Pretoria. By the beginning of May he mustered some 70,000 men and 178 guns north of the Orange River. At Kimberley Methuen's 1st Division (9th and 20th Brigades) had been joined by a newly-constituted 10th Division under Hunter, formerly White's Chief of Staff, made up of Hart's and Barton's brigades sent round from Natal. In Natal Buller had three mounted brigades, Clery's 2nd Division (2nd and 4th Brigades), Lyttleton's 4th Division (chiefly composed of the Ladysmith garrison now formed into 7th and 8th Brigades), and the 5th, commanded by Hildyard in place of Warren, who had been sent off to deal with the rebellion in the northwest Cape.

Roberts intended to leave Kelly-Kenny's 6th Division to garrison Bloemfontein, with Gatacre's successor, Chermside, and 3rd Division deployed to the south. The main advance up the line was to have French's Cavalry Division on the left flank, Tucker's 7th and Pole-Carew's new 11th (1st (Guards) and 18th Brigades) astride the railway, preceded by Hutton's 1st MI Brigade,[46] and on the right a force commanded by Ian Hamilton of Broadwood's Cavalry Brigade, Ridley's 2nd MI Brigade,[47] Smith-Dorrien's 19th and Bruce Hamilton's 21st Brigades. Hamilton's column was to be followed by Colvile's 9th Division, which now contained only the Highland Brigade and some MI, apart from artillery and engineers. Rundle's 8th and Brabant's Colonial Divisions were to sweep up the Eastern Free State after the main advance had gone forward to prevent any attack on its rear.

From Kimberley, Hunter was to march north and enter the Transvaal from the west, while Methuen was to advance north-east, ready to support either Hunter or the main army; both divisions had battalions of Imperial Yeomanry attached as MI. At the same time Colonel Mahon, with the ILH from Natal, the Kimberley MI and 100 of Barton's Fusiliers, was to relieve Mafeking in conjunction with Colonel

Group of typical mounted Boers. All seem to be mature men except for two youths in the centre.

Plumer's column of Rhodesians, Queenslanders and Canadians coming down from Rhodesia. Another force from Rhodesia of Yeomanry, Australians and New Zealanders under General Carrington was to invade the Transvaal from the north; in the event this never happened and Carrington's force was later sent to the Western Transvaal.

As for the large force in Natal, Roberts wanted Buller merely to contain the Boers holding the Biggarsberg while breaking out into the Free State through Van Reenan's Pass to assist his own advance. However Buller claimed it was more important first to clear Northern Natal and the Durban-Johannesburg railway, on which he depended for supplies. Unwilling to overrule the former commander-in-chief, Roberts gave Buller the benefit of the doubt. Thus from Kimberley in the west to Ladysmith in the east, a frontage of 350 miles, 100,000 Empire troops—Regulars, Colonials, Volunteers, Militia and Yeomanry[48]—would be confronting some 30,000 Boers, about half of whom were positioned or on their way to oppose Roberts' main advance.

Although the British had a preponderance of numbers and artillery, they would be operating in hostile country and dependent on a single supply line which, as De Wet had foreseen, would become increasingly vulnerable the further they advanced, requiring the dropping off of guards and garrisons to secure the rear areas. On the other hand, the commandos, being among their own people, could find supplies, shelter and reinforcements and could range freely almost anywhere they chose in the huge spaces of the Republics. Unlike the British they had, at this stage, no overall strategic plan.

On 3 May the great advance began, though Buller was to make no move until the 11th. Pretoria lay 300 miles from Bloemfontein, with Kroonstadt about half-way in between and the Johannesburg gold-mines only 40 miles from the capital. Across the line of advance flowed certain rivers, the Vet, Zand, Vaalsch, Rhenoster and the Vaal, where the Boers prepared to stand. But always outnumbered, and with Roberts' mounted troops riding wide to find the open flank, the best the Boers could do was to delay the advance as long as possible and then fall back to

8th Battery RFA and RE observation balloon en route for Johannesburg. Four balloon sections were employed during the war, each requiring seven carts. They achieved only limited success but had some morale effect on the Boers. Note the RFA driver's right leg guard, foreground.

1st (Guards) Brigade marching in column during Roberts' advance north. Unlike the Scots Guards and most of the army, the Grenadiers and Coldstream did not use helmet covers. Note ox wagons on skyline.

avoid being outflanked and surrounded, blowing the bridges and railway track behind them. Such fighting as there was fell mainly on the cavalry and MI of French, Hutton and Hamilton, the infantry having little to do but plod on mile after mile. Private Waller of the CIV battalion in Hamilton's column wrote home that he and his comrades thought 'going into action was nothing ... but they are sick of the incessant tramp over miles of plain without anything to vary the monotony, nothing but the burnt up grass to look at. You cannot distract your thoughts for a moment. It is no good talking for it dries one up'.

On the 12th Roberts entered Kroonstadt. He then had to halt for ten days to repair the damaged railway, bring up supplies, evacuate his sick and rest the mounted troops, whose horses, many of them unacclimatized, had covered greater distances than the infantry and suffered accordingly.

Meanwhile Buller reached Dundee, where the war had begun,on the 15th, having forced the Boers to evacuate the Biggarsberg by outflanking them to the east. In the west Hunter entered the Transvaal and Methuen was approaching Hoopstadt, midway

between Hunter and Roberts, neither having encountered much opposition. On the same day, by a skilful choice of route and his infantry's hard marching, Mahon's 900 men linked up with Plumer's 700 from the north, having covered 226 miles in 12 days, fighting one engagement. Plumer's Rhodesians had tried to reach Mafeking in early April but had been driven back with heavy loss when only five miles from the town. Now he and Mahon met at a critical time, for they were confronted by De la Rey and 2,000 men sent from the central front by Botha. A stiff fight ensued on the 16th, but after five hours' engagement the Boers gave way and that evening the Imperial Light Horse rode into Mafeking. After seven months' siege, Baden-Powell's little garrison of amateur soldiers[49] was at last relieved.

The news created a storm of emotion in Britain and the Empire, far greater than that provoked by any other incident of the war, and the scenes of rejoicing in London over nearly 48 hours placed a new verb, 'to maffick', in the English language. Yet the euphoric, almost hysterical, response was out of all proportion to the military significance of the event.

Colonel Baden-Powell, defender of Mafeking

Lieutenant-Colonel Mahon, Mafeking relief column (south).

Lieutenant-Colonel Plumer, Mafeking relief column (north).

Major-General Barton, 6th (Fusilier) Brigade.

A redoubt at Mafeking, its defenders in very mixed dress with little to distinguish them from Boers.

2nd Regular MI, with Hamilton's column, crossing the Vaal, 26 May. Note the light transport carts.

Certainly Baden-Powell's guile and spirited leadership, coupled with Boer incompetence at siege warfare, had tied down Cronje and 10,000 burghers in the crucial opening stages of the war, thus rendering a valuable contribution to the field army. But after Cronje's departure in late November to face Methuen, the siege of this little 'dorp' in the middle of nowhere had been marked chiefly by Baden-Powell's efforts to eke out his supplies—largely at the expense of the local Africans—and a lethargic investment by the remaining Boers. Only from Field-Cornet Eloff's dashing attack a mere four days before the relief had the garrison ever been in danger of falling. Nevertheless the dauntless 'pluck and wits' of Baden-Powell and his Colonials had served as a morale-booster to the Empire, particularly during the dark days of defeat, and so, with their well-merited relief coming at a time when victory seemed to be shining on British arms, the Imperial spirit erupted in unbridled jubilation.

When the advance from Kroonstadt was resumed on 22 May, Roberts must indeed have felt that victory was within his grasp. In the west, organized resistance had seemingly ended before Hunter's and Methuen's advance and the latter had been ordered to garrison Kroonstadt. In Natal, Buller had occupied Newcastle, Botha having taken 3,000 over to the central front, but had then halted to mend the

railway and bring up supplies. During the halt at Kroonstadt Hamilton's column had swung out east, through Lindley and Heilbron, after Steyn, De Wet and the Free Staters, and then cut into the railway again north of the Rhenoster river. This march forced the Boers to leave their positions on the Rhenoster, so clearing the way for Roberts, but though it had divorced the Free Staters from the Transvaalers, it had failed to prevent them dispersing to the east. However they could be left to Colvile, Rundle and Brabant sweeping up from the south-east.

There were those on Roberts' staff who thought, like Buller, that failure to round up the Free Staters before proceeding would prolong the war, but Roberts still adhered to his original plan: cross the Vaal, secure the Johannesburg goldfields, then on to Pretoria, annexing the Transvaal as a British colony, so to share the same fate as the Free State, formally proclaimed the Orange River Colony on 28 May. In India and Afghanistan, where all Roberts' previous experience had occurred, the powerful, confident advance by strong columns through hostile territory and the capture of strongholds had usually been sufficient to cow tribal peoples into submission; surely a triumphant entry into Pretoria, whence all Boer intransigence had sprung, would have the same effect, and with the minimum of bloodletting on either side.

Having crossed the Vaal on 24 May, Roberts found Botha and De la Rey holding a range of hills to the west and south of Johannesburg. While he advanced with the infantry against the junction of the Cape and Natal railways east of the city, Hamilton was to cross over to the left, join French and envelop the enemy from the west. Handing over his two mounted brigades for French to press on round the Boer rear, Hamilton launched the 19th and 21st Brigades against the enemy right flank at Doornkop, a place of historic significance for both sides as it was here that Jameson had surrendered in 1896.

The attack, led by the CIV on the left and 1st Gordons on the right, illustrated the different method of Volunteers and Regulars. According to Private Waller, the CIV 'advanced slowly and drove [the enemy] off the top of the kopje with rifle and shell fire and so avoided a big casualty. The Gordons, as usual, wanted to get in with the bayonet so closed up their ranks at 800 yards and prepared to charge. If you consider the weight of our kits (anything between 50 and 70 lbs), it is a physical impossibility to charge 800 yards in anything like a short time, up a hill.' So it was that the Gordons were quite spent and in some confusion when they reached the top—only to find that they had taken a false crest and were now under heavy shell and close-range rifle fire. Their own supporting artillery had ceased fire, and as they

regrouped they were hard hit. Nevertheless, after half an hour, they charged again and the Boers fled. Hamilton was as thrilled by the ultimate, though costly, success of his old regiment's 1st Battalion as he had been by its 2nd Battalion at Elandslaagte, but had he waited for French's turning movement to take effect, the loss of life could probably have been avoided.

On the following day, the 30th, Johannesburg was completely encircled and Roberts demanded its surrender. The Boer commandant, Dr Krause, agreed on condition that, to avoid street-fighting and possible damage to the mines, a day was to elapse before the British entered. Roberts' concurrence ensured that the goldfields would be taken over intact but also permitted the escape of the Transvaal commandos northwards.

Had Roberts not held off after Doornkop he might have encompassed the Transvaalers' surrender. All were in disarray and low spirits, many burghers were going home, and the leaders, even the most redoubtable like Botha and De la Rey, were deeply

City of London Imperial Volunteers advancing by sections prior to extending at the Battle of Doornkop, 29 May. The Boers fired the veldt to show up the infantry's khaki against the blackened ground. Eyewitness sketch by C.E. Fripp.

Roberts taking the salute at the grand march-past in Pretoria, 5 June.

pessimistic. Kruger, tired, old and despondent, left Pretoria with his goverment on the 30th for Middelburg on the Delagoa Bay Railway to the east, leaving orders for the Pretoria forts, built at great expense after the Jameson Raid, to be dismantled, and for Botha to delay the British as long as possible but without seriously engaging his remaining forces, now little more than 2,000 effectives. On 1 June, the day after Roberts entered Johannesburg, the Transvaal leaders were seriously considering surrender. Two days later Roberts resumed the advance, sending French to swing north round Pretoria to the west—thereby leaving the Boers' line of retreat to the east open—and on the evening of the 4th Botha sent in to propose peace talks. Roberts replied he could only accept unconditional surrender, whereupon Botha left for the east, leaving Pretoria undefended.

The next day Roberts entered the Transvaal capital. British prisoners were released, the Union Jack was hoisted and he and Kitchener took the salute as his thousands of sunburnt, war-worn troops marched past. On short rations and in trying weather they had covered the 300 miles from Bloemfontein (nearer 400 for the mounted troops) in 34 days, including halts totalling 16 days, but of the 38,000 who had left Bloemfontein, only 26,000 entered Pretoria. The 14th Brigade had been left to garrison Johannesburg, others had been dropped off as guards, about 3,000 were battle casualties, some had been lost through disease and non-battle wastage, but a high proportion were dismounted cavalrymen or MI left behind because their horses had died or become worn-out. Although their horse-mastership had left much to be desired, the endurance and discipline of those who had marched and fought to Pretoria had been of a high order. Roberts could draw satisfaction from the willing response his leadership had inspired in them, but his march was not to achieve the decisive result he had expected and which had attended his other epic march 20 years before, from Kabul to Kandahar. Indeed the signs that the forecasts of Buller and others would be realized had been emerging since he entered Johannesburg.

12. NEITHER VICTORY NOR DEFEAT

6 JUNE–25 SEPTEMBER 1900

The despairing thoughts of surrender entertained by the Transvaal leaders on 1 June had been brief. The sudden change of heart was due to a furious telegram from President Steyn, castigating the Transvaalers for their weakness and assuring them that the Free Staters would never surrender. His words were speedily reinforced by the actions of Christian De Wet and his brother, Piet. On 31 May Piet had captured at Lindley the 13th Imperial Yeomanry, chiefly Irish but including five noblemen and a company of gentlemen volunteers who had paid their own passage out to South Africa. On 4 June Christian seized a supply convoy and 160 Highlanders near Heilbron and two days later pounced on a raw battalion of Derbyshire Militia guarding a railway bridge over the Rhenoster, taking nearly 500 prisoners and a quantity of ammunition, blowing the bridge and destroying the line. Despite the efforts of Kelly-Kenny, Colvile and Methuen, co-ordinated by Kitchener hurriedly sent south by Roberts, Christian De Wet continued to raid the railway north of Kroonstadt through most of June, his example encouraging similar activity further south.

Chastened by Steyn's rebuke and encouraged by the Free Staters' tenacity, the Transvaalers decided to fight on. While the Free Staters mounted a guerilla campaign against the British rear areas, they would hold the Delagoa Bay Railway, thereby protecting Kruger's goverment, their gold and ammunition reserves, and their only outlet from which outside aid might yet reach them. Botha's peace-feelers and the surrender of Pretoria had yielded a breathing-space to regroup and restore morale. By 8 June Botha had gathered 6,000 men and 23 guns to hold a north-south line of high ground, 25 miles long, astride the railway centred on Diamond Hill, 16 miles east of Pretoria.

Realizing that no surrender was to be forthcoming, Roberts determined to remove this threat so close to Pretoria before Botha could be reinforced by the Boers driven up from Natal by Buller, who had resumed his leisurely advance on 5 June. With Tucker's division guarding Pretoria and Johannesburg, Roberts had only French's Cavalry Division (so reduced by horse losses that the regiments were only of squadron strength and the RHA batteries down to four guns each), Pole-Carew's 11th Division and Hamilton's original column, less Smith-Dorrien's 19th Brigade, sent south with Kitchener, but replaced by Gordon's 3rd Cavalry Brigade; in all some 14,000 men, about a third of them mounted, with six heavy and 64 field guns, a preponderance of only just over two to one, which on past experience was less than favourable odds for an attack against a strong position. Roberts' plan was to demonstrate against the centre with Pole-Carew's infantry, while French and Hamilton turned the Boer right and left flanks respectively.

Since this tactic had become Roberts' usual practice, Botha had anticipated it exactly, strengthening and stretching out his wings at the expense of his centre. Thus when the attack began on 11 June French's two cavalry brigades, supported by Pilcher's and Alderson's MI, soon found themselves pinned down by De la Rey's well-posted burghers, and the outflanking movement reduced to a dismounted fire-fight. On the far right Broadwood's cavalry brigade, flanked to right and left by Gordon and Ridley's MI brigade, became heavily engaged from three sides. To assist him Hamilton ordered Bruce Hamilton's[50] 21st Brigade to attack the Boer left centre on the Diamond Hill plateau itself, but by nightfall the infantry had managed only to take a ridge in front of the plateau.

Next day Bruce Hamilton was ordered to attack again, supported by the Guards Brigade and De Lisle's MI on his right. The CIV, 1st Derbyshire, 1st Royal Sussex and the Guards fought their way up

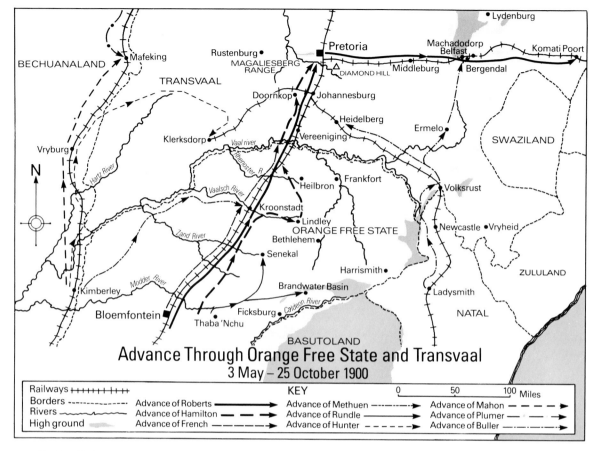

Advance Through Orange Free State and Transvaal
3 May – 25 October 1900

KEY

Railways ++++++++++++	Advance of Roberts ▬▬▬▶	Advance of Methuen -------▶	Advance of Mahon ▬ ▬ ▬▶
Borders -------------	Advance of Hamilton ▬ ▬ ▬▶	Advance of Rundle ▬▬▶	Advance of Plumer ▬▬▬▶
Rivers ~~~~~~	Advance of French ▬ ▬ ▬ ▬▶	Advance of Hunter ▬ ▬ ▬▶	Advance of Buller ▬ · ▬ · ▬▶
High ground ▓▓▓			

0   50   100 Miles

Diamond Hill, but then came under intense fire from hitherto unseen positions further back and from their flanks. Despite two batteries being sent up to them they could no longer advance.

Meanwhile on the far left French's position had grown so precarious that De la Rey informed Botha that, given reinforcements, he could throw French back and fall on Roberts' centre. Botha was in the act of sending the reinforcements when a message from his left made him recall them.

While Bruce Hamilton's battalions were trying to subdue the fire against them, De Lisle had spotted that the key to the position was a kopje at its south-east end. Once his 6th Regular MI had seized a footing at its base, he sent the New South Wales Mounted Rifles, dismounted and with bayonets fixed, swarming up the hill in very open order. Deceived as to their numbers—only 350—the Boers fell back, and the Australians had secured a vital lodgement on the flank of Diamond Hill just as darkness fell.

During the night, unknown to Roberts, Botha withdrew all his men eastwards. By the time this was discovered next morning it was too late to pursue effectively. De Lisle's MI were the most tenacious and in the afternoon his West Australians attacked a Boer rearguard at Bronkhorst Spruit but had to retire for want of support. Curiously the last shots of the penultimate set-piece battle of the war had occurred at the same place as the first shots of the 1881 war.

Neither side could claim Diamond Hill as a victory, though both did. Roberts, preoccupied about his supply lines, reluctant to incur heavy casualties and disappointed by the Boers' resurgence, had allowed the battle to slip out of his grip into separate actions. He had cleared away the threat to Pretoria but Botha's army was still intact, had suffered little, and most of all had regained its self-confidence. Roberts now grasped that the Transvaalers had still to be defeated and hoped for the assistance of the slow-moving Buller, who had at last entered the Transvaal on 12 June after outflanking his opponents holding the 1881 battlefields of Majuba and Laing's Nek. First, however, Roberts had to deal with the growing threat to his rear in the Eastern Free State.

Kitchener had restored the railway and the various formations still in the Free State had garrisons to its east at Heilbron, Lindley (which had already changed hands seven times), Senekal and Ficksburg on the Basutoland border.[51] Beyond this arc, up to the Natal-Johannesburg Railway, the Free Staters roamed at will, mounting their operations from such towns as Frankfort, Bethlehem and Harrismith. They had frequently pierced the arc of garrisons towards the central railway but had been unable to break out southwards through the line firmly held by Rundle's 8th Division between Senekal and Ficksburg.

Roberts planned, while maintaining the garrisons, for three columns to drive all the Free State commandos against the mountains forming the boundary with Basutoland and Natal; Buller's advance up the Natal railway towards Standerton and Heidelberg should prevent them breaking out

north-east to join the Transvaalers. Rundle was to press them from the south-west, Clements with his 12th Brigade was to link up with Paget's 20th Brigade at Lindley and capture Bethlehem, and Hamilton's much-worked column was to come down from Pretoria, pick up MacDonald's Highland Brigade from Heilbron and advance on Bethlehem from the north. Hamilton had the same force as at Diamond Hill and the other formations had a proportion of mounted troops, either Colonials or Yeomanry, including the Lovat Scouts, attached to MacDonald and raised in Scotland from Highland ghillies. At the last moment Hamilton was incapacitated by a fall and his column was given to Hunter, whose 10th Division had been

CIVs manhandling their Maxim into action at the Battle of Diamond Hill during 21st Brigade's attack on 11 June. Skyline marked 'Main Boer Position' is the Diamond Hill feature, the nearer marked position that taken by the evening of the 11th. Sketch by C.E. Fripp.

131

Australian mounted infantry of the New South Wales contingent advancing dismounted in open order with bayonets fixed.

broken up into garrisons holding the Western Transvaal.

By 9 July, Hunter and MacDonald reached Bethlehem, which had been captured two days before by Clements and Paget, and Hunter assumed command of all columns. The Free Staters, 7,500 strong, with Steyn, the De Wets and all their commandants, fell back to the Brandwater Basin, a natural fortress formed by a 75-mile long semi-circle of tangled and jagged mountains enclosing a tract of land along the Caledon River on the Basutoland border, which could be entered only by four passes: Commando Nek to the south-west, Slabbert's and Retief's Nek in the centre, and Naauwpoort Nek to the north-east. However, no sooner had they reached it than dissension began to surface among the leaders. It struck De Wet that what they had thought to be an impregnable sanctuary could equally become a trap, if and when the British seized the passes. They therefore decided to break out again in four groups, starting on 15 July.

Meanwhile Hunter had been delayed at Bethlehem for six days by the need to bring up supplies from his distant bases and to acquire information about the Brandwater Basin, which was very inadequately mapped. Thus the troops were on their way to, but had not reached, the passes the very night that De Wet, with Steyn, 2,600 men and 400 wagons, came out of Slabbert's and slipped unheard past the British bivouacs, heading back towards Lindley. When this

was realized next day, Broadwood's cavalry and Ridley's MI went off in pursuit but De Wet, a master of rearguard tactics, held them off while sending his wagons on ahead.

Deprived of his dominant leadership the remaining Boers, unable to agree who was now in command, abandoned their plan and barred the passes. Aided by the Lovat Scouts' masterly reconnaissances, MacDonald's Highlanders forced their way through Retief's Nek while Clements and Paget fought through Slabbert's and Rundle entered the Basin via Commando Nek. By the 26th all four passes were secured. The Boers had eventually elected the elderly Marthinus Prinsloo as leader, but it was too late to break out. On the 29th Prinsloo surrendered with 4,500 men and several thousand sheep, cattle and horses. Only 1,500 with a number of commandants managed to escape over an unguarded track to the east. This was a considerable achievement by Hunter's troops and the biggest haul of Boer prisoners since Paardeberg. Unfortunately the most determined fighters had got away, including of course the very incarnations of resistance, Steyn and Christian De Wet. For a month after their escape thousands of troops were to be employed in trying to catch them as they ran, fought and feinted, first north, then west, then north again across the Free State and into the Transvaal.

Despite Hunter's qualified success, Roberts in July and early August was beset by trouble. Apart from the De Wet hunt, which he handed over to Kitchener, he had to plan and regroup to smash Botha's army, capture his stores, supplies and, if possible, Kruger, now installed further east at Machadodorp among the mountains, and deprive the Transvaalers of the

Marthinus Steyn, President, Orange Free State.

General Christian De Wet, C-in-C Free State forces.

Lieutenant-General Sir Archibald Hunter.

Major-General Clements.

Delagoa Bay Railway up to Komati Poort on the Portuguese East African frontier. All this he was making more difficult for himself by failing to insist that Buller strike north-east towards that railway, instead of continuing up the Natal line towards Johannesburg. As a first step he sent Hutton's MI brigade to clear his right flank, prior to a general advance on Middleburg. Hutton not only met stiff resistance but on 11 July Roberts was forced to postpone the advance. Out of the blue fighting erupted in the hitherto pacified country west of Pretoria.

After Diamond Hill, in greatest secrecy, De la Rey and Jan Smuts took 7,000 Western Transvaalers with 19 guns, pom-poms and Maxims on a wide detour north of Pretoria and established themselves in the Magaliesberg range, stretching for 60 miles west of the capital. There were few troops in this area other than Baden-Powell with the defenders and relievers

of Mafeking at Rustenburg, half Barton's Fusilier Brigade at Klerksdorp, the end of a branch line from Johannesburg, and some other small posts. On 11 July De la Rey struck simultaneously at three points, at one capturing three companies of Lincolns and some Scots Greys, and thereafter kept the region around Pretoria in a ferment. Concerned for the security of the capital, where a plot to kidnap him had been discovered, Roberts recalled French from the east, summoned up Methuen from the Free State and formed a new division from recently-arrived reinforcements for the now-recovered Hamilton. Notwithstanding their efforts to catch him, De la Rey continued to attack where opportunities offered, but he failed to overcome a post at Eland's River where Colonel Hore of Mafeking's Protectorate Regiment with 500 Australians and Rhodesians won the admiration of their attackers by holding out for eleven days until relieved.

On 16 July Botha struck in the east as a diversion to aid De la Rey, sending Viljoen with 2,000 men against Hutton. The 2nd Royal Irish Fusiliers and New Zealand Mounted Rifles became hard pressed but managed to hold on until a magnificent counter-

36th (West Kent) Company of 11th Imperial Yeomanry, serving with Rundle's 8th Division, leaving camp to reconnoitre in the Eastern Free State.

attack by the Canadian Mounted Rifles restored the situation; in their final charge fell Lieutenant Borden, a son of Canada's Militia Minister who had had responsibility for the Dominion's first two contingents.[52]

De la Rey had not concerted his operations with this diversion and Roberts was now more confident about the security of Pretoria, even though he had had to evacuate much of the country to its west to safeguard it. De Wet's escape from Brandwater on 15 July was worrying in case he marched to join Botha, but when Roberts heard he was moving west he decided to resume his advance along the Delagoa Bay Railway with French and Hutton. Botha fell back and on 27 July Roberts occupied Middelburg, halting there until Buller, now at Heidelberg, was ready to co-operate. In the meantime there remained the problem of De Wet.

By early August, having crossed the central railway, De Wet had eluded all pursuit and reached the Vaal. His aim was to enable Steyn to reach Kruger and to evade capture himself so as to continue his guerilla campaign. Kitchener had 11,000 men in five columns advancing from the south to prevent him from doubling back into the Free State and to drive him north against three successive lines: Methuen on the Vaal, Smith-Dorrien on the Klerksdorp-Johannesburg railway, and Ian Hamilton on the Magaliesberg, a further 18,000 men. Despite the dogged endurance and tenacity of his pursuers, the wily De Wet managed to keep ahead of them, twisting and turning in his route, always finding an unguarded gap or one blocked too late, supplying himself from friendly farms, and maintaining the strictest discipline over his burghers. Throughout the hunt De Wet benefited from his hunters' poor intelligence and tardy communications, and the superior scouting of his own men, particularly that of a corps of foreigners, most ably led by Danie Theron, as strict a disciplinarian as De Wet himself, who had first distinguished himself at Paardeberg by carrying messages between De Wet and Cronje through the British lines. By 14 August De Wet had reached the Magaliesberg and nipped through Olifant's Nek a few hours before Hamilton arrived to block it. Methuen had been hard on De Wet's heels but, believing Hamilton was safely in position, had swung left-handed to block any escape westwards, enabling De Wet to get clear away eastwards into the region dominated by De la Rey. Having despatched Steyn with an escort to Kruger, he broke up his force into smaller groups and returned by devious routes to the Vaal, whence he again began raiding the railway.

Deprived of one formidable opponent, Roberts once more turned his attention to Botha and Kruger. For the first time in the three months since the grand offensive began Buller was co-operating with the main army around Middelburg. He had left one cavalry brigade and two divisions to hold the railway

Mounted Infantry clearing the Brandwater Basin.

135

General Koos De la Rey, commanding in the Western Transvaal, perhaps the most outstanding Boer leader, both as a tactician and as a personality.

from Heidelberg back to Natal so that he had only Lyttleton's 4th Division and Dundonald's and Brocklehurst's mounted brigades. By 15 August he had made contact with French's cavalry some 30 miles south-east of Middelburg. The eight commandos who had opposed his advance fell back eastwards to the south of the new positions taken up by Botha.

Between Middelburg and a point 80 miles short of the Portuguese border the Delagoa Bay Railway ran through a tangled range, the northern Drakensberg, about 50 miles wide and reaching from the far north of the Transvaal down to the Swaziland border. On these heights Botha deployed his 6,000 men to protect Kruger, sitting in his railway carriage on the line, as well as the towns of Lydenburg and Barberton, north and south of the railway, where stores had been accumulated for the continuance of the war by guerilla means. The morale of his men was generally not high, but the safe arrival of Steyn and his dynamic personality did much to encourage them.

French urged Roberts to let him take his own and Buller's cavalry and make a wide sweep southwards via Barberton to cut the Boers' line of retreat. However Roberts thought this too risky, and with Buller refusing to hand over his mounted men and making other difficulties, what could have been a bold turning movement offering high dividends degenerated into a ponderous advance on the Boer centre around Belfast, with French, Buller and Pole-Carew all bunched up near the railway.

On 25 August Roberts moved French over to the north of the railway to break through the Boer right, prior to striking the line at Machadodorp, while Pole-Carew's infantry was to protect French's right by engaging the Boer right centre. Buller was to advance eastwards south of the railway, through the enemy left centre to meet French at Machadodorp.

French made good progress on the 26th and the next day was joined by Pole-Carew, who had marched to meet him with the Guards, leaving 18th Brigade confronting the enemy right centre. Meanwhile Buller had advanced 4th Division with a mounted brigade on either flank but was halted by five commandos with two heavy guns holding a line of hills running south-east for nearly six miles from the railway. A cavalry patrol reported that the right of this position was a kopje just in front of Bergendal Farm alongside the railway. Buller determined to break through there, rather than continuing due east. Unknown to him, the Bergendal kopje was only an outpost thrown forward from the Boer line, which continued north of the railway, and was held by only 75 Johannesburg policemen—the Zarps; to their left and right rear were two groups of foreign volunteers.

At 11 a.m. on the 27th what was to be the last set-piece attack of the war began. For three hours Buller's 38 guns laid down a preliminary bombardment on and around Bergendal. Such was the weight of fire that no reinforcements could reach the Zarps, nor could they retire even if they had wished to. Grimly they lay low in their trenches and waited for the infantry attack, realizing that the noise of the bombardment was worse than its actual damage and confident in their perfect field of fire over the approaches. As soon as the leading infantry appeared they opened a heavy fire with rifles, a Maxim and a pom-pom, despite the gunfire which continued to cover the infantry forward. The left battalion, 2nd Rifle Brigade, advanced across the open in short rushes but soon began to sustain casualties from the Zarps and the hitherto unseen foreign detachment behind. They kept going, alternately running forward and firing, while the reserve companies successively extended the line towards the right battalion, 1st Inniskillings. Nearing the objective, a Rifles officer, Lieutenant Aspinall, recalled that as they 'rose for the last time, they gave a savage yell and the language—Corporal Porter, a good judge, said he never heard worse—as they all raced up the slope and over the kopje'. The gallant Zarps continued firing right to the end and though some fled as the bayonets closed in, over 40 were killed, wounded or captured, including their brave commandant, Philip Oosthuizen. The Rifle Brigade lost 15 killed and 68 wounded, including their colonel, and the Inniskillings 17 wounded.

Officers of 1st Canadian Mounted Rifles (Royal Canadian Dragoons). Seated left is Major Williams, commanding. Second left, standing, is Lieutenant Borden, killed during Viljoen's attack on 16 July. Standing right is Lieutenant Turner, awarded the VC as were Lieutenant Cockburn and Sergeant Holland of the same regiment, for gallantry at Komati River on 7 November.

Buller's infantry advancing in the Transvaal. An imperfect photograph but taken in action. It shows the much wider intervals men now adopted than earlier in the war.

1st Scots Guards of Pole-Carew's division advancing on Komati Poort. They have adopted slouch hats with regimental dicing instead of helmets and the subaltern nearest camera wears a guardsman's equipment and carries a rifle.

This well-led and spirited attack against a courageously defended but small post surprisingly caused the collapse of the entire Boer position, north and south of the railway, though yet again most of the commandos got away untroubled by pursuit. As the Boers retreated eastwards, Roberts' columns tramped after them, but it was now clear to both sides that the end of conventional fighting was near. The Boers had agreed that Kruger should go to Europe to rally support. On 11 September he entered Portuguese territory and a month later he sailed for Holland. Steyn took a circuitous route back to the Free State. Freed of responsibility for Kruger's safety, Botha and the more active leaders divided up 4,000 of

the most stalwart burghers into small groups and made off to the north through the mountains before the converging columns could trap them against the border, ready to continue the struggle as De Wet and De la Rey were doing. Some 3,000 of the weaker spirits and most of the foreigners formed a rearguard at Komati Poort but, as the British approached, the majority sought refuge in Portuguese territory, taking as much of their armaments with them as they could and destroying their supplies. When Pole-Carew reached Komati Poort on 24 September, he found it almost deserted.

The Boers had been thrown back from Cape Colony and Natal, had seen their Republics annexed and their towns occupied, and were finally cut off from the outside world. Yet the fighting spirit of their men remaining under arms was undimmed and they had the whole of South Africa, from the Limpopo to the Cape, in which to ride and strike at will.

13. KITCHENER TAKES COMMAND

1 OCTOBER 1900–15 MAY 1901

In early October the Natal army ceased to exist as a separate force and Sir Redvers Buller, much to the sorrow of the men he had led from the Tugela, sailed for England to receive a hero's welcome from the crowds, but no honours from the Government. Lord Roberts, confident of several, anticipated being not long behind him for, with the Transvaal annexed as a Crown Colony, he pronounced the war to be 'practically over'. He would shortly hand over to Kitchener, who should have no difficulty in mopping up the burghers still at large, since the recently instituted policy of farm-burning would deprive any would-be guerillas of food and shelter. Their surrender was further to be hastened by a proclamation that any doing so would not be sent out of South Africa. With the railways and centres of population garrisoned, and the countryside scoured by flying columns, Kitchener would surely be faced only with a police operation. Thus, Roberts told the Government, the field army could be gradually reduced and replaced by a South African Constabulary, to be recruited in Britain and the Empire by Baden-Powell.

How misplaced was Roberts' confidence would soon be demonstrated, even before he handed over. The disappointing results of his capture of the capitals should have revealed to him how he had underestimated the resilient toughness of the Boers and how unimportant such places were to them. True, his operations had scattered their forces and some surrenders had been taken, but he seemed blind to the fact that the majority of armed Boers, and the best of them at that, remained undefeated and unrepentant, still free to roam the veldt and easily able to outdistance the pursuing columns which, far from 'flying', were predominantly composed of infantry and artillery and encumbered with slow-moving ox wagons. Furthermore the shared endeavours of a year's fighting had honed the spirit of

Boer nationalism and the burghers were about to embark on a mode of warfare for which they were far better suited by character and tradition than the conventional fighting they had largely pursued hitherto.

In late October, Botha and Steyn met to consider future policy. To keep the burghers in the field it was agreed that the commandos should, in the main, operate from their own home areas under regional commanders and that, for the moment, they should rest and regroup while losing no chance of striking at opportunity targets, as indeed De Wet was already doing in the Free State. However such pin-prick attacks would not by themselves win the war and the likely reprisals therefrom—the destruction of places thought to be harbouring commandos—would bear heavily on their families. It was therefore resolved to carry the fight into Cape Colony and Natal, where the authorities could not permit farm-burning, and the Afrikaner element, already encouraged by Roberts' failure to pacify the Republics, hostile to the annexations, and resentful of Government measures against rebels, might yet be incited to major insurrection.

From this meeting Botha returned to organize the Transvaal commandos, allocating the west to De la Rey and Smuts, the north-east to Ben Viljoen and the north to Beyers, retaining the south-east for himself as well as exercising overall command. Steyn went south to brief De Wet who, since his escape from Methuen in August, had been galvanizing the Free Staters into action and attacking the railway. He had recently been repulsed by Barton's Fusiliers at Frederikstadt and was being hunted by an all-mounted column led by Knox, the former commander of 13th Brigade.

By 31 October, when Steyn and De Wet met, Knox had temporarily lost the scent and the two Free Staters moved on to De Wet's laager near Bothaville

Farm-burning, a policy instituted by Roberts in September 1900, which failed to intimidate and strengthened the Boers' determination to fight on.

to discuss the invasion of the Cape. The plan nearly collapsed before it had even begun. At dawn on 6 November the enterprising Colonel Le Gallais' Regular MI from Knox's column surprised the sleeping laager. The Boers panicked and Steyn and De Wet fled with some of their burghers, leaving the rest to fight it out. In a vicious four-hour action at close range, Le Gallais was mortally wounded but his men, inspired by his example, battled it out and finally charged with the bayonet. De Wet rallied his men to return, only to be driven off by De Lisle's MI which had galloped to the scene of the fighting. Steyn and De Wet got away but all their guns, supply wagons and over a hundred burghers were captured.

Undeterred by this reverse, De Wet called out 1,500 more men and set off towards the Orange River. Having avoided the line of fortified posts round Thaba 'Nchu between Bloemfontein and Basutoland, he captured the four-company garrison of Dewetsdorp, the town named after his father. Taking with him 450 prisoners, who were to endure severe privations and some brutality, he rode on to co-

ordinate his invasion of the Eastern Cape from Bethulie with Judge Herzog, who was to invade from the west.

The Dewetsdorp attack had elicited little response from the nearest British forces but from 23 November it was again Knox, now with three columns, who was sent in pursuit, while at the same time the line of the Orange was strengthened. For the next three weeks Knox kept close at De Wet's heels but the latter always managed to keep ahead, dodging this way and that, making the best use of darkness and ground, and allowing his men nothing but their rifles and ammunition. Finding the Orange drifts blocked and the river impassable, he doubled back north again and by mid-December had drawn clear from all pursuit. He had failed to enter the Colony but, by attracting all British columns towards himself, he had enabled Herzog and another group under Kritzinger and Scheepers (a Cape rebel) to cross the Orange and threaten places like De Aar and Naauwpoort junctions, which had not featured in the war for nearly a year.

Meanwhile, far to the north, De la Rey, Smuts and Beyers had been causing anxiety with their attacks west of Pretoria which culminated in a dawn raid on Clements' unsuspecting column, camped in a gorge at Nooitgedacht. Through the Boer failure to exploit the surprise achieved, Clements was able to extricate his command but not before he had lost 637 men, over a third of his strength.

The vigour with which the second De Wet hunt was, albeit unsuccessfully, pursued and the retaliatory measures instigated against De la Rey after Nooitgedacht were due to the forcefulness of Kitchener, who had taken over from Roberts on 29 November. He had inherited the problem of fighting an entirely new kind of war for which his commanders and troops were neither trained nor organized and whose deployment and capability had been impaired by the past operations and Robert's optimism.

Despite having lost some 20,000 killed, captured or interned, the Boers could still muster 60,000 men of military age, including Cape rebels and foreigners, though less than a quarter might actually be in the field at any one time. Kitchener had 210,000 troops in South Africa, but over half were deployed in static duties, guarding the railways and isolated garrisons, while more were detached at bases and headquarters on countless minor duties, or had been left behind by their units for some purpose during the long advance of 1900, or were in hospital. Thus, not only were the numbers available for anti-guerilla operations greatly reduced, but the numbers of mounted men vital for the prosecution of such operations were diminishing. The Yeomanry had been developing with experience into useful soldiers, but their recruitment had been stopped following Roberts' recommendations and the first contingent were nearing the end of their year's contract. So too were the even more valuable Empire contingents which, as an Australian corporal had justifiably boasted, had shown the Regulars 'how to scout, how to take cover, how to ride, how to shoot, how, in short, to play this particular game as it should be played.[53] The Regular cavalry, trained for years in shock tactics with sword and lance, had been slow to learn these lessons, overloaded their horses in comparison with the Boers, and, though Kitchener abolished lances in favour of infantry rifles, many cavalrymen resented this attack, as they saw it, on 'the cavalry spirit'. Of more use were the Regular MI, but their men and horses were reduced from over-work, their horsemastership lacked expertise, the purchase of horses abroad had been stopped and infantry battalions were reluctant to draft their best men to this arm.

The 10,000 South African Constabulary then being raised would go some way to offsetting this mounted deficiency, and Kitchener appealed for more volunteers from the Empire, from British-born South Africans, for the renewal of Yeomanry recruitment, for more cavalry regiments and for reinforcements from the MI School at Aldershot, setting up a similar school and depot in South Africa. He even asked for Indian cavalry regiments but this 'the-white-man's-war' policy would not permit. It would, however, be four or five months before new mounted drafts could take the field and even then they would be inexperienced. He had the rear areas combed out for unproductive hands and evacuated isolated garrisons, particularly those far from a railway. The divisional organization used hitherto was broken up and the components re-distributed into brigades and columns, some with a proportion of mounted troops, a few entirely mounted, each with their own area of responsibility. To command them Kitchener appointed the best men available, regardless of seniority, thus bringing to the fore some men who

Ox-wagons crossing the Vaal. Though oxen only required grazing for subsistence, their pace of 2–2½ m.p.h. either retarded a column's speed or necessitated the detachment of strong escorts. Mule-drawn transport afforded greater mobility but needed forage.

would become household names fifteen years on—Rawlinson, Allenby, Plumer, Byng, Gough and Douglas Haig.[54]

Sir Alfred Milner, whose High Commissionership now embraced the Transvaal and the former Free State, wanted Kitchener to subdue the guerillas by the systematic pacification and subsequent protection of one district at a time, thus sparing the country further devastation, allowing those who wished to return to their peacetime occupations unpestered by

Captured Boers at a dockside awaiting embarkation. They were among the 24,000 prisoners of war shipped to camps in Bermuda, St Helena, India and Ceylon.

guerillas and avoiding future bitterness. Kitchener, however, believed in holding fast to the communications and their centres, while ruthlessly harrying the commandos across the veldt in conjunction with the denial of food and shelter through farm-burning, and another measure which was to have far-reaching consequences: the removal of men, women and children, together with their native servants, from all the worst guerilla-infested districts to camps located near to railway lines for protective and supply purposes. Any burghers surrendering voluntarily would be allowed to live with their families in the camps until the cessation of guerilla activity permitted them to return home. By this means Kitchener hoped to deprive commandos of support, hasten surrenders and, not least, protect isolated women on outlying farms from roving natives.

This policy, as a means of shortening the war, was urged on Kitchener by surrendered and moderate Boers who, anxious to see an end to hostilities, had formed a Burghers Peace Committee. Kitchener was as keen as anyone to finish the war as not only would its protraction cause difficulties and benefit neither Briton nor Boer, but he also feared it might cost him the chief command in India, on which he had set his heart, and which had fallen vacant prematurely owing to the death of the present incumbent. He therefore gave every encouragement to the Peace Committee, assuring its representatives of his determination to allow voluntary submissions without conditions and to see a just and progressive government after the war, giving a wide circulation to this pronouncement which was to be carried to the commandos by emissaries.

Meanwhile the fighting spilled over into 1901 and, as Queen Victoria's long reign drew to a close, success favoured the Boers. Since early December, Botha had been harassing posts near the Natal border and along the Natal railway and he now concerted attacks with Viljoen against the Delagoa Bay line. Westwards, De la Rey, Beyers and Smuts were ambushing and raiding convoys, railway stations and garrisons. In the Cape, despite urgent measures to form town guards and raise local forces, followed by the imposition of martial law, Herzog and Kritzinger were advancing deeper into the Colony, evading the columns sent in pursuit. Herzog was making for the Atlantic coast to rendezvous with a ship from Europe carrying munitions and volunteers, and sent back reports of his high hopes for a rebellion by the Cape Dutch. Encouraged by these reports, the Boer leaders formulated a plan: De la Rey was to prepare to support the Cape invasion if opportunity offered, or to distract attention from Botha, who would invade Natal with 5,000 men and Durban as his ultimate objective. De Wet, with 2,200, would again enter the Colony, link up with Herzog, exploit the hoped-for rebellion and ride for Cape Town.

Botha's aggressive activities in the Eastern Transvaal had so forced the British on to the defensive that Kitchener had planned a counter-offensive against him to be led by French. But then his intelligence service, which he had been strenuously trying to improve, discovered De Wet's projected invasion of the Cape and he hastily assembled twelve columns, making maximum use of the railways, to prevent De Wet crossing the Orange, placing the whole operation under Lyttleton. French, with a reduced force, was to contain Botha, while Methuen watched the Western Transvaal.

From 27 January the third great De Wet hunt began. Displaying all his usual cunning and speed, De Wet again dodged through the Thaba 'Nchu line of posts. By sending scouts far ahead he discovered that the Orange was strongly held southwards around Bethulie. Feinting in that direction, he then altered course to the west and crossed the Orange unopposed on 10 February at Sand Drift, north of Colesberg, but 800 of his men refused to leave the Free State. Finding they had been gulled, Knox and Bruce Hamilton pounded westwards along the north bank, reaching Sand Drift only 15 hours after De Wet's rearguard, but then were unable to cross owing to the river flooding. Lyttleton meanwhile, poised to the south at Naauwpoort with four columns, learned that De Wet was heading west and launched a pursuit. Foremost was Plumer's entirely mounted column chiefly composed of Australians and New Zealanders, which soon picked up the trail and by dogged riding forced De Wet to head north-west. Both quarry and hunters

Five of De Wet's men. The two in front hold captured Lee-Enfields; the man in the dark jacket has also a British webbing bandolier, as issued to many Yeomanry and Volunteers.

were hampered by torrential rain-storms which churned the veldt into a sea of mud but De Wet, though losing many horses and wagons through his merciless driving of his men, managed to keep just ahead of his pursuers and crossed the De Aar-Kimberley railway on the night of 14 February, still heading west to join Herzog.

The rebellion optimistically forecast by Herzog had not materialized and his rendezvous with the munitions ship had been thwarted by a Royal Navy warship. Three columns, including De Lisle's formidable MI, had gone after him and driven him back north-east towards the area De Wet was now approaching. Kritzinger, meanwhile, had headed for the Cape Midlands, east of Naauwpoort, but had since been hunted by four columns under Haig and so was in no position to assist De Wet or Herzog.

On 16 February, Kitchener, having arrived to take over the hunt himself, made a new plan with the aim of preventing De Wet from marching south and

6th New South Wales Imperial Bushmen behind cover. Chiefly volunteers from the outback, Citizen Bushmen contingents were raised under private arrangements in Australia. Imperial Bushmen were paid for by the British Government.

driving him and Herzog away to the barren north-west. From Orange River Station, southwards for 160 miles along the Cape railway, he deployed 15 columns, each averaging 1,000 men and all facing west. Plumer was to continue the direct pursuit of De Wet but the others were to be ready to march west in succession from the north to head off De Wet should he break south. If a column lost touch, it was to return to the railway to be ferried further south, thus continuing the line.

In the event none of this proved necessary. On the 19th De Wet, harried by Plumer, then Knox, then Plumer again, and conscious of his men's fatigue from the endless marches in atrocious weather and his loss of horses, decided to abandon the expedition. He turned east again, following the south bank of the Orange, vainly looking for a passable ford across the swollen river. By the 24th he had managed to re-cross the railway but was now penned in a quadrilateral formed by the Orange and three railways along which Kitchener hastily re-distributed

his cordon. With columns closing in and Sand Drift, his entry point, flooded, there remained only one drift, Botha's, the fifteenth he had tried, before he was baulked by the Central Railway. Then his luck turned. On the 27th he was joined by Herzog, who had been marching roughly parallel, and they rode on together towards Botha's Drift. Owing to congestion on the railways only 200 men of Byng's column had arrived to guard this stretch of river and they had to be spread over 25 miles. At dawn on the 28th De Wet and Herzog swam their horses across unopposed, their burghers swearing they would never go south of the Orange again. They headed north, dispersing their men as they went. Plumer's dauntless Australians again gave chase but De Wet's lead was too great and by 11 March he reached sanctuary near Senekal. In 43 days he had covered at least 800 miles, evading the best efforts of 15,000 troops, further enhancing his reputation. Against this, his plan to set the Colony aflame had failed, there had been assistance but no rising, and he had been driven back, if not with ignominy, with nothing to show for his desperate attempt. Kritzinger, however, remained in the Cape Midlands, defying all Haig's endeavours to trap him.

While all this was going on, French in the Eastern Transvaal had been sweeping the country between

144

Boer non-combatants, the chief sufferers from the devastation policy.

the Delagoa Bay and Natal railways with a view to surrounding Botha or driving him against the Swaziland and Zululand borders. French deployed some 14,000 men, of which just over a half were mounted, including nine Regular cavalry regiments. They were divided into five columns, who were to advance due east, being joined successively by two more advancing south from the Delagoa line. The countryside was to be stripped of all food, horses and transport and families sent back to the railway.

The westernmost columns moved on 28 January, followed by the northern on 3 February. Progress was necessarily slow and most of the population fled before the columns. By the 5th, French was starting to encircle Ermelo, to which Botha had fallen back, but the gaps between some columns had become dangerously wide. Botha saw his chance and, having detached 1,500 men to cover the refugee families' flight eastwards, attacked the isolated camp of Smith-Dorrien's column with 2,000 men under cover of darkness and fog. Stampeding the cavalry horses

towards the outposts, he initially had some success. However the troops recovered and repulsed the attack, though they were unable to prevent the Boers breaking through the cordon to the rear of French's sweep and making their escape.

The great drive continued eastwards until mid-April with much hardship for troops and horses. Though large quantities of ammunition, wagons, horses and livestock were taken, only just over a thousand burghers were accounted for. Nevertheless Botha's plan to invade Natal had been thwarted and the Boers' grand design for early 1901 had not borne fruit.

Neither had Kitchener's schemes for ending the war by other means. The Burgher Peace Committee's emissaries had received a grim reception from the fighting Boers who, regarding them as traitors,

Boer women from the Eastern Transvaal singing the 'Volkslied' under the 'Vierkleur' national flag at Elandsfontein, prior to entraining for a concentration camp.

Mounted Infantry stripping a Boer farm. The men in Stetson hats are Canadian Mounted Rifles. Drawing by C.E. Fripp.

executed one, sentenced two others to death and flogged a fourth prior to shooting him. The concentration camps had imposed a heavy and unpleasant burden on the troops and, as will be seen, were to prove counter-productive. Kitchener had also initiated a meeting between Botha and himself, using Mrs Botha as intermediary, to discuss terms for ending the war. Kitchener believed that, though the Republics must forgo their independence, a conciliatory attitude, particularly over what was to prove the most critical issue—an amnesty for Cape and Natal Afrikaners who had taken up arms—might end the war speedily. Neither Milner, who disagreed altogether with talk over terms, nor the Government approved Kitchener's line. Thus, when Kitchener met Botha at Middelburg on 28 February, he was able only to offer stiffer terms than he had intended, with no amnesty for Cape and Natal rebels. Despite

this, the meeting was cordial and Botha agreed to consider the terms. On 16 March, however, he reported that they were unacceptable, chiefly on the amnesty point. Even if Kitchener had been allowed to dictate his own terms, Botha probably could not have persuaded the intransigent Free Staters to give up the fight. So it was back to military means for both sides.

The South African winter would soon inhibit further operations, but before its onset Kitchener ordered a drive into the region north of the

The Middelburg Conference, 28 February 1901. From left, seated: N De Wet (Botha's secretary), Botha, Kitchener, Colonel H.I.W. Hamilton (Military Secretary). Standing: Colonel Henderson (Director of Intelligence), D. Van Velden (Transvaal Government secretary), Major Watson, H. Fraser, Captain 'Brat' Maxwell VC (ADC), A. De Jager. Hamilton was Bruce Hamilton's brother.

Regular MI (Seaforth Highlanders) watering their horses. The rifle was carried in a butt-bucket with a short arm-sling attached to the muzzle.

Magaliesberg-Pretoria-Delagoa line, where British forces had scarcely penetrated hitherto. His objectives were Schalk Burger's caretaker Transvaal Government, lying low near Lydenburg, Ben Viljeon's commandos and the continuation of the devastation policy begun by French in the east. While six columns marched up under Sir Bindon Blood, an experienced campaigner from the Indian Frontier, the ubiquitous Plumer rode in from the northwest towards them via Pietersburg.[55] Schalk Burger made a rapid getaway to join Botha, who had returned to Ermelo,but Viljoen, closely pursued, his

men growing mutinous, only escaped by burning his wagons and taking to very thick and steep country. Making a wide sweep westwards he too joined Botha. Though the prime targets had not been captured, the region was thoroughly stripped of resources and the inhabitants packed off to camps.

In the west, De la Rey had been suffering from a scarcity of horses and a reluctance by the local burghers to take the field. When he heard of De Wet's failure in the Colony he gave up any idea of a march south. In early March he realized that the search by the few British troops in the area for the bands of Smuts and Kemp had left the garrison of Lichtenburg dangerously exposed and he therefore attacked it. The defenders, Northumberland Fusiliers and Yeomanry, made a fierce resistance and drove off De la Rey's men. Throughout March and April the columns marched hither and thither in search of De la Rey, now joined by Kemp, but although some minor successes were achieved, the guerillas simply dissolved into small groups whenever a column appeared. In early May, Kitchener launched a five-column operation under Methuen between Lichtenburg and Klerksdorp but, with inadequate communications between columns and false information spread by the Boers, the weary troops achieved nothing but the usual destruction of resources.

Thus with the coming of winter and the close of Kitchener's first six months in command, although the Boer plan of carrying the war into British territory had been foiled, the commandos were everywhere still active and dangerous. The outlying areas away from the railways had been stripped but not pacified, and there was no sign of an end to the fighting.

14. THE BITTER END

16 MAY 1901–9 APRIL 1902

As the cold winter winds blew over the grassless and devastated veldt, Kitchener still launched his columns against the commandos, who scattered before them to find what sanctuaries they could. The mounted reinforcements he had asked for in December had now arrived;[56] together with the 26,000 Regular cavalry and MI still in the field, he had a mounted strength of some 80,000, one-third of his total force. Many of these had little military training or knowledge of horsemastership, but Kitchener put them straight into operations, with consequent waste of horses and easy pickings for the alert and war-hardened commandos, who by now were short of clothing, horses, rifles and ammunition. Thus, despite their general policy of simply surviving the winter, the Boers were able to inflict some reverses on the columns during May and June, usually upon the green Yeomanry or the columns' ponderous supply wagons escorted by infantry. In one such action, at Vlakfontein, Kemp caused 179 casualties by use of a new tactic: firing the veldt and charging through the smoke at a Yeomanry screen, his men shooting from the saddle. Only the determined resistance of some infantry prevented a worse disaster.

Between, behind and around the scouring columns the leaders of both Republics were making their way to a meeting. At the beginning of May the Transvaal leaders, disappointed by the results of six months' guerilla warfare, concerned at the plight of their country and pessimistic as to the future, had sought, with Kitchener's blessing, the views of the exiled Kruger about continuing the war. Informed of this, to him, defeatist stance, Steyn was incensed that the Transvaalers, who after all had started the war and whom the Free State had loyally supported, should be contemplating betraying him and their allies in the Colony. He demanded that all the chief men should discuss a joint policy. Notwithstanding the difficulties of assembling such a meeting, particularly at a time when Kitchener was deploying 12 columns in the Eastern Transvaal with the express intention of capturing Schalk Burger's Government, the leading Boers came together at Standerton on 20 June.

Steyn and De Wet, who were implacably opposed to submission, found that the Transvaalers' despondency had changed. Ordered by Kruger to fight on and heartened by such successes as Vlakfontein and, more recently, the overrunning of a new Australian unit under an unpopular British commander at Wilmansrust, they had come round to the view that, despite the great odds against them, the experience and hardihood of the fighting burghers might yet wear down the will of their opponents. All were agreed, then, to continue the guerilla campaign, but until the spring rains revived the grass on which their horses depended they must lie low and survive. Only in one area might more positive action be taken: in Cape Colony, where Kritzinger and others were still at large, where there was no devastation or deportation and where at least succour, at best armed assistance, might be found. Jan Smuts undertook to lead a commando of Western Transvaalers into the Colony to carry on the work begun by the Free Staters.

As the delegates dispersed to their own areas they were beset by Kitchener's columns, particularly in the Free State where big drives had been planned for July and August. On 10 July Broadwood's column made a night raid on the town of Reitz, capturing the entire Free State Government, its papers and treasury, except for the biggest prizes of all, Steyn himself, who just escaped, and De Wet, who was sleeping elsewhere. As the columns transferred to the north-west Free State, they picked up the scent of Smuts who, having collected 340 Transvaalers, was riding south through troop-infested country. Sur-

149

Imperial Yeomanry taking it easy during a halt. The condition of their clothing suggests that they are recent arrivals.

prised by some South Australians, he got away, though not without losing men and horses, but had to keep doubling back to get behind the pursuit. Twice more he was attacked, suffering more losses, but at last he reached the Cape border, having taken 43 days to cover a distance of 260 miles and with his force reduced to 250 men.

After De Wet's departure from the Colony in February, the nuisance value of Kritzinger's and other bands had been out of all proportion to their numbers, due to food, shelter, intelligence and, not infrequently, recruits received from the Cape Dutch. They were helped by the mediocre performance of their pursuers, largely the Colony's local forces, Kitchener needing to keep the more experienced Regulars and Colonials for operations in the north—a policy he would henceforth have to alter. In late May, Kritzinger had obtained reinforcements from the Free State and, thus encouraged, local adherents swelled his ranks. Haig, hitherto in command of mobile operations, had managed to contain the situation but, with disaffection spreading, Kitchener decided in June to place French in overall command in the Colony.

French organized his 5,000 mounted troops into nine columns, with his best troops—the 9th, 16th and 17th Lancers and two Regular Cape corps, the Police and Cape Mounted Rifles—spread among the inexperienced Colony irregulars and recently arrived Yeomanry. In mid-July he began a major drive to push the Boers north of the Orange. Kritzinger was

forced out of the Colony, but so extensive and difficult was the ground that the other bands, notably two led by Cape rebels, Lotter and Scheepers, filtered back through the columns.

On 15 August, Kritzinger joined Smuts to plan their joint re-entry, an enterprise that should relieve the pressure in the north and ultimately pave the way for a larger incursion by De la Rey by inciting the long-hoped-for uprising of the Cape Boers. Crossing the border on 3 September and heading south-west, Smuts soon found himself in trouble, first from hostile Africans, next from French's cordon which began to close round him. French's aim was to prevent any concentration of the Boer groups and to keep them constantly on the move, thus depriving them of rest and the chance to collect recruits and fresh horses. The day after Smuts' entry, Scobell's column, of 9th Lancers and CMR, which rivalled any commando in its scouting and mobility, surprised and destroyed Lotter's group, Lotter himself being captured and later executed.[57] A fortnight later, Smuts avenged the loss of this dangerous band. Harried by five columns, his men and horses suffered terribly from the spring rains and icy nights as they rode, or marched, to join the bands active in the Cape Midlands. Across their path lay nine miles of the Eland's River, its drifts guarded by the 17th Lancers. Warned by a friendly farmer, Smuts surrounded a squadron under cover of fog, inflicted 71 casualties and made off westwards to join Scheepers with the stores, arms and horses he so urgently needed. By mid-October he had linked up with Scheepers' commando (though Scheepers himself was captured and later suffered the same fate as Lotter). He rode away out of the Midlands well to the west of the

A more war-worn group of Yeomanry or Colonials taking cover prior to moving against the farm in the right background.

Cape-Kimberley railway where three other bands were lurking.

This renewal of hostile activity in the Colony allied, as will shortly be seen, with a new threat to Natal, not only forced Kitchener to divert troops from his drives in the Transvaal and Free State, but also demonstrated the failure of a propaganda attempt to shorten the war. On 7 August, while the big Free State drives were in progress, Kitchener had issued a proclamation demanding the surrender of all Boers by 15 September, after which all captured leaders down to the rank of field-cornet would face perpetual banishment from South Africa and all burghers would have charges levied on their property for the maintenance of their families in British camps.

Concurrently he increased the military pressure by stepping up the activity of the sweeping columns, whose radius and speed of action had hitherto been restricted by their infantry elements and slow-moving transport. Henceforth each column was to have a small, lightly-equipped mounted group, capable of moving rapidly over long distances without heavy transport, while the remainder of the column cleared the country and escorted the wagons. In addition special columns, acting independently of the larger columns which worked in unison over an area, were formed to carry out raids, mostly by night, on specific targets. Most Boers had little fear of the columns, which they could usually outpace or outwit, but being caught asleep in their laagers was an unnerving experience. Soon one raider in particular, Colonel Benson RA, who had navigated the night advance at Magersfontein, was earning a fearsome reputation in the Eastern Transvaal with his column of three mounted units[58] and 1st Argylls to guard his base and transport. Successful raiding needed good intelligence which Benson acquired from a band of scouts, part African, part Boer, led by the Uitlander and former Jameson Raider, Colonel Woolls-Sampson, who had raised the ILH at the start of the war.

The work of drives and raids was, from mid-1901,

151

5th South Australian Imperial Bushmen (325 strong) with a heliograph, the chief means of communication, using Morse, between columns and well suited to South African conditions. Also much used by the Boers, often with captured instruments.

increasingly facilitated by two static aids: barbed wire and the blockhouse. Earlier the ineffective system of protecting the railways by trenches around vital points like stations and bridges, with mounted patrols in between, had been replaced by lining the tracks at intervals with stone forts and corrugated iron blockhouses manned by permanent garrisons; all were connected by telephone and barbed-wire fencing and armoured trains patrolled the line. With the invention, by Major Rice RE, of a cheap, mass-produced, easily erected blockhouse, the intervals between each were reduced to about a mile and a half and later to as little as 200 yards on some sections. Devised first for railway protection, the blockhouse lines then became used as barriers to restrict Boer movement during the drives. From July the lines began to be constructed across country, serving a dual purpose: the better protection of roads and the carving-up of the vast countryside into areas of more manageable size in which to round up the commandos.

With the onset of spring in September, the

extension of the blockhouse system was still in its early stages and neither it, nor the measures to improve mobile operations, were as yet seriously deterring the Boers from taking the field again. Prisoners had been taken, particularly in the night raids, but these frequently turned out to be the weaker brethren, the best and most determined managing to escape. Nor were the latter impelled by Kitchener's proclamation to anything but renewed defiance, as witnessed firstly by Smuts' expedition, and second by Botha's long-nurtured but deferred plan for carrying the war into Natal.

Despite his relative proximity to Benson's energetic raiding, Botha had been gathering men throughout August. By mid-September he had 2,000 in the inverted wedge-shape of the South-East Transvaal between Natal, Zululand and Swaziland. He intended to strike first at Dundee. Rumours of his march had reached Kitchener and columns moved south and east to intercept him but at a far slower speed than his. At the same time Lyttleton, commanding in Natal, was alerted. Intelligence opinion about Botha's objective was divided between Dundee and the northern tip of Natal, so both eventualities had to be covered. Even knowledge of Botha's precise whereabouts was lacking. Thus, when Gough's MI, sent to escort an empty convoy from Vryheid back to Dundee, spotted some Boers resting, they charged, only to be counter-charged from the rear by Botha's main body and completely overwhelmed.[59]

Natal, though strongly held, was ill-prepared for a Botha hunt since all its troops were tied down in small static garrisons. Mobile columns had to be hurriedly diverted from their work in the Republics but on arrival found themselves in terrain with which they were unfamiliar and under a command structure which was unsuited for and unpractised in mobile operations. Thus their slow deployment, together with poor intelligence, never seriously threatened Botha.

He too was facing difficulties. The spring rains were weakening his horses, the Buffalo river guarding Natal was flooded, no rebellion nor even support could be expected in Natal, and his escape routes back to the Eastern Transvaal would soon be blocked. After fruitlessly attacking two stoutly-held posts on the Buffalo he turned for home. Avoiding the trap set for him by abandoning his transport and

Colonel G.E. Benson RA, the successful night-raider in the Eastern Transvaal, August–October 1901. He also navigated the Highland Brigade's advance at Magersfontein, December 1899.

wounded and died that evening. The day's fighting cost the column 238 casualties and the whole might have perished had not Benson's fight allowed time for Woolls-Sampson to laager the wagons and entrench. Having lost a hundred of his own best men, Botha was disinclined to venture further and rode off. The virtual loss of his best column was a serious blow to Kitchener, coming as it did after the failure to catch Botha in Natal, Smuts' continued survival in the Cape and, a month before, the losses inflicted by De la Rey's surprise of Kekewich's column, which nevertheless had stood its ground and beaten off the attack.

Furthermore these Boer actions, small though they were, had caused three times the casualties they had themselves sustained. Despite 64 columns being ranged against them throughout September–October, these had only accounted for an average of about one Boer per column per day. Notwithstanding the improvement in Kitchener's mounted troops, the Boers still had cause to believe that, man for man, they remained tactically superior and thus to continue the fight might still retain them their independence.

using mountain tracks, he reached safety in his own territory a month after he had set out.

Though he had failed in his aim, the diversion of columns to Natal had assisted Boer activities in the Cape, the Western Transvaal and the Southern Free State. De Wet, however, had chosen to remain inactive. On the other hand Botha found that the men he had left behind under Viljoen to keep resistance alive in the Eastern Transvaal had become increasingly demoralized by Benson's relentless harrying, and his help was urgently needed to deal with this menace.

His chance came on 30 October when, with no other columns in the area, Benson was returning to the Delagoa Bay railway to replenish his supplies, his rearguard being harassed by Grobler's commando near Bakenlaagte.[60] Summoned by Grobler from 70 miles away, Botha covered the last 30 without a halt and attacked Benson's 180-strong rearguard from three sides with 800 men. Despite a heroic resistance most gallantly directed by Benson himself, the Boers took the position but not before all but 17 of the rearguard were killed or wounded; Benson was twice

1st Argyll and Sutherland Highlanders, Benson's infantry battalion, replaced in October by 2nd Buffs. Compare with photograph on page 75 of same battalion in 1899. Slouch hats and short puttees have superseded helmets and gaiters.

As the war entered its third year Kitchener felt he was making progress, though both the Government at home and Milner were far less confident. With an average of 2,000 Boers dealt with every month since March, his intelligence staff calculated only some 10,000 could remain in the field (an estimate that was to prove wide of the mark). The way to cope with these, Kitchener now saw, was to deny them the use of the vast spaces which enabled them to escape the drives and raids. This had already begun with the blockhouse system which was expanding apace all over the country; each blockhouse was manned by seven infantrymen with armed African scouts patrolling around and in the intervals. Eventually 3,700 miles would be guarded by 8,000 inter-connected blockhouses manned by 50,000 troops and 16,000 Africans. The latter's use, incidentally, showed how flexibly the 'white-man's-war' policy was now being interpreted. By progressively enclosing the country and then sweeping it, starting with Bloemfontein, Johannesburg and Pretoria and working outwards, areas would be first cleared of, then protected from, guerillas, permitting normal civilian life to resume. Kitchener was coming round to the policy advocated by Milner, but the methods were his.

The blockhouses, though bullet-proof, were not shell-proof but, as the Boers had practically given up using artillery, this was unimportant. Kitchener, too, realized he had far more artillery than he required for this type of warfare and took the opportunity of increasing his mounted troops by converting batteries into the Royal Artillery Mounted Rifles, ultimately 2,300 strong.

In conjunction with his new policy of protected areas, Kitchener in December stopped the deportation of Boer families into camps. The appalling fatalities of women and children, due to overcrowding, poor hygiene and lack of medical facilities, first reported by Miss Emily Hobhouse, had raised a storm of protest in England, particularly among Radical elements and sections of the Liberal Opposition, who had been vociferously pro-Boer all along. This had resulted in the establishment of a Ladies' Commission led by Mrs Fawcett. Its balanced report and sensible recommendations had greatly improved conditions in the camps from October onwards. These considerations apart, the rounding-up and transportation of the families had been wasteful of military manpower. Furthermore, though the Boers had been bitterly

Stone fort guarding the lines of communication. Substantial structures like this were usually confined to vulnerable points like bridges.

Corrugated-iron blockhouse of Major Rice's pattern, with turf wall, under construction. Besides the surrounding barbed wire, each had a water tank, alarm signals, flare lights, fixed rifle batteries and sometimes land mines. 8,000 blockhouses were constructed by Royal Engineers by the end of hostilities.

Regular MI (2nd Northamptons) halted in the Eastern Transvaal. Each man wears two 50-round bandoliers and some have newly-issued slouch hats. This detachment was one of the original components of 3rd Regular MI, formed from 1st Division battalions.

enraged by the fatalities, they were realistic enough to appreciate that the removal of responsibility from them for their families' sustenance and security greatly assisted their military capability. Henceforth that responsibility would be theirs.

That there were surrendered or captured Boers who, however stoutly they may have fought in 1899, now regarded the guerilla war as ultimately destructive of their Republics, had been demonstrated by the Burgher Peace Committee. Having failed to persuade their countrymen by argument, their willingness to help end the war manifested itself in the formation of fighting levies known as the National Scouts. Though their numbers were never large, and their military value chiefly confined to reconnaissance, their propaganda value tended to sway disillusioned fighting burghers, if not towards joining them, at least towards surrender; a trend that was increasingly to worry the Boer leaders. Many burghers now had to choose whether to join the 'hands-uppers' or remain among the 'bitter-enders'.

Of further help to Kitchener was the appointment, in December, as Chief of Staff of Ian Hamilton, who had returned to South Africa after going home with Roberts. Kitchener's strength was his painstaking and driving energy; a weakness, one which hitherto had inhibited all operations, was his inability and unwillingness to delegate. Hamilton, whom he trusted and had indeed asked for, would be able to relieve some of the burden Kitchener had imposed upon himself, though acting not so much as a true Chief of Staff, but more as a deputy and a semi-autonomous commander as occasion required. Moreover, having the ear of Roberts, now Commander-in-Chief, he would be able to maintain better liaison than had existed previously between Kitchener and the War Office, and through it, with the Government.

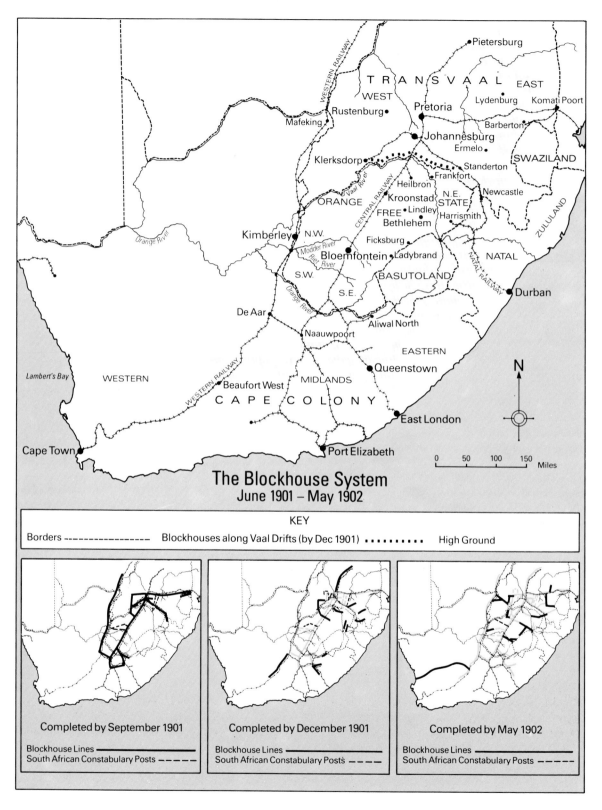

The Blockhouse System
June 1901 – May 1902

KEY

Borders ------------ Blockhouses along Vaal Drifts (by Dec 1901) •••••••••• High Ground

Completed by September 1901

Blockhouse Lines ————
South African Constabulary Posts – – – – –

Completed by December 1901

Blockhouse Lines ————
South African Constabulary Posts – – – – –

Completed by May 1902

Blockhouse Lines ————
South African Constabulary Posts – – – – –

156

11th Imperial Yeomanry crossing the Caledon River. They have exchanged hats for helmets (see photograph on page 136). This was the regiment surprised by De Wet at Tweefontein on Christmas Day 1901.

planned to contain him and concentrate his mobile forces in the east to work in conjunction with the blockhouse lines.

Throughout November and December, 14 columns drove this way and that across a quadrilateral area of De Wet's territory about the size of Yorkshire, Lancashire and half Cumbria combined. Here the blockhouse line was complete only down the western side, along the Central Railway, though other lines were reaching out into its centre from west and east. Stung into action by a letter from Botha suggesting that peace talks might be advisable, De Wet, who had been inactive since February, called out his men. By limiting his movements to an area out of reach of the blockhouses, he managed not only to avoid the drives, but to find and attack isolated British units, culminating in a devastating blow on the 11th Imperial Yeomanry at Tweefontein on Christmas Day, before dispersing his men as the year changed.

The simultaneous operations by Bruce Hamilton against Botha in an area roughly the size of Holland began with a sweep by 12 columns towards the Swaziland border, very similar in concept to French's in February, but with the columns backed by continuous blockhouse lines along the Delagoa Bay and Natal railways, and by another line closing the exit into the south-east corner of the Transvaal and one under construction between Standerton and Ermelo through the heart of the district.

Beyond driving the enemy eastwards this sweep achieved little; indeed Botha was able to escort the

From November onwards the most troublesome areas, apart from the Cape where Smuts' activities were confined to the far west, were the Western Transvaal under De la Rey, the Eastern under Botha and, contiguous with the latter, the North-East Free State under De Wet. With De la Rey now separated from the other two by the cleared and protected area around Pretoria and Johannesburg, Kitchener

Pom-pom section with Rawlinson's column. These automatic guns fired a 1-1b. shell in belts of 25 rounds, with a maximum range of 4,500 yards. Their adoption was copied from the Boers.

8th Regular MI of Rawlinson's column returning to camp in the Eastern Transvaal. This MI was drawn from the South Wales Borderers, Cheshire, East Lancashire and North Staffordshire Regiments, but there is little to distinguish them from Boers.

Transvaal Government across the Delagoa blockhouse line to safety in the north-east, before himself returning to the Ermelo district on which the columns were converging. Bruce Hamilton now changed tactics. Aided by Woolls-Sampson's corps of Boer and African scouts and informers, he mounted throughout December and January a series of night raids of the Benson pattern. The establishment of a permanent and protected base at Ermelo permitted the columns to dispense with their heavy wagons,

which had been Benson's undoing, and to ride swiftly through the night over long distances towards targets pin-pointed by Woolls-Sampson, rushing a sleeping laager at dawn. One of the most successful columns was Rawlinson's of Regular MI and Cape irregulars, which took 300 prisoners and in one raid narrowly missed Botha himself. Botha, however, remained as quick as ever to spot an opportunity to pounce on an isolated or unwary detachment, even such experienced men as Plumer's well-tried Colonials, half of whom were overwhelmed in early January.

Nevertheless Hamilton's work accounted for nearly 700 Boers in six weeks and, more important, the nervous strain imposed by the night raids and the relentlessness of the columns was wearing down the

The 10th Hussars in Cape Colony. This was the regiment that captured Kritzinger after a pursuit in conjunction with the 5th Lancers lasting all day and covering some 80 miles.

morale of Botha's burghers, many of whom, unable to see any future in continued resistance, were scattering or breaking up into small, ineffective groups. Furthermore the main towns of the area were firmly in British hands and by February the Standerton-Ermelo blockhouse line had been extended to the Delagoa Bay Railway, thus cutting Botha's domain in two. With only 500 of his best men remaining, Botha slipped away to sanctuary in the mountains between Vryheid and Zululand.

Everywhere Kitchener's iron will was increasing the pressure on the commandos, whose casualties were starting to include their senior men. Opperman, one of the heroes of Spion Kop, had been killed in the Transvaal, Ben Viljoen captured near Lydenburg, and Kritzinger, who had re-entered the Cape Midlands

in mid-December, was pursued and taken on a blockhouse line by the 10th Hussars. However De la Rey was soon to show how formidable he still was, and the most uncompromising and elusive of all, Steyn and De Wet, had yet to be brought to book from their Free State lairs east of the Central Railway.

Since the failure of December's drives, two west-east blockhouse lines now traversed that country between the railway and the Drakensberg: from Wolvehoek via Heilbron and Frankfort, 120 miles long, and from Kroonstadt via Bethlehem and

159

Harrismith, 135 miles, one being between 30–80 miles from the other. With supply depots around the periphery and 8,000 troops deployed either in the blockhouses or as stop columns in support, Kitchener planned to sweep up De Wet's commandos with mobile columns, reinforced from the Transvaal, totalling 9,000 men. Whereas previous sweeps had resembled a big-game drive, now the analogy was to be a fish-trawl: a tightly-controlled, systematic advance by an unbroken line of horsemen at 12-yard intervals between the blockhouse lines, searching every yard of veldt by day, entrenching a continuous line of picquets by night.

From February onwards these massive drill movements went on, westwards, eastwards, then southwards and eastwards combined. But however painstaking the manoeuvres, there was always the human error or irregularities of terrain disrupting the trawl. Twice De Wet broke through: once taking advantage of lack of vigilance by a blockhouse guard, once in a massed night charge of a thousand burghers, wagons and a herd of cattle through a weakly-held part of the cordon. By early March the columns were tiring from lack of rest but De Wet had lost 1,200 men and the morale of his survivors was weakening under the unceasing pressure. He also had to get treatment for Steyn, who was suffering from an eye infection, so they left the Free State and headed for De la Rey.

Not only did they find safety and a doctor, but De la Rey greeted them with news of one of the biggest coups of the guerilla war, to cheer De Wet before he returned to the Free State. Because of a shortage of horses and ammunition, De la Rey had been limited to minor actions and, with so many troops in the east, had not been unduly harassed. Only three columns were active in the Western Transvaal and the blockhouse system was underdeveloped. By late February De la Rey recognized that a diversion was essential if the critical situation in the east was to be eased. On 25 February he ambushed a convoy of Methuen's, capturing all the horses and ammunition he needed and causing heavy casualties. The next day he rode north.

Methuen was the last of the senior generals who had been out since the beginning without a break. Senior even to Kitchener, with his command far smaller than in 1899—sometimes no more than a weak column—he had nonetheless remained constant to his duty in the Western Transvaal. Now, hearing of the convoy's loss, he quickly assembled a makeshift column of very mixed units and variable quality and marched in pursuit. On 7 March, at Tweebosch, he was utterly overwhelmed by De la Rey. His 300 Regular infantry, Northumberlands and Loyals, who had been under him since the start of the war, and some Cape Police fought it out to the end, but the rest of the column was no match for the burghers. Seriously wounded and with the position hopeless, Methuen surrendered. Two hundred of his men had been killed or wounded and 600 were taken. Disregarding the burghers' clamour to hold such a senior general hostage, De la Rey chivalrously had Methuen escorted to the nearest British hospital, and sent a telegram to Lady Methuen, expressing his concern about her husband's wounds. Such conduct, at a stage in the war when not only were the Boers under great pressure but acts of brutality towards prisoners on both sides were increasing, speaks highly for the character of De la Rey.

Kitchener was prostrated by the news for 36 hours but, after a huge meal, threw himself into transferring 16,000 troops from east to west to round up De la Rey. The large drives seen in the Free State began on 23 March but, with a scarcity of blockhouse lines, scanty intelligence and poor co-ordination between columns, little was achieved and indeed some reverses were suffered at the hands of the 2,500 men De la Rey had mustered. At the same time Kitchener launched a hunt for Botha in the South-East Transvaal and another drive in the Free State; he also had other pressing matters on his mind. On 5 April he despatched Ian Hamilton to take overall charge in the west. Hamilton immediately gathered the reins into a firm hand and ordered a big semi-circular sweep for the 9th. Whatever the outcome it would not catch De la Rey himself. On the same day he and all the chief Transvaal and Free State 'bitter-enders' were meeting, under British protection, at Hamilton's own headquarters, Klerksdorp.

15. GOOD FRIENDS NOW

10 APRIL–31 MAY 1902

Since the failure of his conference with Botha at Middelburg in February 1901, Kitchener had rigorously prosecuted the military campaign but had always been ready to discuss with the fighting Boers fair and just terms for peace. In January 1902 the Netherlands Government, with Kruger's approval, had suggested they should mediate between the Boers and the British Government. The latter had declined, suggesting that the most appropriate way of reaching a settlement lay in direct contact between the Boer leaders and Kitchener. This correspondence was sent in March by Kitchener, without comment, to the Transvaal Government. Encouraged by the implied suggestion that terms, rather than unconditional surrender, might be offered, Schalk Burger asked for safe conducts for all Boer leaders to meet and discuss peace proposals. Kitchener agreed. Though his troops continued their unremitting operations, Burger, Botha and De la Rey for the Transvaal and Steyn, De Wet and Herzog for the Free State, having met at Klerksdorp, decided to go to Pretoria to negotiate. Here they were joined by Smuts, brought up from the Cape where, having been driven to the far west by French's columns, he had been attacking the copper-mining town of O'okiep; though constantly harassed he had increased his strength to 3,000, mostly Cape rebels, and tied down a large number of troops whom Kitchener could otherwise have deployed in the north.

Though the Boer leaders still entertained no thoughts of surrender, the opening negotiations were overcast for them by news of Ian Hamilton's defeat and pursuit of Kemp, De la Rey's second-in-command. Outmanoeuvred by Hamilton, Kemp had charged a thin MI screen, only to come under heavy fire from Kekewich's column, mainly Scottish Horse and Yeomanry, deployed along a ridge near Roodewal. Kemp lost 110, including his lieutenant, Potgieter, who fell at the head of his men. Persistent-

ly pursued by Kekewich and Rawlinson, Kemp eventually escaped by splitting his force but lost more in the process.

Notwithstanding this reverse in a hitherto unsubdued region, and the devastation and drives continuing elsewhere, the Boers approached the negotiations conscious they were not yet defeated and still had their best men in the field. To Kitchener. they offered concessions, including votes for Uitlanders, but stood out for retention of their Republics' independence. Surprised, but determined to keep the talks going, Kitchener telegraphed the Boer proposals to London. They were rejected. Then, additionally confronted by the far less conciliatory Milner, the Boers enquired of the British proposals. Back to London went the enquiry, accompanied by strong representations from Milner that nothing more lenient than the Middelburg terms should be offered, and that no date should be mentioned for the eventual self-government of the former Republics after an indefinite period as Crown Colonies.[61] The Government replied that the Middelburg terms still stood but that concessions might be made on the amnesty question. Thereupon the Boers asked for a general armistice and safe passage for their representatives from Europe. Kitchener denied both requests but undertook to allow the leaders to canvass the commandos in the field. Thereafter they were to re-assemble with 30 delegates from each Republic at Vereeniging on 15 May. So for a month a curious situation ensued—the fighting burghers were hunted with undiminished vigour by Ian and Bruce Hamilton, while their leaders progressed around under safe conduct.

The Vereeniging Conference was, on the face of it, between two parties, Britain and the fighting Boers; the surrendered Boers, who had taken the oath of allegiance and in some cases even fought for the British, were to find themselves cold-shouldered by

camps were receiving proper medical treatment and education; and the Rand mines, which would finance his vision of a future South Africa, were back in operation, already producing a third of their pre-war output. It was British skill that was restoring the embattled Republics to life and it was a British-dominated South Africa, guided by him, that Milner wished to see. There must be no return to the bad old Boer ways and only unconditional surrender could ensure this.

Among the Boers, the more pragmatic Transvaalers, like Burger and Botha, conscious of the devastation, the sufferings of families still on the veldt, and the falling morale of their starving, ragged burghers, sensed that continued resistance would only increase the numbers of 'hands-uppers' out of sheer desperation; consequently better to accept terms now than abject surrender later. Though equally aware of conditions on the veldt, the indomitable Steyn, tired and ill though he was, refused any compromise over independence, being strengthened in his resolve by a pledge to that effect extracted by De Wet from all Free State commandos, and similar views expressed by some Transvaalers.

When the Boer delegates came together on 15 May, these contradictory viewpoints were expounded, to which were added Smuts' report that while his men in the Cape were sound, no rebellion was likely, and a new factor, the danger that some African tribes were preparing to pay off old scores. Botha spoke for peace, De Wet for war. De la Rey, whose military position was strongest, listened impassively but eventually seconded Botha. It was agreed to offer the Rand and control of the Republics' foreign relations to Britain, provided they retained their independence. Botha, De la Rey, De Wet, with the lawyers Smuts and Herzog, were nominated to negotiate this proposal with the British and, if turned down, to negotiate on any other basis they thought acceptable, but the final terms would have to be ratified by all delegates.

It was turned down, the British insisting that terms

both parties. It soon appeared that neither party spoke with one voice. Kitchener believed that, despite the blows he had inflicted on them and their willingness to discuss peace, the Boers, particularly the hard-line 'bitter-enders' like Steyn and De Wet, were capable of dragging out the guerilla war until war-weariness forced the Government to concede their independence. Moreover he and many of his officers had come to respect, even admire, their opponents' strength and resilience, at the expense of sympathy for the Uitlanders and Cape Loyalist politicians, especially those whom Ian Hamilton called the 'Jewburghers', the Rand magnates, whose professed loyalty to the Crown was motivated, as the soldiers saw it, by concern for their profits, which in turn depended on the crushing of Afrikanerdom. If the Army had fought to achieve a unified South Africa within the British Empire, then Briton and Boer must be reconciled to work together in rebuilding the country. Therefore reasonable terms must be offered to encourage these stout-hearted men to that end, rather than alienating them.

Milner, on the other hand, believed that the Boers were as good as beaten and that the coming winter would finish them off. Already the protected areas were being restored to sound administration by his 'Kindergarten', brilliant young graduates imported specially from England; the deported families in the

The last drives in Western Transvaal. 1st Australian Commonwealth Horse with De Lisle's column. The last Australian contingents to arrive, from March 1902, no longer had State designations, following the federation of Australia in January 1901.

were dependent on the basic issue of the Boers surrendering independence. In the discussion that followed it was De Wet and Milner who were the chief obstacles to agreement, the Boer unable to stomach the idea of allegiance to the Crown, the High Commissioner unwilling to concede anything and seeing De Wet as the best chance of the talks failing, ensuring thereby the collapse of the Boers which he believed must follow.

But the tide was running against Milner, not only at the negotiations, but with the Government and public opinion at home, which wanted an end to the war. By dint of Smuts' legal skill and Kitchener's diplomacy a formula was arrived at. Subject to the Boers acknowledging the King as their lawful sovereign, self-government would follow when circumstances permitted. An amnesty would be granted for all acts of war committed in good faith, and Cape rebels, except for leaders, would be disenfranchised but not imprisoned. The Dutch language would be allowed in schools and law courts. No war tax would be levied on Boer property, £3 million would be given by Britain towards restoring damage and loss caused by both sides, as well as loans on generous terms. An important point concerned the

black populations of the former Republics. A British war aim had been to achieve for them the same political rights as existed in the Cape and Natal. Despite this, and at Milner's instigation, the question of the native franchise was to be deferred until after the grant of self-government, which in effect meant never. On this at least Milner and the Boers saw eye to eye. The Colonial Office had demurred but the Cabinet allowed Milner his way. Notwithstanding the original 'white-man's-war' policy, by the end of hostilities many thousands of armed Africans had been assisting the British and many more had been employed by both sides as non-combatants. Neither Briton nor Boer, however, was prepared to risk white dominance in South Africa.

Though Milner was dissatisfied with these terms, the Government agreed them but insisted they were not negotiable, requiring a straight acceptance or refusal from the Boer delegates convened at Vereeniging by midnight, 31 May. When shown to the ailing Steyn, he bitterly denounced them and resigned as President, nominating De Wet in his place. For two days the 60-strong convention agonized over all the old arguments, the leading Transvaalers urging acceptance, De Wet still hostile. Then suddenly, after a private appeal to him by Botha and De la Rey, he changed his mind and recommended acceptance, subject to the production of a document justifying to the burghers why such a course was inevitable. A vote was taken: 54 for acceptance, six against. At 11.55 p.m., 31 May, the Treaty of Vereeniging was signed, ending the war after two years and eight months. Kitchener shook hands with all the Boer leaders, saying 'We are good friends now'.

The war had cost Britain approximately £220 million. Of just under 450,000 troops who had served in South Africa, 357,500 were British Regulars, Militia, Yeomanry and Volunteers.[62] Australia had contributed 16,715, New Zealand 6,400, and Canada 6,000. South Africa had raised 52,000 and the South African Constabulary, recruited from all over the Empire, had totalled 8,500. There had been 21,000 fatalities (62 per cent from disease, a sad commentary on inadequate hospital facilities and the shortage of nurses, particularly up to 1901) and 52,000 other casualties, so that in all about one man in six had been a casualty. Over half a million horses had been provided, from England, South America, Canada, USA, Australasia, Hungary, India and South Africa itself, of which 67 per cent were lost during the war, which amply demonstrates how much it had been a mounted man's war and the terrible demands made on horses, which were frequently unacclimatized, often ill-fed and less than well-cared-for.

French's operations in the Cape had ended with the relief of O'okiep on 3 May and the last drives by the two Hamiltons had continued until 11 May. When the tattered, emaciated commandos rode in from the veldt to surrender their arms and take the oath, over 20,000 of them were counted; about half their fighting strength of a year before, but still nearly double the estimate of British Intelligence in November (though the latter's task was bedevilled by the constantly fluctuating numbers actually in the field at any one time). The estimated total number of Boers engaged throughout the war varies from 87,365 to 65,000.[63] In either case, for a greatly outnumbered army, without formal discipline and organization, to have as many combatants under arms after two and a half years' hostilities and still, in most cases, ready to continue fighting despite grievous shortages of food, clothing and munitions, is a magnificent testimonial to the Boers' fighting skill, endurance and devotion to their cause. Their struggle cost them about 4,000 killed in action, and the appalling loss of some 20,000 in the concentration camps from disease.

That the Boers had survived so long reflected little credit on the British Army as organized and trained in 1899, nor on its first two field commanders, Buller and Roberts. The pointers to what might be expected from the Boers had been demonstrated in 1881, but the lessons had been overlaid by subsequent victories over spear-and-sword armies. The discipline and courage of regimental officers and men had, on the whole, been as sound as ever, but those qualities had not been enough to overcome a fast-moving, quick-thinking race bred to horse and rifle since childhood. Buller had held Natal and Roberts had turned the tide, but the latter's over-confidence and misjudgement of his enemy had saddled Kitchener with his difficult task, which his great energy, persistence, grasp of events and diplomatic skill finally brought to a successful conclusion. It could not have been accomplished without the loyalty and adaptability of troops who, predominantly infantry at the start of the war, learned from their enemies and Colonial brothers-in-arms to turn themselves into mounted riflemen capable, in the latter stages, of engaging the Boers on equal terms.

Transvaal delegates leaving the Vereeniging Peace Conference after the final sitting, 31 May 1902.

Two British nurses at a hospital on the veldt. In 1899 there were only 176 Regular and Reserve Army nurses worldwide. The number of female nurses was greatly increased after June 1900, including volunteers from the Colonies and private institutions.

The Army's experience in the war resulted in major reforms in organization, administration, tactics and weapons affecting the whole service, Regulars and part-timers alike, and from top to bottom: from the replacement of the Commander-in-Chief's office by the Army Council, the reorganization of the War Office and creation of a General Staff, down to the re-design of the soldier's uniform and personal equipment. From these reforms emerged the Expeditionary Force of 1914, 'the best trained, best organized and best equipped British Army that ever went forth to war', which, man for man, was the equal of, if not superior to, any in Europe, though its first commander, French, did not fulfil his South African promise.

The widespread use of mounted troops in South Africa was not helpful for the future. Several commanders had been cavalrymen, like French and Haig to name but two, whose success brought them to prominence in the Army where they became upholders of the mounted arm, forgetting that the war-winners had been mounted riflemen, not sword-and-lance cavalry. Furthermore, although the cavalryman now had a rifle and was trained (though still reluctantly) to produce a musketry as accurate and rapid as the infantry's, he also retained his sword and the belief in shock action persisted; indeed in 1909 the lance was restored as an offensive weapon.

The guerilla war, with its downgrading of infantry and artillery, was unlikely to be repeated in European warfare but the South African experience generally had not diminished the Army's faith in attack over defence. What it failed to appreciate fully was that modern artillery, machine-guns and magazine rifles, used in conjunction with trenches and barbed wire, now gave the advantage in war to the defender, a lesson the Germans were to remind them of with a vengeance.

The Great War was to see the erstwhile confederates, Botha, Smuts and De Wet on opposite sides. After the peace of Vereeniging a great and lasting work of reconstruction was done by Milner and his 'Kindergarten', but his dream of outnumbering the Boers by a flood of British immigrants never materialized, and he even lost the support of the existing Uitlanders by importing Chinese labour to work the mines. In 1905 he resigned. The following year a Liberal Government took office; as Kitchener

Gunner Isaac Lodge's VC, one of four won by Q Battery RHA at Sannah's Post, with his Queen's South Africa, George V Coronation, and Long Service and Good Conduct medals. 78 VCs were awarded in the war: 59 British (including 2 to non-Regulars), 8 South Africans, 6 Australians, 4 Canadians, and 1 New Zealander.

had forecast to Smuts during Vereeniging, the Liberals soon granted the old Republics the status of self-governing colonies. At the first election the party founded by Botha and Smuts, supported by many Uitlanders, came to power. In 1910 the four former colonies were granted full independence within the British Empire as the Union of South Africa, with Botha as Prime Minister.

De Wet retired from public life before the Union and in 1914, with Kemp, led a rebellion which was crushed by Botha and Smuts, who also waged a successful campaign against German South-West Africa.[64] Smuts went on to command all British forces

in German East Africa, later becoming a member of the Imperial War Cabinet, subsequently Prime Minister of South Africa, and a world statesman, high in Allied councils during the Second World War. Despite certain pro-German elements in the Union, troops of both white races fought alongside Imperial forces in both World Wars.

Botha and Smuts with their South African Party, later joined by the Unionist Party mainly of British-born voters, remained loyal in their allegiance to the British Empire and the cause of racial peace and unity between whites in South Africa. There were still Afrikaner irreconcilables—the disciples of Kruger, Steyn and De Wet[65]—who through their Nationalist Party sought separation from the Empire and the

Reverse of Queen's and King's South Africa medals, to Private Richews, Royal Munster Fusiliers. Ribbon colours are: red/blue/sand and green/white/sand.

The type of soldier that dominated the war on both sides, the mounted rifleman.

A sign of reconciliation. Memorial erected by 1st Gordon Highlanders to Transvaalers of the Standerton, Heidelberg and Carolina Commandos, killed at Belfast, 8 January 1901.

ascendancy of Afrikanerdom. Led by Herzog the Nationalists achieved power in 1924, but their majority was too weak to pursue a separatist policy. On the outbreak of the Second World War the Nationalists voted for neutrality but were defeated in Parliament and Smuts again became Prime Minister. However in 1948 the Nationalists regained power, which they have held ever since, and in 1961 Dr Verwoerd took South Africa out of the Commonwealth, proclaiming a Republic.

The two Anglo-Boer Wars are known to the Afrikaners as the First and Second Wars of Independence. The first they most certainly won, though the result nurtured the seeds of future conflict. Thirty-nine years after apparently losing the second they eventually won that, not only imposing their ascendancy over their heartlands of the Transvaal and the Free State, but regaining the Cape and Natal from which they had made the Great Trek over a century before. That exodus had been inspired by their resentment of liberal British policy towards the black Africans, whom the Afrikaners viewed as

undeserving and incapable of exercising any political rights, a basic tenet to which they have adhered consistently ever since. Afrikaner Nationalism finally separated itself from the British Crown but, to maintain its dominance, also had to separate itself from the majority of its country's inhabitants, with the results seen today.

Kitchener's assertion about 'good friends' proved true up to a point. But today, beset by a nationalism as insistent on its rights as their own, the Afrikaners are again under fire from Britain, no longer from soldiers and Imperialist statesmen, but television pundits, churchmen and politicians. Many are the political heirs of those who, during the Anglo-Boer Wars, were, if not exactly pro-Boer, sympathetic to the Boer cause. Yet the Boers of then and now remain essentially the same.

ENDNOTES

Chapter 1

1. An Imperial regiment, but locally enlisted from Hottentots with a proportion of British Regulars who eventually predominated; became a Colonial unit after 1878.
2. Three 6-pounders, Royal Artillery; detachment, Royal Engineers; two companies each 45th, 91st Regiments, 1st Rifle Brigade; four companies, Cape Mounted Rifles.
3. As the newly created High Commissioner for South-East Africa (Transvaal, Natal and Zululand).
4. *See* page 10.

Chapter 2

5. Boer version of sangars, stone-built defences.
6. Some Boers had the same Martini-Henry rifles as the British, but most had Westley-Richards. Both types were single-shot breech-loaders.
7. These Colours remained in service with the 58th's successors until 1960, the centenary of their presentation. They are now displayed in the National Army Museum. Colours were never again taken into action by British infantry.
8. Boer casualties at Laing's Nek were only 14 killed and 27 wounded; the British lost 83 killed and 111 wounded.
9. Though his local rank of major-general made Colley the senior in South Africa, their true Army ranks of colonel both dated from 1 April 1874, Wood being one place ahead of Colley in the Army List.

Chapter 3

10. Later killed while commanding the Desert Column during the Gordon Relief Expedition in 1885.
11. He had only recently rejoined his regiment after recuperating in England from wounds received during the Zulu War.
12. 92 killed, 134 wounded, 59 prisoners.

Chapter 4

13. The Transvaal Parliament.
14. Both German Jews, naturalized British.

Chapter 5

15. Four sections (each of 25 men under a sergeant) formed a company. Two sections formed a half-company under a subaltern.
16. Predecessors of the Territorial Army.
17. Offers of aid also came from the non-white Empire: from Malays, West Indians, Nigerians, Canadian Indians, Maoris, Indian princes, Pathan tribesmen and, of course, the native Indian Army. None could be accepted for political reasons. At this stage the same reasons debarred the use as combatants (except in defence of their tribal lands) of Swazis, Zulus, Basutos and Bechuanas, whose sympathies were anti-Boer.
18. Diary of Lieutenant C.W.Barton, 2nd Northamptons. Captain Slocum, US Military Attaché in South Africa, made a similar observation.
19. 1st King's Liverpool, 1st Leicesters, 1st and 2nd KRRC and 2nd Royal Dublin Fusiliers.
20. Variously called the Battle of Ladysmith, Lombard's Kop or Farquhar's Farm.

Chapter 6

21. 3rd Grenadiers, 1st and 2nd Coldstream and 1st Scots Guards.
22. Its casualties were only six per cent of the total (one killed, 16 wounded).
23. Also called the Battle of Enslin.
24. This was the home battalion. The 2nd, under White in Ladysmith, had come from India.
25. On the North-West Frontier, in the Tirah Campaign of 1897.

Chapter 7

26. While acting as war correspondent for *The Morning Post*.

27. The Composite Regiment consisted of one company 2/60th Rifles, one section 2nd Dublins and one squadron each ILH and Natal Carbineers. Thorneycroft's had been raised in Natal from colonial volunteers.

28. For this single incident VCs were awarded to Babtie, Schofield, Congreve, Reed, Roberts, Nurse and Private Ravenhill 2nd RSF, one of the guns' infantry escorts. Eighteen NCOs and drivers RFA received the Distinguished Conduct Medal.

Chapter 8

29. In which a Victoria Cross was won by Lieutenant Masterson.

30. Lord Kitchener's younger brother, then commanding 2nd West Yorkshire in Hildyard's Brigade.

31. Mostly Uitlanders, the infantry equivalent of the ILH.

32. Having escaped from Pretoria, he was now combining the duties of war correspondent with those of subaltern in the SALH. He had gone up to Spion Kop to see for himself.

33. 2nd Scottish Rifles (Cameronians), 3rd 60th Rifles, 1st Durham Light Infantry and 1st Rifle Brigade.

Chapter 9

34. Queensland MI, New South Wales Mounted Rifles and New Zealand Mounted Rifles.

35. 2nd Buffs, 2nd Gloucesters, 1st Duke of Wellington's and 1st Oxfordshire Light Infantry.

36. Household Cavalry, 10th Hussars, 12th Lancers and G and P Batteries RHA.

37. 4th, 5th and 6th Regular MI, two squadrons Kitchener's Horse and one squadron New South Wales Mounted Rifles.

38. Then designated Princess of Wales's Own (Yorkshire Regiment), but colloquially known as Green Howards, a title formally adopted in 1920.

39. His fourth battalion, 2nd DCLI, had earlier sent four of its eight companies to reinforce the Highland Brigade and the remaining four were on baggage guard.

40. The Cavalry Division was brought across the Modder via Koodoosrand Drift in the early hours of the 21st.

41. Each of two battalions, Regular MI, and 3–4 squadrons of Colonials (Australians, New Zealanders, South Africans, Ceylon Europeans), Burma MI (Regulars) and CIV MI, under Colonels Alderson, Le Gallais, Martyr and Ridley.

Chapter 10

42. Two each from 2nd, 4th and 6th Brigades.

43. Hamilton, like White, was a Roberts supporter or 'Indian' in the feud with Wolseley and his 'Africans', of whom Buller was a leading figure.

Chapter 11

44. He died ten days later.

45. 1st and 2nd Brabant's Horse, Kaffrarian Rifles, Cape Mounted Rifles, Driscoll's Scouts and one company Royal Scots MI.

46. Of four 'corps' of mixed Regulars, Australians and New Zealanders and two battalions of Canadian Mounted Rifles. It also included Lumsden's Horse, made up of British volunteers from India, chiefly tea planters.

47. Of four 'corps' of mixed Regulars, West Australians, South Africans and the CIV MI.

48. Three Militia battalions had joined 1st Division and four had joined 3rd Division. Twenty-three battalions were guarding lines of communication in Cape Colony. Thirteen battalions of Imperial Yeomanry were in the field, the remaining seven on the lines of communications or under training.

49. 470 Protectorate Regiment, 90 British South Africa Police, 100 Cape Police, 70 Bechuanaland Rifles, 400 Town Guard and 400 armed Africans.

Chapter 12

50. The Hamiltons were not related. Bruce Hamilton was the brother-in-law of the ill-fated Colley (see page 30).

51. In the interests of keeping the conflict 'a white men's war' and to avoid any native uprisings, both sides respected the neutrality of Basutoland, an independent native territory under British protection.

52. The two battalions of Mounted Rifles had formed part of Canada's second contingent; the 1st was later redesignated Royal Canadian Dragoons. Another Canadian unit, Strathcona's Horse, then serving with Buller, had been raised at Lord Strathcona's personal expense.

Chapter 13

53. Corporal J.H.M. Abbott, 1st Australian Horse (serving with 1st Cavalry Brigade), in *Tommy Cornstalk* (London, 1902).
54. Rawlinson, General, 1914 IV Corps, 1916–18 Fourth Army. Allenby, FM, 1915 V Corps, Third Army, 1917–18 C-in-C Palestine. Plumer, FM, 1914 II Corps, 1915 and 1918 Second Army, 1917 C-in-C Allied Forces Italy. Byng, FM, 1915 Cavalry Corps, 1916–17 Canadian Corps, 1917–18 Third Army. Gough, General, 1915 I Corps, 1916–18 Fifth Army. Haig, FM, 1914 I Corps, 1915 First Army, 1915–18 C-in-C Western Front, vice FM Sir John French. Others who achieved high command included Ian Hamilton, General, 1915 C-in-C Gallipoli; Smith-Dorrien, General, 1914 II Corps; De Lisle, General, 1918 XV Corps; and Mahon, General, 1915–16 C-in-C Salonika.
55. His column now included the volunteer unit known as Bushveld Carbineers, later notorious for the court-martial of the Anglo-Australian 'Breaker' Morant and three other officers for the murder of Boer prisoners. Morant and another officer, Handcock, were executed on Kitchener's orders, notwithstanding their previous excellent records and their plea that they had acted in reprisal for similar murders committed by the Boers.

Chapter 14

56. Fifty-five per cent were South Africans, Australians and New Zealanders; the remainder were Imperial Yeomanry (second contingent) and South African Constabulary. The original Canadian contingents had gone home and, save for individuals and a battery, no more Canadians arrived until early 1902.
57. At his trial, for murder and treason, he unsuccessfully claimed Free State citizenship.
58. 18th and 19th Regular MI and 2nd Scottish Horse (recruited from Scotsmen, South Africans and Australians).
59. The same Gough who had been first into Ladysmith. Though taken prisoner, he subsequently escaped. *See also* page 143 and note 54.
60. Benson's column had been reconstituted into 3rd and 25th Regular MI, 2nd Scottish Horse, 2nd Buffs and 84th Battery RFA.

Chapter 15

61. The Middelburg proposals had offered self-government 'as soon as circumstances permit'.
62. Regulars and Reservists 256,000; Militia 45,000; Yeomanry 26,500; Volunteers 20,000.
63. *Official History* and *The Times History* respectively.
64. De la Rey, whose loyalties were uncertain, was accidentally killed during the rebellion.
65. Kruger died in 1904, Steyn in 1916 and De Wet in 1922.

PICTURE CREDITS

Africana Museum: 33. Australian War Memorial: 132, 144, 152, 163. Author: 10, 17, 21, 36, 38 (left), 40, 45–47, 49, 63 (top), 67, 69, 70, 83, 85, 87, 88 (bottom), 90 (right), 92, 94 (top), 101, 103, 117, 125, 127, 133. Canadian War Museum: 53, 54, 137 (top). Imperial War Museum: 124, 142, 145, 148, 151, 153 (bottom), 168 (left). Killie Campbell Library: 12, 13. National Army Museum: 9, 11, 14–16, 18, 20, 23–26, 29, 30, 34, 35, 37, 38 (right), 39, 41, 42, 52, 56, 59 (bottom), 60, 63 (bottom), 74–78, 82, 84, 86, 88 (top), 89, 90 (left), 93 (right), 95–98, 107, 109–111, 114, 115, 118, 119, 121–123, 126 (right), 128, 131, 134, 135, 140–143, 146, 147, 150, 153 (top), 154, 157, 158, 159, 162, 164–168 (right). Navy and Army Illustrated: 55, 58, 62, 72, 81, 93 (left), 126 (left), 136, 137 (bottom). Northamptonshire Regiment Museum: 27, 155. R.J. Marrion: 59 (top), 71, 73, 79, 138. Royal Green Jackets Museum: 31. Royal Photographic Society: 57, 61, 64, 94 (bottom).

BIBLIOGRAPHY

The literature on the Boer Wars, particularly of 1899–1902, is extensive. The following works are those that have been the most useful in the compilation of this book.

Amery, L.S. (Ed) THE TIMES HISTORY OF THE WAR IN SOUTH AFRICA (7 vols) Sampson Low, 1900–09

Belfield, Eversley THE BOER WAR Leo Cooper, 1975

Bellairs, Lady B. St J. (Ed) THE TRANSVAAL WAR 1880–81 William Blackwood, 1885

Butler, Lt-Gen. Sir W.F. THE LIFE OF SIR GEORGE POMEROY-COLLEY John Murray, 1899

Carter, T.F. A NARRATIVE OF THE BOER WAR Cape Town, 1896

Churchill, Winston S. MY EARLY LIFE (1930) Fontana, London, 1959

Duxbury, G.R. THE FIRST WAR OF INDEPENDENCE 1880–81 South African National Museum of Military History, Johannesburg, 1981

Duxbury, G.R. BATTLES OF THE ANGLO-BOER WAR 1899–1902 (Series) South African National Museum of Military History, Johannesburg, 1979

Emery, Frank MARCHING OVER AFRICA: LETTERS FROM VICTORIAN SOLDIERS Hodder and Stoughton, 1986

Firkins, Peter THE AUSTRALIANS IN NINE WARS Robert Hale, 1972

Goodspeed, Lt-Col D.J. THE ARMED FORCES OF CANADA 1867–1967 Directorate of History, Canadian Armed Forces, Ottawa, 1967

Griffiths, Kenneth THANK GOD WE KEPT THE FLAG FLYING Hutchinson, 1974

Hamilton, Gen. Sir Ian LISTENING FOR THE DRUMS Faber, 1944

Hamilton, Ian THE HAPPY WARRIOR; A LIFE OF GEN. SIR I. HAMILTON Cassell, 1966

Hannah, W.H. BOBS: THE LIFE OF FM EARL ROBERTS OF KANDAHAR VC Leo Cooper, 1972

Kruger, Rayne GOODBYE DOLLY GRAY Cassell, 1959

Lee, Emanoel TO THE BITTER END Viking, 1985

Lehmann, Joseph THE FIRST BOER WAR Jonathan Cape, 1972

Longford, Elizabeth JAMESON'S RAID Weidenfeld and Nicolson, 1982

Magnus, Philip KITCHENER: PORTRAIT OF AN IMPERIALIST John Murray, 1958

Marling, Capt. P.S. RIFLEMAN AND HUSSAR John Murray, 1931

Maurice, Maj-Gen. Sir F. and Grant, M.H. OFFICIAL HISTORY OF THE WAR IN SOUTH AFRICA (4 vols) H.M.S.O., 1906–10

Pakenham, Thomas THE BOER WAR Weidenfeld and Nicolson, 1979

Pemberton, W. Baring BATTLES OF THE BOER WAR Batsford, 1964

Ransford, Oliver THE BATTLE OF MAJUBA HILL John Murray, 1967

Ransford, Oliver THE BATTLE OF SPION KOP John Murray, 1969

Reitz, Deneys COMMANDO Faber, 1929

Stanley, George F. CANADA'S SOLDIERS Macmillan Co. of Canada, Toronto, 1960

Symons, Julian BULLER'S CAMPAIGN Cresset Press, 1963

Wilson, H.W. WITH THE FLAG TO PRETORIA (2 vols) Harmsworth, 1900–01

Wilson, H.W. AFTER PRETORIA, THE GUERILLA WAR (2 vols) Amalgamated Press, 1902

Wilson, Monica & Thompson, Leonard (Eds) THE OXFORD HISTORY OF SOUTH AFRICA (Vol II) Clarendon Press, 1971

Wood, FM Sir Evelyn FROM MIDSHIPMAN TO FIELD MARSHAL (Vol II) Methuen, 1906

Articles

THE CANADIAN MAGAZINE War Number, August 1900

JOURNAL OF THE AUSTRALIAN WAR MEMORIAL April 1985: Burness, P. 'The Australian Horse'. Chamberlain, M. 'The Wilmansrust Affair'

JOURNAL OF THE SOCIETY FOR ARMY HISTORICAL RESEARCH: Tylden, Maj. G. 'The 27th Regiment in Natal. 1841–45' (Vol XXIX, 106); 'The British Army in the Orange River Colony, 1842–54' (Vol XVIII, 67); 'Boomplats, 1848' (Vol XVI, 207); 'The British Army and the Transvaal, 1875–85' (Vol XXX, 159); 'Majuba 1881: A Boer Account' (Vol XVII, 6); 'A Study in Attack: Majuba' (Vol XXXIX, 27). Ward, S.G.P. (Ed) 'Diary of Colonel Bond, 58th Regt' (Vol LIII, 87). A.W. 'Battle of Magersfontein' (Vol XX, 198). Carter-Campbell, D.N. 'Diary of Major G.T.C. Carter-Campbell, 2nd Scottish Rifles, 23 October 1899–2 March 1900 (Vol LV, 138). Spiers, Edward. 'The British Cavalry 1902–1914' (Vol LVII, 71); 'Reforming the Infantry 1900–1914' (Vol LIX, 82).

JOURNAL OF THE NORTHAMPTONSHIRE REGIMENT: Lovegrove, Capt. F. 'Battle of Laing's Nek' (Vol I, 79)

JOURNAL OF THE VICTORIAN MILITARY SOCIETY: Crouch, John and Knight, I.J. (Eds) 'Forged in Strong Fires: Transvaal War 1881' (1981)

Other Periodicals

THE NAVY AND ARMY ILLUSTRATED (1899–1902)
THE BLACK AND WHITE BUDGET (1899–1900)
THE GRAPHIC (1881)
THE ILLUSTRATED LONDON NEWS (1881, 1899–1902)

Manuscripts

Barton, Lieutenant C.W., 2nd Northamptonshire Regiment *Diary, 1899–1900*

Tuck, Private M., 58th Regiment *Diary, 1879–82*

Waller, Private A.E., City Imperial Volunteers *Letters, 1900*

INDEX

174

176